MEMBERS OF THE LONG PARLIAMENT

MEMBERS OF THE LONG PARLIAMENT

D. Brunton

and

D. H. Pennington

INTRODUCTION BY
R. H. TAWNEY

ARCHON BOOKS

1968

Reprinted by permission of
George Allen & Unwin, Ltd.
in an unaltered and unabridged edition

SBN: 208 00686 9
Library of Congress Catalog Card Number: 68-8014
Printed in the United States of America

DOUGLAS BRUNTON was born in 1917 and was educated at Winchester and Wadham College, Oxford. He served in the army for a short time and after discharge on the ground of ill-health was employed in Portugal under the British Council. He was an assistant lecturer in the University of Manchester in 1946-7, and lecturer in History at King's College in the University of Durham from October 1947 until his death in a road accident on 16 May 1952. These are the bare facts, and in going a little beyond them I am conscious of his own dislike of anything which smacked of grandiloquence. But this book, written in collaboration with Mr. Pennington and almost complete when he died, will indicate the loss which we have suffered by his death. He had got into his stride, a little more slowly than some, more surely than most. His interests were wide: in military and naval history, for instance, particularly in the American Civil War; and in European History, on which he had begun to write. He was teaching with increasing confidence and success, endlessly helpful and patient, tolerant of everything except humbug and pretentiousness. These he discerned almost infallibly and punctured with a wit which we recall eagerly, even now. I am speaking for all his friends and colleagues here when I say that our sense of loss has not diminished but has grown since the first shock of his death. There are not many men who take their work as seriously and themselves as lightly as he did.

W. L. BURN

King's College
Newcastle-upon-Tyne

PREFACE

THE research on which this book is based was begun at the suggestion of Professor Namier in 1947, when both the authors were Assistant Lecturers in History at Manchester University. While it was in progress we heard of two other works in the same field. In 1951 the revival in a new form of the project for an official History of Parliament brought hope of the eventual publication of far fuller and more accurate biographical information than could be collected by individual workers; but it seems likely to be some years before the seventeenth-century volumes are even begun. Meanwhile Mrs. Mary Keeler was preparing in America a large-scale biographical study of the original members of the Long Parliament, which we have not seen but which may soon become available. Partly because of these works we abandoned the idea of printing, even in outline, all the biographies from which our statistics and conclusions are derived, and confined ourselves to alphabetical and geographical lists, with a few tabulated classifications.

In May 1952, when our work was in its final stages, there came the sudden death of my friend and collaborator, Douglas Brunton. In the difficult task of joint research and writing no colleague could have been more helpful and patient. It is not for me to speak of his many high qualities as a historian, to which by the nature of this book the parts of it that are his cannot altogether bear adequate witness. For the assembling of biographical information we made a roughly equal geographic division, and Mr. Brunton collected the material for all our regions except the south-east and south-west. Chapter V was written entirely by him, and Chapter I almost entirely; the rest of the book draws heavily on his researches and ideas, and occasionally on his words.

At the time of Mr. Brunton's death unexpected obstacles were delaying the appearance of the volume. The financial risks which necessarily impede the handling of works of this character by commercial publishers have since been removed by a most generous grant from King's College, Newcastle-upon-Tyne, who had already contributed to the expenses of the research, and who have in this way made possible the publication of the main original work on which Mr. Brunton was engaged during his years with them. To the College and to Professor W. L. Burn I extend the thanks which Mr. Brunton would have wished to express.

To mention individually all those who have helped us would be to add another long list of names to a book already over-burdened with them. Information about many members and sources has been supplied, often at considerable trouble, by people with special knowledge of them. For the County of Dorset in particular many gaps in our biographies were filled by such means. Mr. Ivan Roots, Mrs. Marjorie Cox, Mr. George Yule, and members of the Department of History at Manchester have contributed in a variety of ways. To Sir Lewis Namier we owe even more gratitude than do most students of Parliamentary history. Professor R. H. Tawney's Introduction adds to the book the comments of a scholar with a lifetime's knowledge of territory to which we were hesitant newcomers. His suggestions for re-arrangements and additions have made the work in its present form a considerable improvement on earlier drafts, and his advice and support in arranging publication and seeing the book through the press have been invaluable. Lastly I must offer inadequate thanks to my wife and mother for their help with many of the more unattractive tasks, and to Mrs. Kathleen Brunton who, both before and after her husband's death, played a large part in the making of the book.

D. H. PENNINGTON

Manchester, March, 1953

CONTENTS

INTRODUCTION

BY R. H. TAWNEY

THE following pages contain an analysis of the Commons' House of the Long Parliament, from the opening of that assembly on 3 November 1640, to its expulsion by Cromwell on 20 April 1653. The aim of Mr. Pennington and Mr. Brunton is not to advance or rebut a theory of the influences determining the political attitudes of members. It is to answer a prior and more elementary question. The House was not a homogeneous block. It included diversities, not only of opinion, but of social status, occupational interest, education, age and political experience. A knowledge of these traits is not a key to unlock all doors; but it facilitates a more realistic view of a famous institution at a famous period than is possible without it. Classified with reference to them, what kind of pattern does the membership of the House reveal?

Parliament passed in these twelve and a half years through a succession of crises. A reply to that question involves, therefore, an examination of its composition at more than one date. It occupies the authors' three opening chapters, of which the first is devoted to the 552 original members sitting before the resort to arms in August, 1642; the second to the 275 'Recruiters' elected in or after 1645 to replace 'disabled' Royalists and to fill seats vacated by death; the third to the Rump, of whose nominal total of something over 200 rarely more than 50 to 70 appear to have taken part in divisions. Contemporary opinion distinguished, side by side with a predominant landed interest, two minor, but not unimportant, groups. One, the practising barristers, irrepressible on paper as in life, is prominent, in different connections, at intervals throughout the book. The other, the slightly, though only slightly, smaller category of merchants actively

xi

engaged in trade, embraced a variety of dissimilar types, and is the subject of a special chapter. In order to understand the play of personalities on the parliamentary stage, it is not sufficient to observe the actors as, before the footlights, they appear. It is necessary also to follow them home; to catch a glimpse of the rocks from which, in different regions, they were hewn; to discern some, at least, of the threads composing the social webs, within which, in their native surroundings, they lived and moved. On these intriguing topics the authors have much of interest to say; but a full-length picture of the varying provincial backgrounds of members—'our countries' as they called them —would demand several volumes, not one. They have rightly preferred, therefore, to a superficial panorama the intensive exploration of two critical and contrasted areas, the results of which are presented in Chapters V and VI. The note of modest inquiry, on which the book opens, is sustained to the end. Its final chapter offers, not a summary of confident conclusions, but an indication of the problems which, in the light of the evidence adduced in the preceding pages, may most profitably be pondered, together with a hint that, not only some conventional solutions of these enigmas, but the categories employed in formulating them, might with advantage be revised. The reader will find it convenient, after studying the introductory chapter, to turn to the issues which Mr. Pennington and Mr. Brunton, in taking their leave, invite him to consider.

The *personnel* of Parliament, long a neglected theme, has begun in recent years to come into its own. No previous work, however, has examined in detail the membership of the House of Commons which entered and emerged from the Civil War; nor, when due allowance has been made for the statistical uncertainties to which the authors call attention, is it easy to point to one providing for any period before the nineteenth century information comparable in range and precision with that here supplied. Certain of the features revealed by it need not be more than noted. The age-distribution of members—half of those sitting in the critical first two years under forty and only a fifth over fifty—arrests the reader's eye; but, seen in the setting of the low expectation of life characteristic of the pre-industrial era, it should not cause surprise. The minority of a little over one-third with a parliamentary experience extending behind the spring of 1640 is also striking. It is better regarded, perhaps, as another aspect of the same demographic facts than as a symptom of any exceptional immaturity in a Parliament described by Clarendon as differing little in *personnel*, though much in temper, from its immediate predecessor. Twenty years were to elapse before the comments of Hobbes on young gentlemen corrupted by a University education saw the light, nor do we know whether the reflections prompting them had long been in his mind. It appears, however, from the estimates here supplied that rather more than half the House had breathed the infected air of the nurseries of sedition later indicted by him; while a higher proportion had in London, 'the third university of England', read law, or so much of it as seemed serviceable to prospective land-owners, at one or other of the Inns of Court. Such touches add vitality and colour to the authors' picture; but the subjects claiming the lion's share of their attention lie on an obscurer and more controversial plane, where figures, when available, suggest questions, but can hardly answer them. They include the character of the different social groups composing the House; the causes which, during the preceding century, had accelerated or retarded their growth; and the degree to which, when the hour of decision struck, not only personal convictions, but factors of a more external kind, whether family connections, regional loyalties, or economic interests, determined political alignments.

Professor Neale, in his admirable work on the Elizabethan House of Commons, has described the social configuration of the House of 1584. Half-a-century later the pattern has in some important details changed. In the unpropitious climate of the autumn of 1640, the cluster of royal and ecclesiastical officials, which had supplied nearly a sixth of the earlier total, has withered. The handful of noblemen's servants has gone the same way. The legal membership has risen. Commerce, to which he rarely refers, had been vocal in the later parliaments of James, and has now entered in some strength. The larger outlines of the parliamentary landscape remain, in essentials, however, those depicted by him. On the eve of the breakdown, as in the later years of the great Queen, the House is an assembly consisting, to the extent of one-half to two-thirds, of country gentlemen, flanked by increased minorities of approximately eighty barristers and—though the designation is ambiguous—some fifty to seventy merchants.

Into the debate of recent years on the first, largest and politically most important of these groups it is needless here to enter. The vicissitudes of landed fortunes interest Mr. Pennington and Mr. Brunton less as a chapter of social history than on account of the clues to the composition and conduct of Parliament offered by them. Surveying the scene from their vantage-point in the unchartered frontier-region where political and economic interests meet, they suggest some sobering reflections, of which specialists in either field may profitably take account. Clearly, in the first place, an active land-market had been a recurrent feature of the preceding century, and not less clearly strokes of public policy had at times brought fresh grist to the voracious mill. But the mobilisation of estates neither began with the Dissolution nor continued merely or mainly through the improvidence of the Crown in dissipating its domains. The significance of these spectacular transactions, of which contemporaries made much, must not be under-estimated; but to forget, in contemplating them, the inconspicuous, but continuous, effect of private dealings in land, of recurrent failures of male heirs in breaking properties up, and of matrimonial alliances in carrying them, or part of them, away is, the authors hint, to falsify perspectives. It is to sacrifice to the occasional melodrama of life the sober realities of its daily prose. In so far as the decline of old families and rise of new is connected with changes in the distribution of land, the hero or villain of the piece is less often, in their view, the greed or prodigality of rulers richly endowed with both than the impersonal fluctuations of the marriage-market, births, and deaths. It is primarily factors of this pedestrian kind which prompt their remark that the continuance of an estate in the same name for as much as two centuries is an exception, and which make the House of Commons investigated by them an assembly predominantly recruited from families with less than three generations of eminence behind them.

It is evident, in the second place, that landed wealth not infrequently owes its origin and survival to sources of income other than land. Our knowledge of the histories of substantial estates is, as yet, too restricted to permit a confident verdict on the relative importance of the parts played in their formation by the rents and profits of properties already owned and by resources derived from some extraneous source; but the impression left by the present work is that, in the period covered by it, the latter counted for much. The Court, with its golden rain of offices and concessions bestowed by royal favour, is one prolific source of funds later invested in land. In an age when litigation was a passion, and the ever-growing swarm of practitioners battening on it a constant complaint, legal fortunes provide another. City money, though, on the authors' view, less important in founding landed families than, when rough weather is encountered, in caulking their leaks and keeping them afloat, is a third. Nor, of course, does capital move only one way. Not only are leading country gentry interested in local industries, but they invest in commercial ventures launched in London and apprentice their sons to City firms. As the family histories here summarised reveal, marriages, other personal connections and economic inter-dependence cause land, law and commerce to be inextricably intertwined.

A less familiar aspect of the subject is studied at some length in Chapters V and VI. The England of the early Stuarts was marked by a wealth of diversities of local interest, tradition, and sentiment, which tempts one at times to describe its political system as a unitary state in—to use a metaphor—a quasi-federal society. The strength of regional, as distinct from national, loyalties is difficult for modern minds to grasp; but, unless that trait is remembered, both the social life and the politics of the age must remain closed books. The economic preponderance of the capital was, it is true, unchallenged. Litigation brought its unhappy hordes to Westminster. The Court was a magnet to those to whom Courts appeal. Something like a season had set in, and, among the richer gentry, the habit of keeping town-houses had taken root. The fact remains that the strata from which members were drawn consisted predominantly, not of Londoners who sought repose in country seats, but of country-men, some of whom might or might not have a *pied-à-terre* in London, but of whom the majority visited it only when their occasions called them there, or, like Clarendon's father during the last thirty years of his life, did not visit it at all. Nor, even if they were members of Parliament, had it till recently been necess-ary for their resorts to the capital to be frequent or prolonged. When under James and Charles Parliament met, its sessions had rarely exceeded four to five months per year. It was not so long since Ben Jonson's allusion to the theatre-goer who looked in 'once in five years, at a parliament time' had been a jest which hit the mark.

In a society so decentralised and loosely-knit, local concerns and obligations were the common stuff of life, and affairs of wider import an intermittent addition to them. Provincial patriotism was a power. The score or so of studies devoted, in the half-century before the Civil War, to the history and antiquities of different counties suggests that culture was not unaffected by it. Political groupings naturally conformed to the pattern fixed by the same regional moulds. There had been occasions in the recent past when the divergent interests of different districts—agricultural and manufacturing, cereal and pastoral—had found vigorous expression in the debates of the House. The aspect of the subject emphasised here is different. It is the constructive part played by local sympathies in sup-plying the basis for political organisation. The units which count for most, the authors remark, are two, the family and the county. A thorough investigation of the family connections of members of the Long Parliament has still, it appears, to be made. The criss-cross of ramifying relationships between the East Anglian parliamentary families here studied suggests that such an inquiry would not be labour wasted. The second key-position deserves equal attention. The county—the arena where

family influence makes itself first and most continuously felt—
is still, in a sense, a community. It possesses, in addition to its
own administrative system, recognised political leaders, and
speaks at times with a collective voice. The members representing it need not necessarily belong, though often they do, to
families outstanding in antiquity or wealth; but they must have
local roots, in the shape, if not of residence in the county, at
least of property owned in it. The outsider in a county seat is
rare; and, though in boroughs the carpet-bagger has a better
chance, there too he is the exception. These local and regional
bonds—'connections', to use a later term—based on neighbour-
hood, kinship, and, at times, the semi-dynastic influence wielded
by a local magnate, are, in the authors' view, more potent than
most other grounds of union or division. They set the political
styles of different regions, and do much to decide, when the
ways divide, which road each shall take. It is to them, it is suggested, that most of the tracks uncovered by the historian in the
end lead back.

Within a year of the meeting of the Long Parliament the faint
beginnings of the parties soon to be at each other's throats can
be dimly discerned, and less than twelve months later the first
battle has been fought. The reader of this work will naturally
inquire what clues, if any, are offered by it to the causes determining the alignment of the opposing forces. Only a charlatan
will dogmatise on the welter of conflicting motives which
find their agonising issue in the choice of allegiances in a Civil
War. Possessing the humility in the presence of tragic events
which all men, and in particular historians, should feel, Mr.
Pennington and Mr. Brunton disclaim the pretension to pluck
the heart out of such mysteries. They contribute to light, not by
adding one more formula to those already in the field, but by
dispelling some conventional illusions which have bedevilled
the search for it.

It is clear, in the first place, from the evidence here assembled
that the correlation sometimes suggested between the political
attitudes and class connections of members demands a more
critical scrutiny than commonly it receives. If to dismiss it as a

mare's-nest would be premature, it is, at least, an hypothesis requiring qualifications so extensive as to leave little of the scientific cogency claimed for it intact. On that point the authors' analysis of the *personnel* of the House is decisive. It shows that in one feature, that of comparative youth, Royalists have the advantage over Parliamentarians, but that in other respects the contrasts between the contending parties are less striking than the similarities. Royalists and Parliamentarians alike include country gentlemen, lawyers, and merchants. Representatives of old families and new, greater and lesser gentry, conservative and improving landlords, metropolitan and provincial traders and financiers, are found among both. Both contain much the same proportion of members educated at Universities and Inns of Court. Naturally, persons with Court connections and bene-ficiaries of royal favours tended to enlist in the Royalist ranks. Those excluded as monopolists also became supporters of the King; while the remainder of the London commercial members chose the Parliamentary side. Such minorities apart, the two parties appear, on the basis of the statistics here presented, to be economically and socially much of a piece. Nor, in those respects, do the Recruiters and the Rump differ greatly from the original members. It is a question whether the expectation that an Independent will probably be—ambiguous phrase—a *petit bourgeois* is, in fact, better founded than the doctrine that all merchants were Whigs.

It is true, of course, that the general categories here employed mask a variety of social sub-divisions, and that, in considering political sympathies, not at Westminster, but in the country as a whole, these minor species must be taken into account. The gentry included not only well-to-do squires, but small land-owners economically nearer to the yeomen than to their pros-perous relatives, and in some regions, it seems, described as yeomen themselves. The affinities between a successful London barrister and the attorney in a country town were obviously remote. Nor was much love lost between provincial business and the metropolitan export kartells, which beat down the prices of Gloucestershire and Yorkshire clothiers, and excluded

Western and Northern merchants from continental markets. It is true, again, as Mr. Pennington and Mr. Brunton observe, that the mere fact that a man was of the standing to be elected to Parliament implied that he was, in some sense, an exception, distinguished by wealth or influence from the common run of his humbler neighbours. Finally, it is obvious, as they also remark, that for these reasons among others, Parliament, whatever its virtues, was not a mirror of the nation. It is arguable, therefore, that affinities between differences of economic position and political attitudes, which find no reflection in the former, were, nevertheless, a power in the latter; and, though generalisations based on the observation of particular districts must, as the authors point out, be received with caution, the well-known comments of Clarendon and Baxter on the temper of the yeomanry and the textile areas lend some colour to that view. As far, however, as the membership of the House of Commons, with which alone the present work deals, is concerned, the inference from the figures contained in it is plain. It is that the division between Royalists and Parliamentarians had little connection with diversities of economic interest and social class. Till equally comprehensive evidence to the contrary is adduced, that conclusion must stand.

To say this is not, of course, to belittle the part played by economic interests in the history of the period. On the contrary, to judge by the preceding twenty years, the rôle of such interests as a factor in the preparation of the crisis had been important. It is the more necessary for that reason that their character and operation should be correctly stated. The venerable legend of a conflict between, on the one side, a monarchy supported by a feudal aristocracy and, on the other, an aspiring *bourgeosie* is given by the authors the short shrift that it deserves. Pardonable in writers employing, in the infancy of economic history, the continental categories familiar to them in order to fit the English revolution into their historical scheme, that interpretation, which can be more easily tested today than when first advanced, has not worn too well. If the word 'fuedal' refers merely to territorial influence, it draws no dividing line between Royalists and Parliamentarians, for such influence was exercised by both. If it is used, as it should be, in a more precise sense, to describe a class dependent wholly or mainly, like the French *noblesse* before 1789, on the revenue from seigneurial rights, it is a solecism; for, unless the rights in question be interpreted to include all or most payments from tenants to landlords, evidence of the existence of such a class in the England of Charles I is still to seek. The student of agrarian history would be happy to add some authentic specimens of it to his collection; and it is possible that, when conditions on northern properties have been more fully investigated, a few such pleasing rarities may come his way. As far, however, as our present knowledge goes, while seigneurial dues of one kind or another continued to figure in estate accounts, their financial significance was rarely great. The backbone of the substantial landowner's income was normally of a more commercial kind. It consisted of leasehold rents, the premiums on entry known as admission fines, and the profits of farming, supplemented, when occasion offered, by sales of timber, the exploitation of minerals, and sometimes urban ground-rents. The significant fact, in such conditions, was the opposite of that sometimes suggested. It was the truth expressed, with, perhaps, some exaggeration, by de Tocqueville when, in referring to the England of the seventeenth century, he wrote of *le système féodal aboli dans sa substance, des classes qui se pénètrent, une noblesse effacée, une aristocratie ouverte, la richesse devenue la puissance.* It was, in short, the relative unimportance of the feudal question, and the facility with which, as a consequence, political co-operation was in this country maintained between classes destined, in parts of continental Europe, to remain for another century and a half irreconcilably divided.

The country gentry in the House were, therefore, predominantly business men. Like the merchants, often themselves large landowners, with whom they worked and inter-married, they had keen eyes, as their speeches in Parliament show, for movements of prices, costs, and markets, and for commercial or financial policies affecting them. Judged by the sources of its income, each of these groups might with almost equal propriety be described as *bourgeois*; and to attempt to distinguish between them by the use of a term applicable to both is to darken counsel. The economic apprehensions aroused in them, as well as in a host of humbler people, by measures regarded as inimical to the security of property and business were, it may be suggested, of an altogether simpler, more obvious, and less recondite kind than some theorists of a social war have been disposed to assume. It is not, after all, surprising that entrepreneurs, great and small, on the alert to make the most of their resources and opportunities, should have resented the disturbance of established expectations by executive action, or that, partly for that reason, they should have preferred to the unpredictable vagaries of conciliar government the lesser, though not negligible, uncertainties of statute and common law. The degree of political importance to be attached to such alarms and antipathies is, of course, a different problem. It is a question whether, in considering it, an even heavier emphasis than is usual ought not to be laid on the familiar contrast between the first and second chapters in the pre-war history of the Long Parliament. In the legislation of 1641, which wound up the old regime, and which future Royalists and Parliamentarians alike supported, economic interests played, as the tenour of the measures passed suggests, an important part. It is possible that similar motives were a power in the second stage, which saw the final rupture of the following year. If so, however, the evidence required to establish that conclusion still remains to be brought to light.

Such random reflections, though suggested by the concluding chapter of the present work, stray beyond its theme. The excuse for them must be the infectious interest of the authors' pages. It is rare, in laying down a book on a subject at first sight so trite as the parliamentary history of the England of the early Stuarts, to be stirred by feelings of mingled gratitude and surprise at the new vistas opened by it. Mr. Pennington and Mr. Brunton have performed that feat. They express more than once the conviction that the key to some of the unresolved enigmas of their subject is to be found in a more thorough study of its regional and local aspects. It may be hoped that the admirable example set by them will encourage future scholars to act upon that hint.

CHAPTER I

THE ORIGINAL MEMBERS

NEVER was the King's party smaller than in the Parliament which put an end to conciliar government in 1641. To save Strafford from execution the King could not rally as many as sixty supporters, and some of these were men who objected to the manifest injustice of the proceedings, but did not lend support to the system of government which was also being condemned. Yet the Grand Remonstrance was passed by only eleven votes, and in 1642, when members were forced to decide for one cause or the other, considerably more than two-fifths of them chose the King's.

Many conflicting explanations have been offered of this rapid development of a Royalist party. It is now commonly agreed that the backbone, at least, of this party consisted of constitutional Royalists as strongly opposed to arbitrary power in the King as they were to arbitrary tendencies in the Commons, but the precise influence of constitutional, religious, and economic motives has been variously assessed. Such speculations can hardly be more than inspired—or more often uninspired—guessing. Men are not usually in the habit of weighing in their minds a pennyworth of political liberty against an ounce of religious freedom and assessing the effect of either on their bank-balances before engaging in an armed struggle, and we can hardly disentangle for them their own confusion of motives. But though it is impossible to enter the minds of Royalists and Parliamentarians, something may be discovered of their status in society and of their families' history before 1640 and after 1660—whether they were landowners, merchants, or lawyers; whether they were old or young, local men or strangers; whether they belonged to 'new' or old-established families. In this chapter an attempt is made to answer such questions about the members who sat in the Long Parliament before the outbreak of war in August 1642.

For the elections in October 1640 writs were sent to 51 counties (Durham was not represented until 1675), 206 cities and boroughs, including the 7 Cinque Ports, and the 2 Universities. In the early months of the Parliament 7 more boroughs (Ashburton, Cockermouth, Honiton, Okehampton, New Malton, Northallerton, and the Cinque Port of Seaford) were 'restored to their ancient privilege' of sending members.[1] The double borough of Weymouth and Melcombe Regis and the City of London each returned four members; the 12 Welsh counties, the 12 Welsh boroughs, and 5 English boroughs (Abingdon, Banbury, Bewdley, Higham Ferrers, and Monmouth) returned one member each; everywhere else returned two. The maximum membership for the whole Parliament was therefore 507, though for one borough, Newport in Cornwall, only one member is known to have been returned. To the members who sat as a result of the first elections we have added for the purpose of our numerical calculations those who were returned at by-elections. This gives a total of 552 men who sat at some time between November 1640 and August 1642, and are called here the 'original' members.

In this total those whose elections were declared invalid are not included, unless they were Royalists who merely had this amenity added to the resolution 'disabling' them, or—like Sir John Melton (Newcastle-on-Tyne)—died before the election dispute was decided. In one or two cases these disputes were not settled by 1642 and the constituency concerned was short of a member until the election of the 'Recruiters'—that is, the members elected from 1645 onwards. Though William Watkins sat at the very beginning of the Parliament for Monmouth, he was charged to cease attendance until his election dispute with Thomas Trevor was decided; in fact neither of them ever gained this seat, for Watkins sat in the 'Oxford Parliament' of Royalist

[1] There is an article by Lady de Villiers on boroughs restored by the House of Commons in *English Historical Review*, Vol. LXVII, p. 175.

M.P.s without really having a right to his seat, while Trevor found his way into the House as Recruiter for Tregony. As Monmouth was one of the single-member constituencies, this meant that it was in effect disfranchised until the younger Thomas Pury was elected as Recruiter. Anthony Ashley Cooper's election was not decided until 1660, but this was a unique occurrence.

In 1640, as in the Parliaments of Elizabeth and, for that matter, in the Parliaments of Victoria, the landed interest was of course dominant. Many of the members came of new families, even if 'new' be taken only to mean families which had acquired their lands or the chief portion of them under Charles or his father. If it be taken to signify families which had risen to importance since the Reformation settlement, the proportion is strikingly high. Generalisation is dangerous, for even a few hundred Members of Parliament do not provide an adequate basis for pronouncements about the class of landed gentry. The majority of landowners did not aspire to the distinction of sitting in the Commons, and those who achieved it attained thereby a certain eminence. At the same time rapid transfer of lands was obviously characteristic of the period. The Reformation settlement, though responsible for a change in ownership of land far larger than in the years just before and after, did not burst on a static market. Again, the sales of monastic property and other Crown lands in response to the financial needs of Elizabeth as well as of her predecessors, important as they were, should not obscure the frequency of land sales by private owners. The Dissolution of the Monasteries, and the Civil Wars with their forfeitures, compositions, debts, and special taxes, marked the two periods in which huge quantities of land were flung on to the market, and sales of Crown lands in financial emergency at many times in the sixteenth and seventeenth centuries produced minor booms in land speculation. Yet even more important than these temporary influences in the rise of new landowning families, and in the sudden emergence of old but comparatively obscure ones, was that failure of the male line which sooner or later struck most such families before they became county dynasties. The heiress, and more particularly the coheiress, was perhaps the most powerful element in breaking up old estates and founding new families. Political or financial catastrophe ruined many landowners, but it is doubtful (so far as this study resulted in an investigation of the question) whether their cumulative effect was equal as an influence in the rise and fall of county families to failure of the male line. In short, of the many branches of the land-market, the marriage-market was the most important.

Whether amid the constantly changing fortunes of the landowners there exists any general difference between those who became Royalists and those who took the side of the Parliament is a question to which there can be no simple answer. In the regional chapters we have shown a little of the kind of evidence from which a study of it could be built up. The most we can say of the country as a whole is that no proof of such a difference among the M.P.s emerges from the easily ascertainable facts about them. So far as titles are an indication of status, they are entirely inconclusive. The majority of both parties were Esquires. A very few whose lack of a claim to this designation left them with the ignominious label 'gent.' are found on both sides.[1] Knighthood was for many an expense to be evaded rather than an honour to be sought. For what the fact is worth the number of both knights and baronets on each side in 1640 was roughly proportionate to the strength of the two sides in the House. There were it is true rather more Royalists among the heirs and younger sons of Peers; but though the relationship gave a link with the more conservative Upper House it did not necessarily indicate greater antiquity or even greater estates.

No one could doubt the pre-eminence of the landed interest; but to assess the extent of the mercantile interest is much more difficult. Any discussion of such a question at once encounters the problem of definition. There is no need to stress the fact that merchants invested their profits in land and that landed gentry increased their wealth through trade and speculation.

---

[1] In theory 'Esquire' was a title that could be acquired by office-holding, and was not necessarily superior to 'Gentleman'. (See *O.E.D.* and Burke, *Landed Gentry*, 4th edn., p. viii); but there was an evident social distinction in practice.

Interest in a colonising project or in the East India Company did not turn a landowner into a merchant. But a man like Sir John Melton, who owned an estate but made most of his money out of coal, or families like the Barnardistons, long established in Suffolk but with important mercantile connections as well, and the Moores, eminent through their antiquity both as a landed family and in the commercial history of Liverpool, are not easy to classify. In a later chapter we shall try to show something of the wide variety of commercial and financial interests, and to discover what basis can be found among the M.P.s for the belief that these interests, or some of them, were associated with the Parliamentary side. But counting of heads can easily reduce itself to absurdity. In any case it cannot give an impression of the representation of trading interests through the close ties of marriage and inheritance that linked land and commerce. The rise of many a landed estate begins with a marriage to the coheiress of a merchant; often its prosperity is maintained by a series of such matches; and younger sons return to the way of life in which maternal grandfathers had made their fortunes.

The lawyers, firmly allied to both gentry and merchants by ties of birth and interest, formed the third powerful factor in what we may, borrowing the term from Professor Namier, call the political nation. Of our 'original' members of the Long Parliament 75 were barristers; 33 of these sided with the King and 42 with the Parliament. Twenty-seven of them were in 1640, or later became, Recorders—all but 4 for the boroughs they represented—and of these the Royalists were in a majority of 17 to 10. From this we might conclude that the lawyers were about evenly divided in proportion to the strength of the two parties in the House. Any deduction about lawyers in general would be a hazardous burden for the evidence to bear, even if we could add information about the type of practice of each individual. The Crown had not been successful in promoting the election of its favoured legal candidates. For the rest the struggle between Common Law and Prerogative was over by 1642, and lawyers were free to choose their side in the war without attention to their natural prejudices in the matter.

There were constitutionalists on both sides, though by 1642 the Royalists probably had the better legal case.

Far more numerous than practising lawyers were the gentlemen who had been to one of the Inns of Court with no intention of being called to the Bar. Opinions differ on the quantity of law most of them imbibed; but the general verdict is probably, as so often with students, a harsh one. There can in any case be no doubt about the extent to which the Inns had been woven into the general life of the country at a time when a high proportion of the gentry sent their sons to one or other of them. This was one of the reasons for the high prestige of the Common Law, though the main one was the vital importance to country gentlemen of what was still mainly land law. Of the members who sat before the outbreak of the Civil War, 310 had been to one of the Inns of Court, 184 Parliamentarians and 120 Royalists.[1] (As explained later a few members have been left unclassified.) The proportion of Parliamentarians is greater than that in the whole House, but not sufficiently so to be of much significance. More members came from Gray's Inn than from any of the other three, and there were twice as many of them for the Parliament as for the King. Only from the Inner Temple was there a tiny Royalist majority. Again, so far as can be judged from the distribution of the members, there was a tendency for certain Inns to be favoured by certain regions. Thus Gray's Inn had more northern members than the rest put together and was also the most favoured by the Midlands and the counties of the Eastern Association, while in Wales and the border counties it shared the preference with Lincoln's Inn. In the counties south of the Thames it was with the Inner Temple the least popular. The Middle Temple on the other hand, which was easily the most popular with the southern counties, had the fewest members from the rest of England. It would be dangerous to ascribe political bias to any of the Inns, as these regional groupings are likely to explain much of the difference, and the attendance of the members concerned was spread over a very long period.

[1] Figures compiled from the Inns of Court admission registers, all four of which are now printed.

The same dangers apply to the examination of attendance at Universities. Two hundred and eighty members, or about half the House, had been to a University, 169 to Oxford and 111 to Cambridge.[1] (About half of those who had been to an Inn or a University had been to both, and of those who attended only one there were rather more at the Inns than at the Universities.) From Oxford there came 73 Royalists and 91 Parliamentarians, from Cambridge 43 Royalists and 66 Parliamentarians. The Eastern Association, which was the most strongly Parliamentarian region, naturally preferred Cambridge—there was only one Oxford man among its members—and the North also sent more men to Cambridge. The other regions, especially the South-west, favoured Oxford.

In their education and usually in their origins the lawyers and the gentry were indistinguishable; but for lawyers, and still more for merchants, the opportunities and methods of entry to Parliament differed from those open to landowners. By far the most important qualification was, however, common to all these groups—to belong to the locality. An overwhelming proportion of the members consisted of men who lived and held estates in the county in which they were elected or near its borders. It was mainly in the larger boroughs that other kinds of local connection counted. In London and Bristol the organised merchant community had a predominant influence on elections; but it was not by any means the rule for merchants to occupy both or even one of the seats in the big towns. Local political service was often a way to Parliament; and the holding of municipal office is no proof of mercantile connections—many gentry seem to have become Mayors and Aldermen. Coventry (where incidentally the Crown normally reckoned on exercising effective influence) and King's Lynn elected merchants; but one of the members for Norwich and one for Shrewsbury was a local gentleman, as were both the members for Chester, though they held municipal office and their families had a long-standing mercantile connection with the city. (Chester again was

---

[1] Figures compiled from J. Foster, *Alumni Oxonienses* and J. and J. A. Venn, *Alumni Cantabrigienses*.

a constituency where the Crown hoped to succeed with its candidates.)

It was of course possible to have a local connection that did not involve residence. Sometimes a Recorder who sat for his borough did not normally live in the county, and sometimes there is a connection through marriage. But there was little opportunity for the carpet-bagger. Apparent exceptions are often due to the exercise of patronage by a great local family. The Herberts, for instance, put their dependants into their Wiltshire boroughs, and the Earl of Northumberland sent his agent, a Cornishman, to represent Berwick. Sir John Clotworthy sat for Maldon, Essex, with which he seems to have had no connection; but his presence in the House was an important aid to the opponents of Strafford, and it would be wrong to suppose from his appearance there that this was a constituency which was normally at the disposal of strangers. The other member for Maldon was the Steward of the borough, Sir Henry Mildmay, who, though he was reckoned to be on the side of the Court during most of the first year of the Parliament, became a Rumper and perhaps a Republican. The Steward had considerable influence within the borough, but whether he used it in this instance in favour of Clotworthy we do not know. Lord Dungarvan at Appleby may be a similar example, though this is by no means certain. He too represented the interests of Irish landowners, though his powerful connections, through his marriage, were with the Court, not, like Clotworthy's, with the Irish Presbyterians and their London backers.

The Duchies of Lancaster and Cornwall were both regions where the Court had formerly been able to find seats for its own candidates. The failure in Cornwall will be dealt with in a later chapter. In Lancashire the surprising feature is not that two southerners sat, one for Lancaster and one for Newton, but the decay of royal influence in the elections, of which it is true there had now long been signs. The Long Parliament cannot be treated as typical in this respect: a number of other constituencies which could normally be relied on to return at least one member in obedience to a recommendation refused to elect Court nominees. But in general the grip of the local gentry had already tightened in the earlier Stuart Parliaments. It is of course a commonplace by now that packing never consisted of more than finding a few seats for those whose presence was considered necessary by the Government, and that no attempt was ever made to affect the composition of the House as a whole; but it was just that endeavour that failed hopelessly on this occasion.

The great national parliamentary families—the Herberts, the Howards, and the Pierreponts to name only three—were still able to control seats in several counties at a considerable distance from each other. For the large majority influence was spread over a single county without extending far beyond it. In the case of boroughs near the edge of a county the boundary was not a rigid barrier. There was no clear line between Norfolk and Suffolk boroughs, nor between some of the Welsh and border counties. (The Harleys, for example, were connected with both Herefordshire and Radnorshire.) But in general the county and the family are the two units in terms of which political rivalries worked themselves out. In many boroughs one seat or both fell normally under the control of a particular local family, and there was sometimes a tradition that a member of that family should sit. But these were less common than those which were open to bargaining among the county gentlemen as a body. Within the county a member of one of the more influential families might sit in the course of his career for two or three different boroughs, and have his turn as the county member too.

The county seats were not monopolised by one or two outstanding names. Knights of the Shire do not in the seventeenth century seem to have differed generally in origin or parliamentary history from borough members. The overwhelming majority of them were country gentlemen of some position in the county, and in most cases of an established county family; but there are exceptions to the rule among the county as among the borough members. The contrast between the Norfolk and the Suffolk Knights of the Shire is noticed in the chapter on the Eastern Association and is an example of the danger of expecting particular rigidity in county membership, for there is no more there than elsewhere. Henry Marten was the son of a wealthy and eminent father when he was chosen as Knight of the Shire for Berkshire, but he was certainly not of an established family; nor was Augustine Skinner, member for Kent, who would certainly have been an unlikely candidate if all the county members had come from prominent older families. Some counties tended to elect men of local esteem but without a family of any parliamentary importance: Shropshire and Worcestershire are examples of this, while the Coningsbys and Harleys of Herefordshire were to be great parliamentary families.

Shropshire Members

One county, Shropshire,[1] can provide a specimen of the original members in which some of these points are illustrated. It is not chosen as a 'typical' county. Indeed if this study has led to any conclusion it is that there is no such thing as a typical county. Each county and each borough has its own history. At the same time much of what is shown here of Shropshire could be shown of the country as a whole from the material on which the figures and generalisations in this chapter are based.

Sir Robert Howard, son of the Earl of Suffolk, did not come of a Shropshire family; but after having Clun Castle settled on him he sat for Bishop's Castle from 1624 onwards. Two of his brothers had also sat in the Commons, one in 1605 and the other in several parliaments before being raised to the peerage as Lord Howard of Escrick—under which title he returned to the Commons as Recruiter for Carlisle in 1649. William Pierrepont, who sat for Wenlock, was second son of the Earl of Kingston and so came of a Nottinghamshire family. His eldest brother was county member in 1629, and a younger brother sat for Nottingham in 1645; but William himself owned an estate at Longueville, Huntingdonshire, and obtained through his wife the Tony estate in Shropshire, of which he had been Sheriff in 1638.

Pierrepont's fellow-member, Thomas Littleton, was son of a

[1] Much of the material that follows comes from the articles on Shropshire M.P.s by H. T. Weyman, *Transactions of the Shropshire Archaeological Society*, 2nd Series, Vols. VII and X; 3rd Series, Vol. II.

local gentleman, related to the more distinguished branch of Littletons of Frankley in Worcestershire, who again were related to the Littletons of Pillaton, a leading family in Staffordshire. Thomas Littleton's father, Sir Adam, was Recorder of Wenlock, which probably accounts for his election. Thomas married a cousin, the daughter of Sir Edward Littleton, who was later Lord Keeper. He fought for the King, sat for Wenlock again in the Cavalier Parliament, and in the Exclusion Parliaments sat in turn for East Grinstead and Yarmouth. His son, who became Speaker, sat for Woodstock for 13 years after the Revolution, and then for Castle Rising, Chichester, and Portsmouth—an impressively long and varied series of constituencies.

William Pierrepont's eldest brother was a Royalist and became Marquess of Dorchester, but William, like his younger brother, Francis, sided with Parliament; he retired after Pride's Purge, refused to sit in 1656 and declined a place in Cromwell's House of Lords, though he was personally on good terms with him. He was again elected for Nottinghamshire in 1660 and sat in the Convention, but retired from politics in 1661 after his defeat in the election to the Cavalier Parliament. He had a great reputation for wisdom, which he had a fine opportunity for transmitting to the House of Lords, as his three sons became in turn the 3rd, 4th, and 5th Earls and 1st Duke of Kingston; one of his daughters married the Earl of Ogle, later Duke of Newcastle, another the 3rd Earl of Clare, and a third became the second wife of the great Marquess of Halifax. A grandson, Gervase, sat for Appleby from 1698 to 1705, becoming an Irish peer in 1703 and an English peer in 1714.

William Spurstow, M.P. for Shrewsbury, was of an old Cheshire family, settled at Spurstow Hall, but he had moved to Shrewsbury, where he was described in 1616 as a draper. He later became a mercer of London. No other member of his family ever sat in Parliament.

His colleague at Shrewsbury, Francis Newport, was a Shropshire landowner like all the remaining Shropshire M.P.s. Sir Richard Newport, the father of Francis, had sat for the county four times and for Shrewsbury once. Both father and son were

2

keen Royalists, and the father, who was extremely rich, bought a peerage in 1642 for £6,000. Together they paid £10,000 to compound for their estates. Richard died in 1651; Francis was an active Royalist during the Interregnum and was twice imprisoned. In 1660 he was made Lord-Lieutenant and later became Comptroller of the Household, a Privy Councillor and Treasurer of the Household; but in 1687 he was deprived of his offices— an apt commentary on James's political crassness. He supported the Seven Bishops and was restored to office by William; in 1694 he became Earl of Bradford. He died in 1708, the last survivor of the Long Parliament. His brother, Andrew, was Knight of the Shire for Montgomery in the Cavalier Parliament, sat for Preston in 1685 and for Shrewsbury from 1689 to 1698, while his son, Richard, who succeeded him as 2nd Earl, sat for the county from 1670 to 1698 with the exception of the 1685 parliament. Another son, Thomas, sat for Ludlow from 1695 to 1700 and for Wenlock in 1715, in which year he was created Baron Torrington. The 3rd Earl, Francis's grandson, sat for Bishop's Castle in 1705, and for the county from 1708 till 1722.

The Newports were one of the great parliamentary families; but neither of the baronets who were Knights of the Shire belonged to families of parliamentary importance. Sir Richard Lee, who voted against Strafford's attainder, had not sat before, and the male line ended with his death in 1660; this was the family's only appearance in the House. Sir John Corbet, a Parliamentarian secluded in 1648, also made his only appearance in 1640; his grandfather had sat for Wenlock and Shrewsbury in the reigns of Henry VIII and Edward VI, and his great-grandson was to represent the county in 1705, 1708, and 1715. Sir John had been Sheriff in 1629 in which year he was imprisoned in the Fleet for resisting the exactions of the government; as he was also one of the Five Knights imprisoned for resisting the forced loan in 1627 and was in the Fleet again in 1635, he had a long and formidable record of opposition to the King's policy, and it is significant that Shropshire, which was one of the most Royalist of counties, should have elected him as Knight of the Shire in 1640. His eldest son, John, was, however, a Royalist and had to compound by a payment of £10,000—a tribute to the wealth and power of the family, but one from which it did not sufficiently recover to take further part in parliamentary affairs.

Richard More, M.P. for Bishop's Castle, had already represented it in 1610 as well as in the Short Parliament, and was one of the older members of the House. He was a Puritan, and one of his sons was Recruiter for Ludlow, while the eldest was excluded by Cromwell after election by the county in 1656, but sat for Bishop's Castle in 1659; his grandson, Richard, sat for the same constituency in 1681, the Convention, and 1695. The Mores, outstanding among the active dissident group which asserted itself so fiercely in a mainly loyalist Shropshire, continued to represent a rather old-fashioned Whig republican tradition in the eighteenth century. The family had held lands in the county since the thirteenth century. Richard was Sheriff in 1619 and Bailiff of Bishop's Castle in 1637. He married the sister of Sir Thomas Harris, an important landowner in Shropshire. Another alliance of the More family turned out badly, and Richard's relations with Isaac Pennington, the influential City member, might have been damaged, had he lived longer, by the breakdown of the marriage of Pennington's daughter.

Both the members for Bridgnorth were Royalists. Edward Acton of Aldenham, ancestor of the historian, was made a baronet in 1644; he died before the Restoration. His son sat for Bridgnorth in the Convention of 1660, his grandson from 1698 to 1705 and his great-grandson in 1710. Thomas Whitmore of Apley (not the Thomas of Ludstone as Mr. Weyman has suggested), a prominent Royalist despite his excuses to the Committee for Compounding, belonged to a family which came to have the most continuous of parliamentary histories.

Also a Royalist was Ralph Goodwin, who had sat for Ludlow since 1624; his father was probably a Bristol man, but was settled at Ludlow Castle, being Deputy Secretary and Clerk of the Council in the Marches. His colleague, Charles Baldwin, was sitting for the first time, but, unlike Goodwin, founded a parliamentary family; he was sixty-seven at the Restoration, but his son, also a Royalist, sat for Ludlow in 1659, his grandson in 1681, the Convention, and 1695, and his great-grandson, Acton Baldwin, from 1705 to 1714, and 1722 to 1727.

In this analysis of the Shropshire members, and in some of the figures already quoted, we have labelled the original members by the clumsy but inescapable terms 'Royalist' and 'Parliamentarian'. The classification raises many problems. Some members who died before the House had even begun to resolve itself into parties of comparable strength cannot be allocated to either side; some dissociated themselves from the struggle as far as they could; some changed their allegiance once or more. In the figures used here 14 members who died in the early months of the Parliament have been left unclassified. Of the remaining 538 there are 236 Royalists and 302 Parliamentarians. For this classification we have adopted the rough and ready method of counting as Royalists all who were 'disabled' from sitting in the House for their desertion of the Parliamentary cause and were not re-admitted. Thus Sir John Fenwick who resumed his seat after changing sides appears as a Parliamentarian, while Sir John Price, though he eventually abandoned the King and became one of the leading figures on the Parliamentary side in Wales, is counted as a Royalist because he was not re-admitted to the House. The Earl of Bedford (William Russell) who never regained his seat in the Lords after he had joined the King is also listed as Royalist. The small number of these arbitrary decisions which might almost as well have gone the other way cannot affect any of our conclusions. Their presence is one of the inevitable drawbacks of a statistical approach, but the advantages of that approach seemed on the whole to outweigh its dangers.

One line of investigation that can only be followed by statistical methods is the possible relation between the members' age and parliamentary experience and their political views. 203 of the classified members—about thirty-eight per cent.—had sat before 1640, of whom 75 became Royalists and 128 Parliamentarians. (In all these calculations the Short Parliament is ignored.) 140 had sat in the Parliament of 1628-9, and of these 49 were afterwards Royalists and 91 Parliamentarians. It is strikingly apparent that the proportion of Parliamentarians to Royalists was much higher among those with previous experience in the House than it was in the House as a whole. This no doubt was an important factor in ensuring a Parliamentarian majority. The organisation provided by Pym, Hampden, and the group of experienced members who had previously been involved together in colonising projects gave the extremists a valuable initial advantage. Later their close association with each other may have lost them support, for the appearance of a cabal was already disliked in the House. ('What this word *Cabal* meaneth I know not,' wrote one of the members for New Romney in 1641; 'some say it signifieth a meeting'.)[1] It would be pleasing to know something of what went on at Fawsley, the residence of Richard Knightley, member for Northampton, where a group of influential members, many of them relatives of Hampden, met—presumably to discuss policy.

It would be unwise to assume from this large superiority in numbers of Parliamentarians who had sat before, that families with parliamentary influence were, for the most part, of that party. The number of those who had sat before has to be compared with the number of those who could have sat before. Of the members known to have been born in or before 1609, and therefore to have had a chance of election to an earlier Parliament, 157 were Royalists and 244 Parliamentarians. (Since most of the 21 Parliamentarians whose ages are not known were almost certainly well over thirty, the number of those who could have sat is probably more like 260.) In short, about half of the Royalists and half of the Parliamentarians who could have sat before did so.

This impression of youth being on the whole on the Royalist side is strongly confirmed by a study of the age-group table to be found at the end of the book. The figures there given are to be treated with some caution: some ages are estimated from the date of entry to a University or to one of the Inns of Court,

[1] Letter from Sir Norton Knatchbull in the possession of Sir Hughe Knatchbull-Hugessen. It appears in his forthcoming history of the family, which he kindly allowed us to see in typescript.

and the members whose ages have not been estimated at all are likely to be older than the average, thus weighting some of the age-groups unfairly; but the proportion of unknown ages and the risk of error are not high enough to damage the validity of the table as a basis of illustration. Little explanation is needed: it is at once clear that in every region the Royalists were younger men than the Parliamentarians. If members above and below forty are compared, the difference is most obvious in the West (Wales and the border) and least obvious, though still strongly marked, in the North and the South-east. The median ages of the two parties for the whole country have been worked out as thirty-six and forty-seven respectively—a very large difference.

Despite their youth, the Royalist members did not prove to have a better chance of living to see the Restoration. 106 of the 236 Royalists and 146 of the 302 Parliamentarians were still alive in 1661. 48 of the Royalist survivors and 25 of the Parliamentarians returned to the House of Commons, nearly all of them in the original Cavalier Parliament or at its numerous by-elections. In addition, 11 Royalists and 7 Parliamentarians sat as Peers. It should be borne in mind that, though an unusually large number of members did sit at a great age in the Cavalier Parliament, many were probably prevented by age from standing for election. Of the 21 Royalists from north of the Thames still alive in 1661 but not elected, one was Chief Justice of the Common Pleas and another became Attorney-General. One was Gentleman of the Bedchamber and Chief Justice of the Brecknock circuit. One, who had been M.P. for Carlisle while his father was county member, had his main residence in Yorkshire not Cumberland. A Westmorland landowner who had sat for a Yorkshire constituency did not sit himself in 1661, but his son was county member. Another, who had gone over to Parliament during the war, was an Irish Peer with his main interests in Ireland. Yet another obtained office as Surveyor of Works at Windsor Castle and Steward of the Forest of Windsor—his old constituency. In two cases representation in 1661 went back to an interest dominant through most of the century; in one of them a member of another branch of the family had sat in the Long Parliament. At Wallingford a member had probably owed his election in 1640 to his father being High Steward of the Borough. In 1661 his father was dead. At Ludlow a member who was accused of procuring his election in 1640 by sumptuous feasting of the burgesses was not elected in 1661. We do not know whether his hospitality was lacking. In one case a father and son who had both been impoverished in the wars may for that reason have been unable to resume the county seat until 1679.

Even this brief discussion of the election to the Cavalier Parliament has led inevitably from the members themselves to their families. At the highest level of politics it was clearly the ability and opportunities of the individual that counted; but at our parliamentary level the family in many ways mattered more. Unfortunately the term is not one that can easily be defined. An answer to the question what, in 1640, was considered to be a family relationship would be a vital contribution to social history, and one that does not seem to have been made by any of the leading historians of the period. Such an investigation would have taken us too far from the members of the Long Parliament, and we were compelled again to draw an arbitrary line. For the purpose of our statistics we decided to define 'relations' as father, sons, brothers, and on the male side only grandfather, grandsons, uncles, and nephews. In the regional studies we have frequently pointed out the importance of the relations of wives and mothers; but to investigate the connections by marriage of every member would be a completely unmanageable task. A calculation of the number of relatives of John Hampden sitting in the Long Parliament soon revealed that he had 80, and probably a good many more, for the project was abandoned when it was discovered that he was distantly related to the King. This *reductio ad absurdum* should not, however, lead us to suppose that the discovery of the extent of relevant relationships in the House is not one of the first jobs to be tackled when working on the biography of any seventeenth-century statesman.

In the Stuart period there were 26 Parliaments, including the Short Parliament of 1640 and the Convention of 1660, which like the Parliaments of the Interregnum are omitted from our tables. About one-third of all the M.P.s elected to the Long Parliament during its first two years belonged to families enjoying representation at least ten times under Stuart rule. The tables showing the parliamentary service of the relations of our members do not reveal any striking difference between the two sides. Allowing for their smaller numbers the Royalist families have rather more continuity than the Parliamentarian, both before and after the Long Parliament. In members whose relations had not sat in earlier Parliaments but continued after the Restoration the two sides are almost equal. It is in families with a Parliamentary record both before and after the war, and in those that had sat before but failed to continue that the Royalists come out best. It would be possible to extract a variety of other conclusions from this table too; but it would be at the risk of making the figures count for more than in our opinion they properly should. It is easy to produce lists of comparative percentages for this and that which would leave the reader breathless, bored, angry, sceptical or convinced according to his attitude towards statistics, but it would all be to very little purpose. One other point may, however, reasonably be made. There are more families with previous parliamentary experience who disappear from national politics in the Civil War period than there are families which came into the House during the Long Parliament and built up a parliamentary tradition after 1660. A survey of the list of returns for the Stuart period leaves the impression that, so far as continuity of political service is concerned, the Long Parliament belongs to the first half of the century. Many families represented regularly in earlier Parliaments disappear from the returns after 1660, and many more after the Cavalier and Exclusion Parliaments. This may often have been the result of impoverishment, as Professor Browning seems to indicate in his address to the Royal Historical Society on party politics in the reign of Charles II;[1] but it was also often the result of failure of the male line.

Analysis, with its artificial isolation of the different factors,

[1] *Transactions of the Royal Historical Society*, 4th Series, Vol. XXX.

may sometimes be an essential part of the historian's work; but if that work is to be complete there remains the further and far more difficult task of re-assembling those factors in such a way as to restore life to the society which is being studied. In short, though anatomy is in history as in medicine an indispensable study, it is desirable that practitioners should be capable of something more than dissection. Lack of evidence is one of the great limitations of the historian's work, and one which he can never entirely overcome, however high he may pile his accumulation of facts. Still, the obstacle is a slight one compared with his inability to penetrate men's minds. Study of motive must always be necessary and always unsuccessful, and it is in his struggle with this problem that the historian is tested. Crude theorising and attempts to assign men to general categories, or endeavours to estimate political, religious, and economic influences in their exact quantitative effect are, as we have already remarked, clearly absurd: how much more foolish then to practise on a large scale what is invalid in dealing with the individual. The study of motive is a delicate matter, and requires a sense of values; this sense the historian must not sacrifice, nor must he evade judgments of value by substituting judgments of quantity.

Inevitably therefore this particular study has a limited and largely negative value. We hope that it helps to clear the ground by disproving some historical legends and throwing doubts on others; but it has no illuminating explanation to put in their place. We tried to find out whether there were striking differences in social position between Royalist and Parliamentarian M.P.s, and what those differences were—whether they enjoyed a different status amongst that extremely large class, the landed gentry; whether in fact merchants and townsmen tended to take, as is often assumed, the side of Parliament rather than of the King. We found that Royalist and Parliamentarian, so far as can be judged from the members of the Long Parliament, were very much the same; that the greater and lesser gentry were not on different sides; that it made no difference whether a member belonged to an 'old' or to a 'new' family; that merchants and lawyers were to be found on both sides, and in such proportions as to make it doubtful whether there was any general hostility to the King amongst provincial merchants and certain that there was none amongst the lawyers. The only significant difference seems to have been that the Royalists were on average ten years younger, and more often belonged to families with a parliamentary history.

Though these discoveries have their importance, the main lesson learned from this investigation was of wider significance. Since Professor F. J. Turner inaugurated a new and successful approach to the history of the Democratic and Republican Parties in the United States,[1] it must have become apparent to more and more students of the history of both countries that investigation of local history might here too hold the key to the enigma of Whig and Tory development. It is hard for any-one born since the time of Jeremy Bentham to realise the extent to which public opinion was formerly a force of local growth and expression. This of course is what makes it so dangerous to accept as true of the whole country opinions which may indeed have been well-grounded but which are only valid for the district which the propounder of them really knew. Thus, for instance, the view of an honest and well-informed man like Baxter has been used as having national authority, when it only expressed his personal impression of what he was able to see for himself. So general is this error that a number of historians, naturally appalled by the difficulties of collecting information on a national scale, very reasonably study a county, or two or three counties, to illustrate, for instance, changes in ownership of land, but then go on most unreasonably to assume that their conclusions are valid for England as a whole. The urgent need in seventeenth-century history is for the investigation of the local origins of developments in national politics, so that the political and constitutional conflicts may be understood in their true setting.

[1] *The Significance of Sections in American History* (1932), and *The United States 1830-50* (1935).

CHAPTER II

THE RECRUITERS

THE question of electing new members to replace the 'disabled' Royalists and to fill the numerous vacancies caused by deaths was raised in the House several times in 1644.[1] London petitioners who asked for new elections were reproved[2] for their presumption; but in December both Whitelocke and the younger Vane suggested that this would be a more effective way of solving the problem of thin attendance than issuing repeated summonses to absent members. While the fighting continued there were obvious difficulties in organising the elections, which would involve almost every county. (Only Middlesex never had a Royalist member, though by 1642 all the Essex members too were on the Parliamentary side.) After Naseby the scheme became more practicable—provided of course that precautions could be taken to ensure that Royalists, avowed or unavowed, were not again elected. On 21 August 1645, in response to a petition from the Borough of Southwark, the House resolved that the first new writs should be issued. Hythe and Bury St. Edmunds received them on the same day, and thereafter they were granted at frequent intervals and without difficulty. By the end of the year nearly 150 vacancies had been dealt with. The year 1646 saw the process of filling the places of the Royalists almost completed, though in some counties, notably Cornwall, there were elections in the first months of 1647. The new members for Fowey were not returned until April and July 1648. Meanwhile there had arisen a few normal vacancies,

[1] C.J. 30 Sept. and 18 Oct. 1644.
[2] C.J. 28 Oct. See also the article on the Recruiters by R. N. Kershaw in *History*, Vol. VIII.

through the deaths of Recruiters or of more original members, and writs for these were usually issued at once. After Pride's Purge there was much more difficulty in holding new elections. Half a dozen members elected under writs already issued were allowed to take their seats, and there were seven new writs in the two years after the Purge. The last member admitted to the Parliament was Anthony Ashley Cooper. His election for Downton in 1640 was disputed, and before it was settled he had joined the King. In 1645, when he had become a supporter of the Parliament, a further report on the election was called for but never made.[1] (His own explanation was that the hostility and influence of Denzil Holles kept him out.) In January 1660 he was admitted without opposition.[2]

With the Recruiters, as with the original members, there are inevitable doubts about the inclusion of men who were returned but cannot be shown with certainty to have taken their seats. It is unlikely that Fairfax would appear in the Rump, and there is no record that he did so, though his election for Cirencester was declared valid in February 1649. A writ for St. Germans, issued in the apparently mistaken belief that the original member, John Moyle, was dead,[3] produced the return of a former Royalist officer, William Scawen, who would certainly have been expelled if he had tried to take his seat.[4] For our statistical purposes we have counted as Recruiters all who first sat in or after 1645, and all who were validly elected in those years and cannot be shown with reasonable certainty to have been refused admittance. This gives a total, including those who replaced other Recruiters and those who were admitted after Pride's Purge, of 275.[5]

The House did not take any extreme measures to control the elections. It ordered that all new members should subscribe to the National League and Covenant, and that no-one who had

---

[1] *C.J.* 1 Sept. 1645.　　　　[2] *C.J.* 12 Jan. 1659-60.

[3] Pink MSS. The election of another John Moyle for E. Looe makes it difficult to be certain about this.

[4] *Western Antiquary*, 1887-8, p. 40.

[5] Including Cooper. Kershaw seems to have put the total between 269 and 274.

been in arms against the Parliament should be allowed to sit.[1] An earlier resolution of 15 May 1643, disfranchising borough electors who had been at war against the Parliament, was still in force; but a proposal to exclude from the right to compound for their estates any Royalists who tried to get in was not carried.[2] Some men with unostentatious sympathies for the Royalist cause may have found their way into the House. The Recruiter for Tiverton, Robert Shapcote, was in 1654 alleged by the 'well-affected inhabitants' to be 'of Royalist leanings'—but he continued to sit in all the Protectorate Parliaments. At a time when 'Royalist' was the obvious political 'smear' word such evidence is not worth much. Only two Royalist Recruiters were brought to the notice of the House. Edmund Hudson was returned for King's Lynn (not Lyme Regis, for which he appears in the Official Return), and was pronounced incapable of sitting because of his part in a Royalist riot in Lynn when he was Mayor.[3] George Devereux, elected for Montgomery, was reported to be under sequestration as a Royalist and suspended from sitting.[4] Apart from the exclusion of such men the House, and the Committee of Privileges under Sir Robert Harley, maintained their practice of fairness to the electors in cases of dispute. The election at Reading was annulled because a poll had been demanded and refused. Ludlow tells how his uncle was returned as a member for Hindon by the principal burgesses and the bailiff; 'yet the rabble of the town, many of whom lived upon the alms of one Mr. George How, pretending that they had chosen the latter, the sheriff returned them both'.[5] How, who got to the House first, was prevented from sitting; but the Committee seems never to have decided the case. Ludlow's account of his own election suggests that the Earl of Pembroke was continuing his activities in the choice of candidates, though the House had ordered that every writ should be accompanied by a reminder of a resolution of December 1641 forbidding Peers to write letters for the purpose of influencing elections.[6]

[1] C.J. 21 Aug. and 1 Sept. 1645.
[2] C.J. 5 July 1647.
[3] C.J. 5 July 1647.
[4] C.J. 15 April 1647.
[5] Ludlow, Memoirs (ed. Firth), Vol. I, p. 132.
[6] C.J. 16 Oct. 1645.

There is little evidence of official pressure on the electors. When the Committee of Safety wrote to the Corporation of Hythe, they were content to urge them to choose 'men of courage, fearing God, and having consciences'.[1]

In the regions that were still under military control it was almost inevitable that there should be at least the suspicion of electoral pressure by army commanders. In November 1645 the House ordered that elections must take place 'without any Interruption or Molestation by any Commander, Governor, Officer, or Soldier, that hath not in the County, City, or Borough, respectively, Right of electing'.[2] The danger was not imaginary. The writs for the elections at Stafford and Newcastle-under-Lyme were taken by the messenger to Sir William Brereton, commander of the Parliamentary forces, who passed them on to the Sheriff. But at Stafford the candidate Brereton most favoured, Sir Richard Skeffington ('whom I should highly commend if he stood not to me in the relation of a brother-in-law') was beaten by one vote. At Newcastle things went even worse; for the Steward, Bradshaw, was defeated, and 'the ill-affected rabbell' carried the election in favour of Samuel Terrick, a London merchant of a local family, whom Brereton described as 'a newter at best'.[3] Colonel Hutchinson as Governor of Nottingham was in his own county. 'The Town', says Mrs. Hutchinson, 'would needs in a compliment make the Governor free in order to elect him to the Parliament,' He accepted the county seat instead, but 'employed his interest in the town . . . and having very many in his regiment that had votes, sent them all home the night before the election'.[4]

Opinions differed on the extent to which the elections and the military influence on them would affect the attitude of the House to the war and the army. Ludlow feared that the electors would choose 'such as were most likely to be for a peace upon

[1] Hythe Corporation MSS. quoted in G. Wilks, *Barons of the Cinque Ports,* p. 82.   [2] *C.J.* 17 Nov. 1645.
[3] Letter-book of Sir William Brereton. Brit. Mus. Add. MSS. 11332, pp. 21, 23, 95-8. See Appendix iii for an account of the election at Stafford.
[4] *Memoirs of the Life of Colonel Hutchinson* (Everyman edn.), p. 230.

any terms'.[1] On the other hand it was widely assumed that the prestige, if not the threats, of the victorious army would lead to the choice of men on the left rather than the right wing of the Parliamentary side. The opponents of the issue of writs were, as Gardiner points out, mainly from the 'Peace' party.[2] Later, and especially after Pride's Purge, pamphleteers developed the idea that the Recruiters were obscure townsmen or upstart colonels. It is true that the number of officers among them was large. It is hardly possible to give relevant figures, since many who called themselves colonels had seen little active service and were certainly civilians by the time they were elected. Then, as now, M.P.s tended to adopt or abandon their military titles as political expediency required. Including militia regiments roughly a quarter of the Recruiters held or had held the rank of colonel or a higher one, and several more were active in the Army as majors or captains. Some of the most prominent officers were elected for boroughs with which they had no connection other than that due to the war. Skippon, who came of a Norfolk family, was returned for Barnstaple; Fairfax and Nathaniel Rich were involved in a dispute at Cirencester with two Gloucestershire landowners. Two of the leaders in the Army's political disputes were also elected as 'outsiders'—Ireton for Appleby and Rainsborough for Droitwich. A few obscure townsmen who had won success in the Army were elected for their local boroughs; a few richer townsmen who could in any case have expected election held office in militia regiments. But the majority of the colonels in Parliament were gentry who had stepped as easily into military leadership during the war as they did into leadership of local affairs in normal times. Their political outlook was not necessarily coloured by their military experience, and they included many strong opponents of the Army's political domination. The course of events makes it clear that the prospect of that domination did not depend on a majority in a free Parliament.

Another complaint of the pamphleteers was that there might

[1] Ludlow, *Memoirs* (ed. Firth), Vol. I, p. 132.
[2] S. R. Gardiner, *History of the Great Civil War*, Vol. II, p. 336.

be an influx of lawyers. This was completely unjustified: the number of barristers among the Recruiters was 33—twelve per cent. compared with just under fourteen per cent. of the original Parliament. Nor was there any appreciable increase in the number of townsmen. Here and there an alderman appeared in place of a member of a Royalist landed family; but in general only the boroughs that had returned townsmen before did so again. They were in some cases townsmen of a lower status than their predecessors.

The great families were by no means unrepresented in the new elections. The Herberts did not quite make up their losses; but three of them entered the House between 1645 and 1649. James, fourth son of the 4th Earl of Pembroke, succeeded to Sir James Thynne's seat for Wiltshire; his brother John sat for Monmouthshire, succeeding a third brother, William, who was disabled as a Royalist, and joining a very distant cousin Henry who had been elected in 1642. Lastly, in April 1649, when the House of Lords had been abolished, the Earl himself found a county seat, for Berkshire.[1] As before, the Herberts took the precaution of distributing their favours between the two sides. James was secluded at the Purge, and afterwards sat with several of his Royalist relations in the Cavalier Parliament; John and the Earl were Rumpers. Another head of a noble and political family who entered the Commons in 1649 was William Cecil, Earl of Salisbury, who had the King's Lynn seat from which William Hudson had been ejected. Altogether we can count 15 Recruiters who were sons of Peers, including 5 who inherited the title. Three others were themselves created Peers, Lord Howard of Escrick before his election in 1649, Edward Montagu and George Booth at the Restoration. Arthur Annesley, who inherited an Irish Peerage, also had an English one conferred at the Restoration.

Thirteen Recruiters were baronets at the time of their election, 8 by creation and 5 by inheritance. This is considerably fewer than in the original Parliament. After the Restoration 14

---

[1] See the account of his delight in Walker, *History of Independency* (1660 edn.), Part II, p. 115.

Recruiters received baronetcies, compared with 13 of the original members—but Restoration baronetcies are little indication of social standing. There were also 8 who inherited baronetcies after their election, 6 before and 2 after the Restoration. The figures for knighthoods show a more marked discrepancy: only 14 Recruiters were knights at the time of their election; 2 more were knighted by the Protector, and 14 by Charles II. In all therefore only fifteen per cent. of them became knights, compared with thirty-four per cent. of the original members. This is not so strong an indication of a lower social status for the Recruiters as might appear. The figures have to be read in conjunction with the dates of birth and the rate at which such titles were being conferred upon—or thrust upon—men of this class at the time when the members in question would normally be eligible to receive them. Many of the knights in the original Parliament were among the exceptionally large number dubbed by James I. Those who came of age or acquired wealth by inheritance or otherwise during the war had little prospect of a new title until 1660, and even then, though many arrears were made up, knighthoods were less common than financial considerations had formerly made them.

The war might also affect figures for the Universities and Inns of Court. Admissions to both fell off sharply after 1642, and the normal careers of those Recruiters who were young enough to have completed their education during the war could easily be interfered with. Nevertheless 75 Recruiters had been to Oxford and 44 to Cambridge. The percentage, forty-six, is only slightly below that of the original members, and incidentally the ratio between the two Universities is almost exactly the same. For the Inns of Court the figures are: Middle Temple 29, Inner Temple 33, Gray's Inn 50, Lincoln's Inn 42, total 154. This is fifty-five per cent., a little higher than the original Royalists and a little lower than the original Parliamentarians.

The fact that the Recruiters were a considerably younger group than the original Parliamentary members is also relevant to the question of their previous parliamentary experience. Nevertheless, 148 of them are known to have been old enough

to sit in or before 1628. Only 17 did so, and only 13 in the
Short Parliament of 1640. Some of these were members of
distinguished families who had a long parliamentary record
and had unexpectedly failed to find a seat at the earlier elections.
Sir John Danvers had sat in every Parliament since his first
election for Arundel in 1610; Sir Edward Spencer, elected for
Middlesex in 1648, had already sat for the county in 1626, and
for the family borough of Brackley in several earlier Parliaments.
Others, such as Nicholas Stoughton (Guildford) had sat in one
or two Parliaments of the 1620s for a borough which other
members of their family frequently represented. But the discrepancy is partly a reflection of the fact that a considerable
number of Recruiters came from families which, though they
held lands and heraldic arms, had not normally sent members
to Westminster. This is borne out by the table of relations in
earlier and later Parliaments. One hundred and nine of the
Recruiters had paternal grandfathers, uncles, fathers, or brothers
who had been M.P.s before 1640—forty per cent. compared with
fifty per cent. of the original Parliamentary and sixty-five per
cent. of the original Royalist members. It is not a big difference, but it is sufficiently large, and sufficiently well-distributed
geographically, to be significant. The discrepancy is greater in
the figures for later Parliaments. Of the 182 surviving Recruiters
32 sat themselves; 82 had sons, nephews, or grandsons who
sat—thirty per cent., compared with forty-five per cent. of the
Parliamentary and fifty-three per cent. of the Royalist members
of the original House. These figures include 46 Recruiters whose
families were in Parliament both before and after the Interregnum. The chances of a Recruiter being the last of a line of
M.P.s were therefore about the same as those of an original
Parliamentary member, his chances of being the first of a line
rather less.

The impression is then that there was a tendency, as we
should expect, for the Recruiters to come in rather greater
numbers than their predecessors from the less prominent of the
county gentry. But the great majority were the same sort of
men from the same sort of families—and often from the same

families—as the original members. The vacant seats were filled by men who lived in or near the county, or who had the same connections with it by marriage or ancestry or property as were found before. Often a Recruiter joined or succeeded a father or brother who had been elected in 1640 for the same place, or for a borough in the same county; and the earlier member was sometimes a Royalist. James Bellingham was returned for Westmorland in place of his father Sir Henry, disabled to sit. Sir Sidney Montagu, disabled and dead, was succeeded by his son, the later Earl of Sandwich. Anthony Hungerford had sat for Malmesbury and joined the Oxford Parliament; his brother Henry was elected for Great Bedwin in 1646. Henry Stapleton, Recruiter for Boroughbridge, was the nephew of the Royalist member for Knaresborough, Sir Henry Slingsby. There were several sons of distinguished Parliamentarians: Francis Holles (Lostwithiel), John Lenthall (Gloucester), Alexander Pym (Newport). But there were also relations of distinguished Royalists. Sir Alexander Carew (Cornwall 1640) was executed for his treachery to the Parliament; his half-brother John Carew (Tregony 1647) was executed at the Restoration as a regicide.

Somerset

Even in areas that were predominantly Royalist in their original membership, and where consequently the number of elections was great and many would-be candidates were likely to be disqualified, the new members came mainly from the same small circle as the old. Somerset had elections for all but 2 of its 16 seats in 1645 or 1646. The county election[1] was a source of many complaints. The story, as pieced together by the Committee of Privileges, follows familiar lines. The High Sheriff, Sir John Horner, summoned the freeholders to Ilchester, and about a thousand of them assembled. Then the Clerk held the County Court in the early morning, when only 20 electors were present, and adjourned it to Queen Camel, where eventually two members were declared elected. After several petitions,

[1] S. W. B. Harbin, *Members of Parliament for the County of Somerset*, p. 150; C.J. 9 Dec. 1645, 1 and 9 Jan. 1645-6, 5 June 1646.

and a report that the election was 'a principal cause of the present distractions in the County', the House declared the return void and issued a new writ. But the same men were re-elected. One of them was George Horner, son of Sir John, and descendant of the John Horner who as Steward of Glastonbury pulled out a rich plum for himself from the Abbey lands. George was suspected of Royalism—'a known neuter if not worse'— and his fellow member John Harrington, a lawyer from another Somerset 'monastic' family, had many Royalist relations.

Of the 12 new members for Somerset boroughs all but one were local men. The exception was Walter Strickland[1] of Boynton, Yorkshire, member for Minehead, who had long been serving as agent in the United Provinces for the Parliamentary government. The other Minehead Recruiter, Colonel Edward Popham,[2] was succeeding his father. Sir Thomas Wroth[3] (Bridgwater) replaced his deceased brother. James Ashe[4] (Bath) was a lawyer whose father and uncle were original members for Wiltshire seats. Both he and the third lawyer Recruiter, Lislibone Long[5] (Wells) had estates near their boroughs. The other local landowners were William Strode[6] (Ilchester), son of a clothier who had bought lands in several parts of the county; Thomas Hodges[7] (Ilchester) of Wedmore; Clement Walker[8] (Wells) whose seat was at Charterhouse, seven miles from the borough; and William Carent[9] (Milborne Port). The second Milborne Port member, Thomas Grove,[10] was one of many elected for that frontier borough who came from a neighbouring county. His seat at Ferne House, Wiltshire, was

---

[1] D.N.B.

[2] Collinson, *Somerset*, I, p. 264; II, p. 483; III, p. 71. Burke, *Landed Gentry*.

[3] Collinson, *Somerset*, III, p. 67.

[4] Hoare, *Wiltshire*, I (ii), p. 118; III (i), p. 41. *Somerset and Dorset Notes and Queries*, III, p. 179. Phillipps, *Visitation of Somerset*, 5. Burke, *Landed Gentry*.

[5] D.N.B. Burke, *Commoners*, IV, p. 65.

[6] *Somerset Archaeological and Natural History Society*, XIII (2), p. 6. *Somerset and Dorset Notes and Queries*, I, p. 236.

[7] *Visitation of Somerset*, pp. 100, 101.

[8] D.N.B.

[9] Collinson, *Somerset*, II, pp. 203, 366, 383; III, p. 207.

[10] Hoare, *Wiltshire*, IV (i), p. 58. Burke, *Landed Gentry*.

15 miles from the borough. He sat for Wiltshire and for Marlborough in the Protectorate Parliaments, and for Shaftesbury, much nearer his home, in 1660. The remaining Recruiters both represented their home towns: John Palmer,[1] the doctor from Taunton who became Warden of All Souls, and Robert Blake[2] the Bridgwater merchant, not yet an admiral but already a colonel.

Hampshire

Hampshire, with only 6 Royalists among its 26 original members, was a county which had no shortage of Parliamentarian gentry to fill the 9 seats that were vacant in 1645. The new county member was Richard Norton[3] ('Idle Dick') of Alresford. He had many parliamentary connections: his father, grandfather, and great-grandfather had all sat for the county before him; his first marriage, to the daughter of Walter Erle of Charborough, brought him into the extensive Fiennes connection; and he took as his second wife the daughter of Lord Say and Sele himself. John Kemp[4] (Christchurch) who had three times been Mayor of the borough he now represented, was one of the Recruiters who had sat in the Short Parliament. He was the first of his line to sit; but through his mother he was related to the Royalist Sheriff Sir John Oglander. Kemp's fellow Recruiter for Christchurch, Richard Edwards,[5] was a barrister and Senior Registrar of Chancery. His father was seated in Bedfordshire, but Richard had married the daughter of Sir Henry Whitehead of Norman Court, Hampshire, whose son, another Richard, was already sitting for the county. Sir John Barrington[6] (Newtown) had just succeeded to the baronetcy. His father and uncle had both sat for Newtown, and his grandfather and great-grandfather for Essex. He was second cousin to Cromwell and was brought into closer touch with the great

[1] Collinson, *Somerset*, I, p. 254. C. Grant Robertson, *All Souls College*, p. 123.

[2] *D.N.B.*   [3] Burke, *Commoners*, IV, p. 79 and *Extinct Baronetage*.

[4] F. Hitchen-Kemp, *History of the Kemp Families*, IV p. 32. We are indebted to the Vicar of Boldre, where Kemp is buried, for further information.

[5] *V.C.H. Beds.* II, pp. 262, 282.

[6] *V.C.H.* V, p. 219. G.E.C. *Baronetage.*

network of Oliver's relations in Parliament when his son married a daughter of Robert Rich, Earl of Warwick. The other Hampshire Recruiters had less distinguished connections. Two of them, John Bulkley[1] (Newtown) and Thomas Hussey[2] (Whitchurch) were minor gentry. Hussey had bought the manor of Laverstoke, a mile or two from his borough, in 1637; after his election he became a considerable purchaser of Hampshire lands, including part of the Bishop of Winchester's huge confiscated estate. Bulkley's ancestors had acquired the manors of Charford and Nether Burgate in the reign of Henry VI, and do not appear to have increased their estate since then. Neither had any close relations in Parliament, but Bulkley had himself sat for Yarmouth in the Short Parliament.

There were two more lawyers. William Stephens[3] (Newport) was Recorder of the borough for which he succeeded to Falkland's seat. His father had been member for Newport in 1593, but unless the compilers of the Crown Office list have made some complicated blunders it was for the other Newport, in Cornwall. William's son and grandson were returned for the Isle of Wight borough in many later Stuart Parliaments. The other barrister, Nicholas Love,[4] was Recorder of Basingstoke and sat for Winchester. His father had been Warden of Winchester College and Chaplain to James I, and Nicholas just before his election achieved a highly lucrative post as one of the six clerks in Chancery. (He had made £20,000 out of it by 1660.) He too was able to share in the distribution of the Bishopric lands. Finally there is Edward Boote[5] (or Boate), Master Shipwright of Portsmouth. We know nothing of his origins except that he seems to have worked at one time in Chatham; but he had been employed by the Parliament in 1644 on a commission for felling the timber on delinquents' estates for the use of the Navy. He was returned as member for Portsmouth in 1646, but took no active part in debates or committees.

---

[1] *V.C.H.* IV, pp. 562, 570.
[2] *V.C.H.* III, p. 349; IV, pp. 209, 213, 302, 513.
[3] *V.C.H.* V, p. 99.   [4] *D.N.B.*
[5] *Notes and Queries*, 31 Aug. 1912.

Berkshire

Berkshire elected 7 Recruiters of widely different origins. For the county sat Sir Francis Pile,[1] 2nd baronet, of Compton Beauchamp, which the family had possessed only since 1617. His grandfather had been Sheriff in 1620 and he was Sheriff himself from 1643 to 1645; he died in 1649 when not much more than thirty. Through his first wife he was a cousin of Edmund Dunch,[2] M.P. for Wallingford; through his second he was son-in-law of a bishop. His baronetcy went to his brother, a Wiltshire landowner—their mother was a Popham—and became extinct in 1761. His death enabled the Earl of Pembroke, head of a vast parliamentary clan, to enter the House of Commons as Knight of the Shire.

William Ball,[3] Recruiter for Abingdon, was one of the four attorneys of the Office of Pleas in the Exchequer Court. He died in 1648 and was succeeded at Abingdon by a much more colourful figure, Henry Neville.[4] The Nevilles of Billingbear were descended from a younger son of Lord Bergavenny who died in 1491. Billingbear had belonged to Wolsey and passed to the Crown by forfeiture; it was alienated to the Nevilles in 1552. Henry's great-grandfather had sat for the county five times, and his grandfather, ambassador to France, had sat for the county and for Windsor. Henry, who was born in 1620, spent most of the war travelling on the Continent. He returned an active Republican, and was elected to the House in April 1649; at the end of 1651 he was on the Council of State, but retired from active politics through hostility to Cromwell. In 1656 he was elected for Reading, and became a vigorous member of Harrington's Republican group. Neville did not share Harrington's rare if limited political genius; but he was a lively writer, and an editor and admirer of Machiavelli. He was imprisoned at the Restoration, but soon released—for he was certainly not dangerous. An elder half-brother, Richard, who had taken the Royalist side, sat for the county in 1670, and a nephew—a Whig—from 1695 to 1710.

---

[1] G.E.C. *Baronetage V.C.H. Berks*, IV, p. 525. [2] *V.C.H.* IV, pp. 382-3.
[3] *V.C.H.* III, pp. 201, 238. [4] *D.N.B., V.C.H.* III, pp. 178-81.

Both the Knollyses who sat for Reading had died by 1648. An election dispute resulted from the first death and when it was eventually resolved the two Recruiters were Tanfield Vachell[1] and Daniel Blagrave.[2] The Vachells were a fourteenth-century family, one of them being Knight of the Shire in 1324; Tanfield Vachell of Coley, the family's main seat, had been pricked as Sheriff by the King. He was related to John Hampden, who married in 1641 his uncle's widow; this aunt was the daughter of Sir Francis Knollys, so that Vachell was succeeding his great-uncle's son. Vachell was secluded in 1648 and died in 1658, his property going to a cousin Thomas; his namesake Tanfield represented Reading at the beginning of the eighteenth century and was probably a Whig, certainly an anti-Tacker. Coley was sold in 1727.

The Blagraves had been an important family in Reading since their acquisition of Southcotes in 1545 and later of Bulmarsh. Daniel, third son of Anthony and of one of the Burlaces of Little Marlow (a borough they tried to represent without success in 1640) was cousin of Sir John Blagrave of Southcotes; his father had been Sheriff in 1603. He is said to have been a barrister, but he is not in the printed register of the Inns of Court, and may be one of several men who were given legal office without proper qualification. He was made Recorder of Reading in 1645 and, though dismissed in 1656, was restored in 1658. He also received the office of Exigenter in the Court of Common Pleas, and that of Master in Chancery. He was a regicide and Rumper and sat for Reading again in 1656 and 1659; at the Restoration, after having on the whole kept in with a succession of governments, he fled abroad. The Southcotes influence remained strong at Reading; Blagrave's nephew sat for it in the Cavalier Parliament and his great-nephew later.

Robert Packer,[3] Recruiter for Wallingford, obtained his estate at Shillingford from his father, who had been Clerk of the Privy Seal in 1604, and later secretary to the Duke of Buckingham. Robert was son-in-law of Edward Stephens, M.P.

[1] V.C.H. III, p. 364.
[2] D.N.B., V.C.H. III, pp. 365-6.   [3] V.C.H. IV, p. 476.

for Tewkesbury, and brother-in-law of John Gell, son of the Parliamentary commander in Derbyshire. He was also brother-in-law of John Browne, who was Clerk of the House of Lords in the Cavalier Parliament. He was secluded and sat again for Wallingford in the Convention, the Cavalier Parliament, and in 1679.

There was little justification then for fears and allegations about the effect of the recruiting on the social structure of the House. It is equally difficult to show any direct effect on the balance of political power. It is true that many prominent and extreme Independents were Recruiters—some of them men who would have been less likely to appear at a normal election. Everyone knows about Rainsborough's politics; and a less celebrated Recruiter, Major Thomas Scott, was also involved in Leveller activities. Scott, who sat for Aldborough, was arrested by order of the House for his part in the Ware mutiny, and died in prison. His namesake the Scoutmaster-General, Recruiter for Aylesbury, was a leading Republican, a member of the chief Rump committees, and a regicide. The Cromwellians among the new members[1] included Oliver's later son-in-law Charles Fleetwood (Marlborough); Oliver's brother-in-law John Jones (Merionethshire); and Oliver's cousin Richard Ingoldsby (Wendover), who having demonstrated that his signature on the Death Warrant must have been a forgery, was made a K.B. at the Coronation and sat in the Cavalier Parliament. Many more names could be listed; but they do not show that the filling of the vacant seats realised the fears of a huge influx of Independents and irreconcilables.

There were indications long before the recruiting approached completion that on religious matters the extreme Presbyterians were having a more difficult time in the House. On 3 February 1645-6 there was a debate on a Declaration, in answer to one of the King's communications, in which the question of religious toleration was involved. The Presbyterians succeeded by a

---

[1] Richard Cromwell appears as Recruiter for Portsmouth in the list in Carlyle's *Cromwell*, but there seems to be no evidence that he sat.

majority of only 7 (105 : 98) in including in it the reservation 'so far as may stand with the word of God and the Peace of the Church and Kingdom'. In April the Presbyterians were defeated by 88 votes to 76 when the Westminster Assembly's petition against appointing Parliamentary Commissioners to judge 'scandalous offences' was voted a breach of privilege.[1] But in matters where the secular jurisdiction of the new Church was raised some members—particularly, as Gardiner suggests, the lawyers—would be likely to support the Independents whatever their doctrinal views. In the large houses of 1646 moderate Presbyterianism and moderate readiness to come to terms with the King had a majority. It was only when considerable numbers of the moderates absented themselves that the Independents and the Army supporters carried their votes. In the first large body of Independents to make themselves known—the 58 signatories of the 'Engagement of the Lords and Commoners that went to the Army'—there were 33 Recruiters.[2] Of the signatories of the King's Death Warrant[3] 44 were M.P.s, and again the Recruiters —28—were in a majority. Of the 209 members we have listed as sitting in the Rump, 118, fifty-seven per cent., were Recruiters. The difference is in any case too small to have much importance; and if we take into account the fact that the number of original members alive and qualified to sit was slightly less than the number of Recruiters—247 compared with 256—it becomes smaller still.

At the return of the Rump the preponderance of Recruiters was rather more marked: there are 77 of them in Masson's list[4] of 122 who sat in the summer of 1659. More than half of them had also sat in one or more of the Protectorate Parliaments; and these too contained considerably more Recruiters than original members. But again the comparative youth—and perhaps the comparative absence of disillusionment—of the Recruiters could account for the difference.

[1] C.J. 11 April 1646.
[2] See below, p. 38.
[3] The names are in Appendix VI, and in Gardiner, Civil War IV, p. 309, which gives also the regicides who were not M.P.s.
[4] Life of Milton, V, p. 453.

The outcome of the elections gave, in short, little cause for alarm either to the left or the right. Independency was perceptibly, but only just perceptibly, stronger among the new members than among the old. Such immediate new strength as the left derived depended not so much on the higher proportion of their supporters among the Recruiters as on the tendency of the Presbyterians and peacemakers to stay away. But in the next 15 years the Recruiters played the increasingly prominent part which their years and the political circumstances would naturally produce. The victory of Independency was not won primarily in Parliament, nor helped appreciably by a change in the kind of men who sat there. How far it was the cause of such a change we can now enquire.

CHAPTER III

THE RUMP

THE 'secluding' of the opponents of the Commonwealth is the only point in the history of the Long Parliament at which we can divide all the members on the Parliamentary side into two opposing sections. For the crucial votes of the pre-war period, such as those on the Root and Branch Bill and the Grand Remonstrance, no lists have been found and it is most unlikely that any ever existed. Nor is it possible during the war to name, apart from the score or so of leaders, the members of the constantly shifting and disintegrating groups. The most we can say is that generally those who can be identified as enthusiasts for the prosecution of the war appear, if they survived, in the Rump.[1] The 58 members[2] who signed the 'Engagement of the Lords and Commons that went to the Army' in 1647, after the Presbyterian City mob had invaded the House, may include the solid core of the civilian Independents. But the voting strength of their side immediately after their return was 94, and in January the Vote of No Addresses had 141 supporters. It was a situation in which, more perhaps than at any other time, the individual Member of Parliament had to decide afresh in each debate how to vote or whether to stay away. His religious allegiance might be unshakable; but it did not necessarily

---

[1] See for instance the Committee for raising a new army, set up in July 1643 in response to a City petition. All but one of its surviving members were Rumpers. (*C.J.* 20 July 1643; Hexter, *The Reign of King Pym*, p. 123.)

[2] The lists of signatories in the *Lords Journals* (Vol. IX p. 385) and in Rushworth, *Historical Collections* (Part IV p. 755) differ slightly from each other and greatly from the list of absentees in H.M.C. Egmont MSS. I, p. 440, though all three contain 58 names. According to Rushworth the signatories include some who sat in the Speaker's absence. Mrs. Hutchinson puts the number of absentees at 100, Walker at about 40.

determine his attitude to the vital constitutional questions that
were constantly under discussion. The terms 'Presbyterian' and
'Independent' became accepted as the political labels for the
right and left wing, and are so used here. Without entering into
the vast question of the relation between religious and political
ideas, it can fairly be claimed that the terms have only a little
more connection with their derivative sense than 'Whig' and
'Tory' a century later. It has been shown[1] that not merely some
but in all probability most of the Independents were also Presbyterians, in the sense that they accepted the Presbyterian
Church and in many cases became its elders. But whatever
names should be applied to the two political sides, members
were almost compelled, between December 1648 and June 1649,
to identify themselves with one or the other. For 'Pride's Purge'
was in fact only the beginning of a process that lasted for nearly
seven months and was even then not quite completed.

On 27 November 1648 the Parliamentary Commissioners,
who ten weeks earlier had been appointed to negotiate with
Charles, left Newport with his 'final' answers. On 5 December
after an all-night sitting 'the question was propounded, That
the Answers of the King to the Propositions of both Houses are
a Ground for the House to proceed for the settlement of the
peace of the Kingdom'. By 129 votes to 83 the motion was
carried. In the afternoon a meeting of Army officers and some of
their supporters in the House discussed the possibility of forcing
a dissolution and a new election; but to this the M.P.s present
would not agree. A Committee of 3 members and 3 officers was
set up to decide what other course could be taken to put a stop
to negotiations with the King. It was on their authority that
Colonel Pride, commander of the regiment of foot that had
taken over the guarding of the House, appeared next morning
with a list of members, who were identified for him as they
arrived by Lord Grey of Groby. Most of those who were refused
admittance went away and were not molested any further;
those who tried to insist on their right to enter the House were
taken into custody; but it is not clear whether Pride had a list of

[1] By J. H. Hexter in *American Historical Review*, No. 44.

members who were to be arrested in any event. Nor do we know how many names in all were on his paper. In the message[1] brought from the General Council of Officers later in the day the demand was for the exclusion of the Eleven Members formerly impeached by the Army, together with those 'to the number of 90 and odd' who had opposed the vote declaring the Scots to be enemies and their supporters traitors. (There were two votes on this, on the 14th and 20th of July, but the Journals do not record a division on either.) The message goes on to invite 'all such faithful members who are innocent in these things' to identify themselves so that the rest could be excluded. A round-up of Independents was urgently necessary, for many members who had not encountered Pride's men had ceased to attend, and there was difficulty in getting the quorum of 40. Accordingly a Committee was set up to make arrangements for members who had been present at the vote on 5 December to declare that they had opposed it. On 20 December about 40 members rose in the House to declare their dissent. Their names were not recorded in the *Journals* (from which the record of the episode was erased in 1660); but a formal Declaration was drafted for signature. In the next few days 43 members put their names to it. On 1 February another 20 names were added, and it was ordered that all who were not present on 5 December but opposed the move for a settlement with the King should record the fact by 1 March. But the House had to balance its zeal for excluding enemies of the Commonwealth against its need for larger numbers, and several absent members were granted an extension of the time limit. On 5 March a new Committee was set up to report on members who gave satisfaction for their failure to enter their dissent by the appointed date, and it made frequent recommendations for admission. On 9 June lists of those who had and those who had not sat since January were presented to the House. A proposal that any more

---

[1] Rushworth, *Historical Collections*, Part IV, Vol. II, p. 1355. Prynne (who was arrested himself) and Walker give this version of the arrests, which is adopted by Masson (III, 606) and Gardiner (IV, 270). Ludlow (I, 210) says it was 'the most suspected' who were seized.

members admitted should be required to make a further declaration approving of the trial of the King was rejected; but a new time limit was fixed. The Committee was to sit every morning until 30 June to consider applications for admission; after that date arrangements would be made for new elections to replace the members still not sitting. No such elections were held, but it is reasonable to suppose that the members who stayed away after the announcement did so with the intention of identifying themselves decisively with the opposition to the Commonwealth. In October it was resolved that all members should take the Engagement 'to be true and faithful to the Commonwealth . . . without a King or House of Lords'. The Committee for admissions was re-established on 10 October 1651; it recommended the admission of Thomas Westrow and Thomas Wodehouse at once, and of two more members, Colonel Norton and John Stephens, on 26 and 27 November.[1]

The names in Prynne, Walker, and the *Commons Journals* of members entering their dissent do not include all the Rumpers. Several contemporary lists have survived: the earliest of them names 89 members sitting in 1649;[2] a folio leaf entitled 'A Perfect List of Rumpers' printed in March 1660 contains 121 names; 'A Catalogue of the Names of the Present Parliament' printed in 1659 has 138. The fullest is a list, over the name of the Clerk of the Commons, of 179 members sitting by 27 May 1652.[3] This coincides very closely with a list we compiled from the *Commons Journals* of members serving on Committees or otherwise shown as sitting, though it sometimes confuses Christian names and has a few who are most unlikely to have sat. From the *Journals* and the lists of dissents to the vote of 5 December we arrived at a total for purposes of analysis of 209 Rumpers—forty-two per cent. of the members sitting in December 1648 or elected later. Nothing like this number normally sat: the divisions show that an ordinary attendance was anything from 30 to 80. Nor did they all return when the

---

[1] See *Commons Journals* for the dates mentioned.
[2] Brit. Mus. Thomason Collection E 536.
[3] Brit. Mus. Thomason Collection E 1246 (2).

Rump was restored in May 1659. Masson, by a similar process of collating the *Journals* with contemporary lists, arrived at 122 as the number then sitting.[1] No Rump division approached the high proportion of the total membership that was sometimes achieved in the pre-war period: 361 members voted on 6 June 1641, and 307 on the Grand Remonstrance in November. But a normal number in 1641-2 was from a quarter to a half of the total membership of 507, and the proportion during the war often fell as low as in the Rump.

While the Independents were thus building up a safe and sizable Parliament, the Secluded Members lost no time in making themselves and their grievances known. On 15 December the House was informed of a 'scandalous Paper intituled "A Solemn Protestation of the Imprisoned and Secluded Members of the Commons House against the Horrid Force and Violence of the Officers and Soldiers of the Army . . .",' and a Committee was set up to find out who was responsible. It cannot have taken them long to suspect the hand of Prynne, who, with his friend Clement Walker, now began an intensive journalistic campaign against the Independents. This first pamphlet did not contain names; but on 20 January Prynne issued anonymously 'A Vindication of the Imprisoned and Secluded Members' which names 45 who were detained and 98 more who were 'secluded'. A much longer list,[2] dated 26 December, had given 214 names; but several are not identifiable as M.P.s at all, and in others there is evident confusion of names. Many of them afterwards 'entered their dissent' and were re-admitted. Presbyterian pamphleteers, naturally wanting the catalogue of victims to be as impressive as possible, included the cautious men who had kept out of trouble but were not committed to either party. In 1660 there was a new spate of pamphlets. One of them, 'edited' by Prynne, names 194 secluded members still alive, and claims that 'above 40' had died since 1648.[3] It is almost the same as an undated list reprinted in

---

[1] Masson, *Life of Milton*, V, p. 453.   [2] Brit. Mus. 669 f. 13 (62).
[3] ' A full Declaration of the True State of the Secluded Members Case.' (Jan. 1659-60).

the *Somers Tracts*[1] of members secluded 'in 1648 and since'. When all these are collated and their errors as far as possible eliminated there remains about a score of members who do not appear in any list. Many of them died during the Commonwealth, and others, elected just before the Purge, may not have sat at all. It will be apparent, from this account of the process and the evidence, that the term 'secluded members' is even more vague than the other main categories. But whatever definitions are accepted we are dealing not with a large body of 'secluded' members and a small minority of Rumpers, but with two lists of comparable size. From these we can ask how far, by the tests already applied to Royalists and Parliamentarians, the 'Independents' differed from the 'Presbyterians'.

An examination of the geographical distribution of the Independent members produces only one clear result: Wales and the western counties (the 'Celtic' region, for those who like racial theories) had an appreciably lower proportion than the rest of the country. The Welsh counties, Devon, Cornwall, and the border counties of Cheshire, Shropshire, Herefordshire, and Monmouthshire had in all 120 seats—twenty-four per cent. of the total. In the Rump they had 29 members—fourteen per cent. of all the Rumpers and twenty-four per cent. of the full number of members from these counties. Some, though by no means all, of this mainly Royalist area had seen comparatively little fighting and had sent few soldiers to other districts. The Civil War in Wales was very largely a settling of private scores rather than an assertion of principle, and the Welsh gentlemen were even more reluctant than most to leave their own battlefields and fight where they were needed. This was true also of the country north of the Tees, and to some extent of Lancashire and Yorkshire as well. (In Northumberland Sir John Fenwick, a notorious land-grabber and law-breaker, sided first with the King and then with the Parliament and showed no sign of caring much for either; and Sir John Price in Wales behaved in much the same way.) But the north, far from sharing the low proportion of Independents of the west, had more than the

[1] Vol. VI, p. 37.

3

average. The 5 counties of Northumberland, Cumberland, Westmorland, Lancashire, and Yorkshire had 38 Royalists among their 62 original members: they now had 36 Independents—nearly sixty per cent. of their membership. This, however, is largely due to the exceptionally high proportion from Yorkshire. With 22 Rumpers from its 30 seats—or rather from 28 seats, since the county by-elections did not take place—it had more than any other county, and a higher proportion than any county with a large enough number of seats for percentages to be significant. Of these Yorkshire Rumpers 12 were Recruiters, and 10 original members. (Only 11 original Parliamentary members were still alive.) Six of the 22 were regicides. All this is the more remarkable when we remember the strong effort that had been made by Yorkshire gentry to establish the county's neutrality at the beginning of the war. And it is not accounted for by outsiders: though the Rumpers from the other northern counties included many 'foreigners', every one of those from Yorkshire was a Yorkshireman by birth or migration. Some of them certainly had personal reasons for violent opposition to the King. The Chaloner brothers believed themselves to have been cheated of a fortune by his action over their father's alum mines; and Sir John Bourchier (one of the Virginia adventurers) had suffered for his opposition to Wentworth. All these attended the Trial, and Bourchier and Thomas Chaloner signed the warrant. One at least of the 22 regretted his decision: Thomas Hoile of York killed himself on the anniversary of the King's death—though he was not a regicide.

A broad belt of counties, extending across the Midlands from Gloucestershire and Wiltshire to Lincolnshire and Norfolk sent 151 members to the original Parliament and 80 to the Rump. Of the other counties only Kent, Somerset, and Sussex come near to the fifty per cent. mark. It could be pointed out that this belt, together with the greater part of Yorkshire, forms the region where open-field agriculture predominated in the seventeenth century. It is also true that Independency was strong among members from the clothing counties, old and new. Yorkshire, Norfolk, Somerset, Gloucestershire, and Wiltshire together have about sixty per cent. of Rumpers among their members—but few of these members had any direct connection with wool or cloth. The differences in numbers are too small and the evidence of a connection between the party allegiance of the M.P.s and the special economic interests of their areas too uncertain for much importance to be attached to figures of this kind.

We have seen that one of the few definable differences between the two sides in the original Parliament was that the Royalist M.P.s were younger. Ages, either exact or near enough to allocate them to a ten-year group, are available for 187 of the Rumpers, and in the table below they are set out together with the total number of original Parliamentary members and Recruiters—including those who died before Pride's Purge. The third line gives the figure in the first line as a percentage of that in the second.

	Born before						
	1580	1580-9	1590-9	1600-9	1610-19	1620-9	Unknown
Rumpers	5	17	57	49	43	16	19
Total excluding Royalists	28	71	133	136	111	51	48
Per cent.	18	24	43	36	39	31	

Death and old age account for the absence from the Rump of many in the oldest groups; and the distribution of those who were under sixty in 1650 does not suggest that Independency can be associated either with the wisdom of middle-age or with the zeal of youth. The median age of the Rumpers in 1650 was forty-seven—two years younger than that of the original Parliamentary members and the Recruiters together. About a quarter of them were younger sons, roughly the same proportion as in the whole Parliament.

When the numerical tests used on the other groups are applied to the Rumpers they produce for the most part the results we should have expected if the 209 members had been picked at random. Thirty per cent. had been to Oxford, twenty per cent. to Cambridge—almost exactly the same as the original

Parliamentary group. Fifty-four per cent. had been to one of
the Inns of Court—very slightly below the figure for the rest of
the Parliament. (Gray's Inn with 46 representatives in the Rump
had about twice as many as each of the other three.) Did the
barristers in the House resist the unconstitutional interference by
the Army? There were 70 of them in 1648, and 33 sat in the
Rump. Was Independency attractive to the townsmen more
than to the countrymen? There were 19 Mayors and Aldermen
among the Rumpers, and we shall show later that a considerable
number of merchants of the various kinds continued to sit; but
the figures are not significantly larger than those on the other
side. The one distinction which might confidently be assumed
between the Rumpers and the rest is in their military service.
The quarrel that produced the Purge was in its most obvious
aspect one between the Army and the civilians; and those officers
who were also M.P.s might be expected to become prominent
in what remained of the House. About a third of the Rumpers
held, or had held, the rank of colonel or a higher one; many of
these were also members of the Councils of State. But the
military men were not on the whole the most prominent in
political disputes or administrative duties. Of some 80 members
who sat on Committees in the first month after the Purge only
about a quarter were then referred to by military titles. There
were many officers who, like Massey, would have nothing to do
with the new régime, and many more who, like Fairfax, were
extremely cautious in their attitude to its more controversial
actions. Two of the New Model colonels who sat in the House
had sided with the Presbyterian majority in 1647, and had been
deprived of their regiments for doing so. On the other hand,
11 were in the Rump, and if they were seldom conspicuous
there it has to be remembered that their military duties prevented them from constant attendance.

If the Rumpers felt that hereditary titles gave their Parliament
an air of respectability they could not complain of the lack of
them. When the Earls of Pembroke and Salisbury entered the
Lower House on the abolition of their own they were joining
sons who were already sitting. Sons of the Earls of Portland and

Leicester were there too. The number of baronets was not far
below the standard of 1640: 10 Rumpers had had the title conferred and 5 had inherited it. The comparative dearth of knights
which we saw among the Recruiters was even more marked in
the Rump. There were only 17 (excluding as before those who
were also baronets)—less than half the number secluded.

The Recruiters, as has already been shown, were slightly
more numerous in the Rump than the original members; and
the factors which reduced their chances of previous parliamentary experience have again to be taken into account in considering the Rumpers from this point of view. 37 of the
Rumpers had sat before 1640, and another 26 in the Short
Parliament. Of the 37 (eighteen per cent. of the Rumpers) all
but 6 were original members. The proportion of original members sitting in the Rump who had been M.P.s before is therefore
not significantly smaller than that of all the original members.
In the parliamentary record of their families the Rumpers
differed from the Presbyterians in about the same proportion
as did the Recruiters from the original members. The number
who came from families previously represented in Parliament
is 88, or forty-two per cent., compared with forty-five per cent.
of the total number of original Parliamentary members and
Recruiters. Seventy-three, or thirty-five per cent. of the Rumpers, compared with thirty-eight per cent. of all the original
Parliamentary members and Recruiters, had successors of their
direct line sitting in Parliament. The obvious political factors
sometimes delayed their reappearance: though several sons of
Rumpers, and indeed a few of the Rumpers themselves, sat in
the Cavalier Parliament, the achievement was only easy for those
with a very firm county or borough connection, or for
families who had feet in more than one camp. We can examine
some specimens.

The Wallops of Farleigh Wallop[1] would not easily allow a
revolution to interfere with their hereditary right to represent
a county where they had held estates since the thirteenth century.
Sir Henry, Lord Justice of Ireland, had founded their political

[1] *V.C.H. Hants* III, p. 365. Several members of the family are in *D.N.B.*

fortunes and greatly increased their material ones. His son, also Sir Henry, was county member in 1640, and had sat in every Parliament since 1597, except that of 1604 when he was Sheriff. The second Sir Henry's son Robert, member for Andover in 1640, had represented that borough or the county since 1621. Robert was a member of the Committee of Both Kingdoms, of the regicide court (though he did not sign the warrant) and of most of the Commonwealth Councils of State. Naturally he had his share of confiscated Winchester lands. He was a fairly outspoken Republican and withdrew from active politics during the Protectorate; but he was back in the House and on the Council of State in May 1659, and would have sat in the Convention Parliament if he had been admitted. The Restoration put an end to his career: he was excepted from pardon, made to stand under the gallows at Tyburn, and imprisoned for life in the Tower. The ancestral estates were confiscated and granted to a good Royalist and distinguished Restoration statesman, Thomas Wriothesley, 4th Earl of Southampton. But the Earl's sister Ann was the wife of Robert Wallop, and their son Henry enjoyed the benefit of the estates. The Hampshire borough of Whitchurch was represented by Henry in the Cavalier Parliament, and by his son in all the Parliaments from 1678 to 1691. And in 1743 John Wallop, former M.P. for Hampshire, was created 1st Earl of Portsmouth.

In the new split, as in the old, many families were divided against themselves. The Bayntons[1] could trace back their descent and some of their Wiltshire estates to a Sir Henry Baynton who was Knight Marshall to Henry II. One or more of them had been in nearly every Parliament since 1545, usually for the boroughs of Calne, Chippenham, and Devizes, which were all within seven miles of their principal estate of Bromham. Sir Edward, who sat in the Long Parliament for Chippenham was well established as one of the leaders of the county. He had been Sheriff—and was accused of injustice and profiteering in the collection of ship-money;[2] he was a J.P.; he had sat in six pre-

[1] Hoare, *Wiltshire*, III (iv), p. 7. G.E.C., *Baronetage*; Burke, *Extinct Baronetage*.
[2] *D'Ewes' Journal*, ed. Notestein, pp. 176-7.

vious Parliaments, sometimes for the county. His sister was the wife of the Royalist member for Gloucestershire, John Dutton of Sherborne, and his family was connected by marriage, inevitably, with the Thynnes and the Hungerfords. He soon identified himself with the extreme war group. For a time, in 1643, he was imprisoned in the Tower for his attacks on Pym. But he was readmitted to the House, named as a commissioner for the trial of the King, and was active in the Rump. His son, also unfortunately called Edward, sat for Devizes and served as a Colonel of Horse in the Parliamentary Army. In 1647 he was suspended from sitting for his part in the Army's attack on the House; but he was re-admitted and was on the lists of Secluded Members.[1] He sat, again for Devizes, in the first Protectorate Parliament. At the Restoration he was able to atone for the deeds of his late father: he returned with the Secluded Members to the Rump (where his old friend at Lincoln's Inn, Anthony Ashley Cooper, was at last sitting for another Wiltshire borough), represented Calne in the Convention Parliament, became a K.B. at the Coronation, and at one of the by-elections to the Cavalier Parliament resumed his duties as member for Devizes. His son Henry sat in due course for Calne and Chippenham.

But such successes were rare among the most serious offenders. At the other extreme from the Wallops and Bayntons are those Rumpers whose families are not found in Parliaments before or since, and whose prosperity did not survive. There was John Downes, elected after a disputed return for Arundel in 1641. He is described as 'a landowner of mean family'—so mean that we know nothing about it; but he became Auditor of the Duchy of Cornwall and a purchaser of Bishops' lands.[2] He too was imprisoned in the Tower as a regicide, and his name is heard no more. The Purys, father and son, enjoyed a brief period of fame. Thomas, Alderman of Gloucester and son of a former Mayor, sat for the town in 1640. He got a place as Clerk of the Petty Bag, became Deputy Lieutenant of Gloucestershire, and bought

[1] Rushworth, *Historical Collections*, IV, p. 800; *C.J.* 3 Sept. 1647.
[2] Rawlinson MS. B 239 gives a list of purchasers of Bishops' lands which includes 39 Independent and 10 Presbyterian M.P.s.

some lands. His lowly origins and his conduct were often reported: 'sometimes a weaver, now an attorney, whom I think nothing hath so much indeered as his Irreverence in Gods House, sitting covered when all the rest sit bare'.[1] He became an active M.P., and sat on many committees, including Grocers' Hall. The younger Pury had been receiver of the King's rents in Gloucestershire and Wiltshire, and was elected for Monmouth in 1646. While the father was helping the cause at Westminster, the son was doing so in the Army—to the extent of becoming a Captain both of Foot and of Horse. Both sat in the Rump, and the elder in the first Protectorate Parliament. They were not regicides; but after the Restoration their lands were sold and they disappear from political history.

Kent and the Cinque Ports.

A territorial specimen of the Independents may make clearer than defective statistics the extent to which county families of the familiar type were colleagues in the Rump of the comparative upstarts. There were 8 Rumpers from the 18 members sent by Kent, its boroughs, and its 4 Cinque Ports. Augustine Skinner,[2] the county member, was seated at Totesham Hall near Maidstone. The Skinners were a recently arrived landed family, and did not last long, though Augustine married the daughter of a Serjeant-at-Law and then the daughter of an Alderman of London, and refused to act in the Trial. He bought lands, but they were mainly Bishops' lands and therefore forfeited at the Restoration. Captain John Nutt[3] of Hackington, Canterbury, came of one of those minor families that occasionally got a representative in Parliament if they lived in or near the right sort of borough. He too declined the invitation to attend the regicide court. The members for Dover were both younger sons. Colonel John Dixwell[4] of Brome, near Folke-

[1] Domestic State Papers (P.R.O.), SP/16/448.

[2] Hasted, *Kent*, II, p. 295. *Archaeologia Cantiana*, XXXIII, p. 145. *Harleian Society*, XLII, p. 122. *C.J.* 2 Feb. 1641-2.

[3] *Harleian Society*, VIII, p. 86. *Archaeologia Cantiana*, XXXV, pp. 45 seq.

[4] *D.N.B.*

stone, came of a Warwickshire family and had a share of some
Kentish estates inherited from a maternal great-uncle. He was
a regicide, and escaped under an assumed name to New England,
where his descendants flourished in the eighteenth century.
Benjamin Weston's[1] father was the Earl of Portland, Chancellor
of the Exchequer under James and Lord Treasurer under
Charles, who saved him from impeachment by dissolving the
1628-9 Parliament. (It is a measure of the Earl's political stature
that he sat for seven different boroughs in the counties of Essex,
Sussex, Hampshire, and Cornwall.) The Westons were one of
the many great landed and political lines founded by Tudor
lawyers: Richard Weston had become a Justice of the Common
Pleas in 1559. Benjamin's elder brother Nicholas, member for
Newtown, was a Royalist; Benjamin himself refused the Trial,
but became a Commissioner of the Treasury in 1649. Queenborough was represented by two men also very different in
status. Sir Michael Livesey[2] was a Baronet, Colonel of Horse,
son of a former Sheriff of Kent and three times Sheriff himself.
His colleague Augustine Garland[3] was the son of a London
attorney who had acquired lands in Essex and at Queenborough.
Both signed the death warrant: Livesey fled for his life to
Holland; Garland was kept under sentence of death in the Tower.

The two Hythe Rumpers differed in their origins in much
the same way. Thomas Westrow was the son of an Alderman
of London, and was, says Walker, 'nothing worth until a
Captain and a Parliament man'.[4] He served under Sir Michael
Livesey, bought Bishops' lands, and married the sister of Arthur
Capel, the Royalist Peer who was executed after the siege of
Colchester. Sir Henry Heyman, Bt. was the son of Sir Peter,
member for Dover until his death in 1641. The Heymans[5] had
a successful history in Kent for a century and a half. They had
acquired Hareng and Otterpool by purchase, Somerfield and

[1] G.E.C. *Peerage*. Burke, *Extinct Peerage*. *Archaeologia Cantiana*, XX, p. 19.
[2] *D.N.B.* Burke, *Extinct Baronetage*. *Archaeologia Cantiana*, XXVI, pp. 326-7.
[3] *D.N.B. Archaeologia Cantiana*, XX, p. 25.
[4] *History of Independency* (1660 edn.), p. 171. Pink MSS.
[5] G.E.C. *Baronetage*, II, p. 135. Wilks, *Barons of the Cinque Ports*, pp. 80 seq.
D.N.B. for Sir Peter.

Wilmington through a coheiress, Claverty from the Crown when one of them was a Gentleman of the Bedchamber to Edward VI, and lands in Ireland for Sir Peter's services there. Sir Peter's mother was daughter and coheiress of a Bishop of Winchester, his wives both coheiresses of London merchants. Lord Zouche as Lord Warden of the Cinque Ports had recommended him to the Mayor and Jurats of Hythe in 1620, and as its member he had spoken against the forced loans. His opposition to the court became so strong that he was sent abroad at his own expense, and in 1629 imprisoned. In 1647 Sir Henry received £5,000 from Parliament for his father's sufferings. He took no part in the Trial; but after the Restoration the family fortunes declined rapidly. His grandson Sir Bartholomew was a Poor Knight of Windsor, and the rest of the baronets earned their living in the Navy or the Church.

The nature of the 'swing to the left' that produced the Commonwealth is not a matter that can be understood by looking only, or even mainly, at the House of Commons. We are concerned here solely with the composition of a House that proved a necessary instrument of the new régime, not so much by making policy as by providing in its Committees the rudiments of a central administrative system. If we expected to find the Rump a collection of upstart colonels, parvenu landgrabbers, and unheard-of townsmen, analysis would soon demolish that illusion. But it does not show the Rump to be in every respect a cross-section of the original Parliament. Each of the two major changes in the membership since 1642 reduced the proportion of old parliamentary families and increased that of the men who seized the opportunity offered by the exceptional conditions. Many who normally would have been too far from the centre of national, county, or town politics now found the way less crowded and obstructed. But, whether for political, economic, or purely personal reasons, few of these established their names on the list of the greater or lesser 'Governing Families of England'.

CHAPTER IV

THE MERCHANTS

THE Merchants of the House, like the Lawyers, were regarded as a distinct group, and were added collectively to Committees concerned with their professional interests. But no-one seems to have drawn up a list of them: for the purposes of the House a merchant was probably anyone who so regarded himself. Between the landowner who marketed his corn and timber, speculated in trading companies, or lent money for interest, and the merchant who invested his profits in land there can be no clear distinction. Among the lesser townsmen lack of information sometimes adds to the difficulty of saying whether an Alderman should be defined as a trader, or where in the range between small shopkeepers and great financiers he came. The number of merchants in the original House has been put as low as 27;[1] but a reasonably cautious count, including some small local men but excluding those who despite interests in trading companies had no mercantile establishment of their own, gives a total of 45-50. If we include speculators too the total could be raised to as much as 70. In the period between the new elections of 1645-6 and Pride's Purge the numbers were a little higher: about 15 had died or been excluded and about 25 elected. But even the most generous estimates hardly justify the description 'a Trading Parliament' quoted in Burton's Diary.[2]

Rigid classification of the merchants is as difficult and misleading as attempts to count them exactly; but we can produce a few categories into which it is possible to fit without too much

[1] M. Ashley, *Financial and Commercial Policy under the Cromwellian Protectorate*, p. 7.   [2] Burton, Vol. I, p. xxv.

strain most of the members whose wealth came chiefly from trade. In the first place there are the few great national figures, the contractors, projectors, farmers of customs and exise duties, and office-holders, whose commercial and financial enterprises covered a wide range and who had close connections with the court. Sir Arthur Ingram,[1] Comptroller of the Customs of the Port of London, a manager of the alum monopoly, and prominent in many City ventures, had been in every Parliament since his election for Stafford in 1609. He had found seats in many different places—New Romney, Appleby, York, New Windsor, and now Callington, as one of the very few outsiders to sit for Cornish boroughs. Despite his close and profitable connection with the King, who stayed at his house in York during his journey in the North in 1642 and would have made him a Peer, Ingram never opposed the Parliamentary leaders, and was on the Committee that drew up the Grand Remonstrance. He died before the outbreak of war. The rest became Royalists of varying enthusiasm. Sir Nicholas Crisp,[2] barrister of the Middle Temple and Attorney-General of the Court of Wards, had a share of the lucrative Guinea Trade monopoly in 1632 and was one of the group of financiers to whom Charles farmed the customs in 1640. He was elected to the Short and Long Parliaments for the seat at Winchelsea controlled by the Warden of the Cinque Ports. He did good service to Charles in buying munitions on the Continent and as a privateer who equipped a small fleet of his own. At the end of the war he fled to France and in successive confiscations much of his wealth came into the hands of the Parliament. But by 1653 he had come to terms with them, and tried to raise a loan for the new government which was to be secured, together with his losses on the royal customs farm, on Crown lands—a total of over half a million pounds. The project failed, and he remained in low water until the Restoration, when he resumed his financial services to the King and his seat for Winchelsea. Another of the

---

[1] D.N.B. See *D'Ewes' Journal* (ed. Coates), p. 108 n. for proof of identity.

[2] D.N.B. G.E.C. *Baronetage. Calendar of the Committee for Compounding*, p. 1651.

customs farmers was Sir John Jacob,[1] who also had a Cinque Ports seat, for Rye. His interests included the tobacco monopoly and the licensing of cloth exports. Jacob was less successful than Crisp in recovering from his losses, and when his estate was restored in 1660 it was seized by his creditors. A fourth member of the group was Sir Thomas Bludworth,[2] or Bludder, member for Reigate in all the Parliaments of Charles I. He became Surveyor-General of Victuals for the Navy, a contractor for the pre-emption of tin, and one of the farmers of the duty on coals. His other enterprises suggest an accurate assessment of the needs of the moment, for he became a middleman between John Evelyn and the Treasury in the supply of gunpowder from the Surrey manufactories, and was also concerned in the sale of Bibles. Bludder compounded for the estate he had bought at Reigate, but it was sold after his death in 1655. Nevertheless his son, a vintner and Alderman of London, and his grandson sat in later Stuart Parliaments.

None of these was altogether a 'self-made man'. Only Ingram, the second son of a linen-draper who had married the daughter of a Lord Mayor and Member of Parliament for York, did not have the usual education at a University or Inn, and he became a member of Gray's Inn later in life. He was also the only one whose successors rose and survived. His son, M.P. for Thirsk, was a Royalist, and his grandson became the first Viscount Irwin. Bludder's father was a knight and was himself a commissioner of victualling; Crisp's had been Sheriff of London and came of a Gloucestershire landed family; Jacob's had a considerable estate in Cambridgeshire. We could perhaps add to the group one member of a well-established landed family whose survival depended on a timely injection of merchant wealth. The Sackvilles had held estates in Sussex since the Conquest, and their rise to the top of the Tudor ladder was begun by Sir Richard, the first cousin of Ann Boleyn, who became

[1] G.E.C. *Baronetage*. Burke, *Extinct Baronetage*. *Calendar of the Committee for Compounding*, p. 680. *V.C.H. Sussex*, IX, p. 52.

[2] *V.C.H. Surrey*, II, p. 317; III, pp. 237, 313. *Harleian Society*, VIII, p. 48. Manning and Bray, *Surrey*, I, p. 306. Pink MSS.

Chancellor of the Court of Augmentations. His son, Sir Thomas, 1st Baron Buckhurst and Earl of Dorset, was among the most brilliant and successful of the Elizabethan court, and eventually succeeded Burleigh as Lord Treasurer. It was he who obtained from the Queen the grant of the reversion of Knole, one of 16 manors he held at his death. But the estate quickly disintegrated under his successors through the familiar combination of extravagance and litigation, and Richard Lord Buckhurst[1] who sat in the Long Parliament for East Grinstead needed all the money he could get from his grant of four shillings a ton on coals and his membership of the Virginia Company. Fortunately he added to his own a far greater mercantile fortune—by his marriage to Frances, daughter and eventually heiress of Lionel Cranfield. He was accordingly able to retrieve Knole and much of the rest from creditors and purchasers. 'No particular interest attaches to Richard Sackville', says Miss Sackville West in her history of the house and family.[2]

The Long Parliament was bound to concern itself early with the familiar grievances of monopolies and the granting of rights to levy customs and excises. It was easier to complain of these than to take effective action against the offenders; but the House could at least penalise those of them who were among its own members. One of its first actions was to order that Projectors and Monopolists, and all 'that have any share or lately have had any share in any Monopolies are disabled to sit in this House';[3] and it invited members who knew of monopolists in the House to denounce them. A committee was set up under George Peard to investigate the question, and the Knights and Citizens of London, and later all the Merchants of the House were added to it. Before it reported one member, William Watkins (Monmouth) was ordered to withdraw as a monopolist, and censured on his knees at the Bar for his refusal. Another, John Harrison, member for his home town of

---

[1] *D.N.B. G.E.C. Peerage. V.C.H. Sussex*, IX, pp. 117, 138. *Calendar of the Committee for Compounding*, p. 1509. Hasted, *Kent*, I, p. 344.

[2] V. Sackville-West, *Knole and the Sackvilles*, p. 112.

[3] *C.J.* 9 Nov. *D'Ewes Journal* (ed. Notestein), p. 20.

Lancaster and a prominent financier and customs official of London, voluntarily forbore to sit on account of the order. On 21 January Peard's committee recommended the expulsion of 4 members: William Sandys (Evesham) for his charges on coals on the River Avon ('12d. a chaldron more than the old tax'); Sir John Jacob (Rye) for his share in the tobacco monopoly; Thomas Webb (New Romney) for his interest in the 'Project and Monopoly concerning the Sealing of Bone Lace'; and Edmund Wyndham for the soap monopoly.[1] The House voted to expel them all and to issue new writs. On 2 February, according to *Diurnal Occurrences* 'fifty monopolists were discovered in the House'. No evidence is offered for this impossible figure, but it suggests an enthusiastic witch-hunt. In fact the committee reported that day against only one member, Nicholas Crisp (Winchelsea), whose sins in holding patents for the sole import of redwood and copperas from Africa were now exposed. He was duly removed and a new writ issued. At the same time George Goring (Portsmouth) satisfied the Committee and the House that he was not concerned in the farm of the tax on tobacco, for which his father, the later Earl of Norwich, paid £1,100 a year.[2]

The soap monopolies had for many years been a bitter topic both among the sufferers and among the rival profiteers, and in August 1641 another Committee under Richard King presented an interim report. Many names of offenders were listed, and on 30 October the only M.P. among them, Fitzwilliam Coningsby (Herefordshire) was expelled. In the following spring a bill was prepared to compel the soap-boilers of Westminster to make restitution for their exactions, and the Serjeant was ordered to take them into custody. Meanwhile Peard's committee had been revived to consider the two Bristol wine-merchants, Humphrey Hooke and Richard Longe. On 12 May 1642 it was voted that they were not projectors, but that they were beneficiaries in the wine project, and accordingly 'not fit to sit'. With the outbreak of war the expulsions came to an end, and the victims of them, naturally enough, took the side of the King. On the whole they

[1] *D'Ewes' Journal* (ed. Notestein), p. 268. *C.J.* 21 Jan. 1640-1.
[2] *C.J.* 2 Feb. 1640-1.

paid heavily for his defeat, though some of them managed to take a modest share of the profits of war. Those members on the winning side who rewarded themselves out of the lands of Royalists did not scorn to take a share of the proceeds of monopolistic trading.

The second main category is that of the London merchants, members of the City Companies and usually, sooner or later, Aldermen. The City itself had 4 members. Sir Thomas Soame,[1] member of the Grocer's Company, the Levant Company, and the East India Company, was the younger son of a Lord Mayor whose family had lands in Norfolk, Kent, and Hertfordshire. Isaac Pennington,[2] Republican and leader of the War Party in the City, succeeded his father as a member of the Fishmongers' Company. Matthew Craddock[3] was a skinner who became the first Governor of the Massachusetts Bay Company, and a member of the Committee of the East India Company. (He came of a Staffordshire landed family, and his father, grandfather, and great-grandfather had all sat for Stafford.) Samuel Vassall,[4] described as a clothworker and merchant, was also a subscriber to the Massachusetts Company. Craddock died in May 1641 and was replaced by a third Massachusetts venturer, John Venn[5] of the Merchant Taylors' Company, who was secluded in 1648, but readmitted. Soame also ceased to sit at Pride's Purge and was formally excluded in 1649 for refusing to attend the proclamation of the abolition of the kingly office. Venn and Pennington both sat as judges of the King, but only Venn signed the death warrant. A sixth City merchant, William Bell, former Warden of the Apothecaries' Company, sat for Westminster until the Purge as the colleague of one of the greatest lawyers on the Parliamentary side, John Glynne. Southwark returned

---

[1] Burke, *Extinct Baronetage*. Pink and Beaven, *Aldermen of London*.

[2] *D.N.B.* *Mercurius Aulicus*, 25 Feb. 1642-3; 22 Jan. 1643-4.

[3] F. Rose Troup, *The Massachusetts Bay Company*, p. 139. Harleian Society, II, p. 149; XV, p. 198. J. Wedgwood, *Staffordshire Parliamentary History*, Vol. II, pp. 66 seq.

[4] Burke, *Commoners*, I, p. 449. F. Rose Troup, *The Massachusetts Bay Co.* Harleian Society, XVII, p. 308.

[5] *D.N.B.* Brit. Mus. Thomason Collection E 181 (21). *Harleian Society*, XVII, p. 308.

two lawyers; one, Edward Bagshawe, was a Royalist; the other, John White,[1] was no stranger to his fellow members from the London area, for he too was a subscriber to the Massachusetts Company and became its legal adviser.

Other Londoners had connections with places far from the capital and found seats there. Some were younger sons of county families, who had turned to trade and now sat in the House with their landed relatives. John Rolle[2] (Truro) was a Turkey merchant; his eldest brother, heir to the monastic estate bought by an earlier merchant, sat for the County of Devon. Edward Ashe, citizen and draper of London, was the second son of James Ashe of Freshford, Somerset, which lies between Bath and the Wiltshire borough of Westbury. John, the heir to the estate, sat for Westbury; his son James became Recorder of Bath and was returned as its member in 1645 and in the Protectorate Parliaments. But it was Edward who established the parliamentary fortunes of the family by buying the estate at Heytesbury which he and his descendants held as a family borough for a century and a half.[3] There are also the men whose trading interests lay in the borough for which they sat as well as in London. William Spurstow, of a family with lands in Cheshire, was a draper of Shrewsbury, which he represented, and later a citizen and mercer of London. George Lowe sat for Calne, where his family had long held the rectory, and was a merchant both there and in London.

At the elections of 1645 and 1646 several Londoners were in the market for borough seats, or were returned by towns with which they were already connected. Lowe was succeeded as member for Calne by Rowland Wilson of the Vintners' Company; Fowey found seats for Gregory Clement, merchant of Plymouth and London, and Nicholas Gould, merchant of London, younger son of a Devon family; Francis Allen, former goldsmith who became Customer of London, Treasurer of the

---

[1] F. Rose Troup, *John White the Patriarch of Dorchester*, has many references to him, though he is not related to the John White of the title.

[2] *D.N.B.* Gilbert, *Parochial History of Cornwall*, I, p. 489.

[3] Hoare, *Wiltshire*, I (ii), p. 118; III (i), p. 41. *Wiltshire Archaeological Magazine*, V, p. 382.

Army, and one of the greatest financiers of the Commonwealth, was admitted to the Cockermouth seat for which he had been named in 1642; Thomas Atkins, Lord Mayor of London and former Warden of the Mercers' Company, sat for his old home town of Norwich; Richard Browne, a woodmonger who was extending his City interests into many other fields, represented High Wycombe. William Crowther, citizen and haberdasher of London, but apparently a native of Ludlow, was returned for Weobley.

All but one of these Londoners were, like the City members, on the Parliamentary side. The exception was George Lowe,[1] who tried hard to explain away his presence in the Oxford Parliament. He had been taken there, he said, by force, and later escaped from it. The story did not cut much ice in Goldsmiths' Hall, where many variations of it had been heard before, and Lowe was fined a total of £1,386. Richard Browne became one of the leading Presbyterians among London politicians, and something of a popular hero to the opponents of Independency. He was secluded in 1648, deprived of his offices of Sheriff and Alderman, and imprisoned. In 1656 he was one of the members excluded from the second Protectorate Parliament for refusing the Engagement to Cromwell; but he sat for London in 1659 and was among the first of the Presbyterians to put his money on Charles. In due course he was rewarded with a knighthood and baronetcy and the office of Lord Mayor. Of the rest Rolle and Spurstow died before 1648; the others, including all the Recruiters, became active Rumpers. Wilson, until his death in 1650, was a member of the Councils of State. Gould and Clement both sat on the important Rump Committees until Clement was expelled for immorality ('lying with his maid'). At the Restoration Clement, who was a regicide, was executed; Gould, who was not a regicide, was made a baronet. Allen also signed the death warrant and in addition to his other activities was a regular attender and committeeman in the Rump. Atkins refused to take part in the trial: he became one of the most

[1] *Wiltshire Archaeological Magazine*, XXIV, p. 310. *Calendar of the Committee for Compounding*, p. 959.

important City politicians on the Independent side, and seems to have turned the hostility of the Presbyterian element among the greater merchants to his own profit. But he saved little more than his life at the Restoration and died in obscurity.

There remains the largest group of merchants—those who sat for the provincial towns in which they traded. The larger towns sent in general, both in 1640 and in the subsequent elections, men who had risen to local prominence in law, municipal government, or trade—sometimes in all three. Bristol and Newcastle each sent two highly successful merchants. The expelled Bristol members, Hooke and Longe,[1] were replaced in 1641 by the Recorder, John Glanville,[2] who had sat in the Short Parliament but was rejected in October after he had been made a King's Serjeant, and the Mayor, John Taylor[3]—another vintner. They too were Royalists and were disabled to sit in 1644. At Newcastle indignation on the subject of monopolies had already been officially expressed. The instructions to the Burgesses serving in the Short Parliament drew their attention to the encroachments on the subjects' freedom 'by monopolies of soap, salt, tobacco, starch, and many such like . . . together with the new great impost on wine, lead, and all other commodities, especially the unparalleled taxation of ship money upon us . . .'. For the Long Parliament one of the seats was disputed between John Blakiston of the Mercers' branch of the local Merchants' Company and Sir John Melton. Melton was a 'foreigner' with estates in Yorkshire, whose only connection with Tyneside was financial and official. Besides reading law and writing books he had made a fortune out of the saltpetre and coal trades, and become Secretary to the Council of the North in 1635, after being a member of it since 1629—an example of the successful combination of the pursuits that were fashionable at the Court of James and Charles. His right to sit was challenged on the grounds of his monopolistic interest in

---

[1] W. R. Williams, *Gloucestershire M.P.s,* J. F. Nicholls and J. Taylor, *Bristol Past and Present,* Vol. I, pp. 293, 296, 318.

[2] *D.N.B. Calendar of the Committee for the Advance of Monies,* p. 408. *Wiltshire Archaeological Magazine,* XXIV, p. 74.   [3] W. R. Williams, *Gloucestershire M.P.s.*

coal; but before the Committee of the House had settled the question he died, and Blakiston was allowed to take his seat. He proved himself a fervent Puritan and eventually a regicide. The other Newcastle member was a moderate Royalist, Sir Henry Anderson, whose father and grandfather had been merchants in the town, and who had himself many mercantile interests, including coal.

There was nothing unique in Newcastle's choice of two merchant members who took opposite sides. Even if we leave out the monopolists, who had obvious reason to support the royal government, and the men who were associated in their enterprises with courtiers, the solid allegiance to Parliament of the Londoners is not found everywhere among provincial merchants. It is true that there were considerably more on the Parliamentary than on the Royal side, and that there were proportionately more Independents than in the Parliament as a whole. But a closer examination of the political allegiance of the provincial merchants does not suggest that commercial interests were in themselves enough to bring a member on to the Parliamentary side. In the north and west the majority for the Parliament among the handful of merchant members is too small to be significant. The Eastern Association, as can be seen in a later chapter, had only Parliamentarians among its merchants; but its Royalists were everywhere in a minority—and one of them was returned by Norwich.

In the country as a whole there probably was a preponderance of Parliamentarian feeling among merchants; but the M.P.s among them have to be considered not simply as representatives of the interests or politics of a class but as part of the complex pattern of borough and county electioneering. In the largest of our regions, the south-west, merchants and Aldermen together were about equally divided between the two sides. The distribution is particularly striking in Devonshire, where there were 26 seats and 12 Royalists. At Barnstaple the Recorder, George Peard,[1] a Puritan and prominent supporter of Pym in the early sessions of the Parliament, had as his colleague a merchant,

[1] *D.N.B.*

Richard Ferris,[1] who was disabled to sit in 1644. At Exeter Robert Walker,[2] Alderman and former Mayor, was a Royalist, and Simon Snow,[2] merchant, a Presbyterian. Dartmouth was represented by a lawyer, Samuel Browne[3] (Oliver St. John's cousin and fellow barrister of Lincoln's Inn), who was secluded in 1648, and a local merchant Roger Matthew,[3] Mayor in 1639, who sat in the Oxford Parliament. Matthew died in 1646 after a spell in the Tower, and his estate was allowed to pass to his sons, who were 'well affected'. He was one of many 1639 Mayors who were returned in 1640 by boroughs that gave seats to townsmen—a fact which in itself suggests the danger of looking for political motives in the choice of members. The original members for Plymouth were both ex-Mayors and sons of ex-Mayors. One of them, John Waddon, sat until 1648; the other, Robert Trelawny, who had been a promoter of American plantations, was reported to have said in March 1642 that the House of Commons had no power to appoint a guard for themselves without the King's consent. For these words, 'accidentally spoken out of the House' he claimed, he was expelled and committed to prison, where he died two years later.[4] A new writ was promptly issued, and Trelawny was succeeded by a Devon landowner, Sir John Young, who also had interests in American colonising. He and his father, the member for Honiton, were secluded in 1648 but Sir John sat again in the Protectorate Parliaments.[5]

Elsewhere local merchants were about as likely to be Independents as to be Presbyterians, though since they were an appreciably older group than the average their chances of surviving to sit in the Rump were smaller. Both the York members, Sir William Allanson, draper and former Lord Mayor of York, and Thomas Hoile,[6] Governor of the Merchants' Company, continued to sit after Pride's Purge. Both the Southampton members, George Gollop and Edmund Exton, Aldermen, were

[1] Burke, *Landed Gentry*, 2nd edn.
[2] J. J. Alexander, *Exeter M.P.s. Transactions of the Devonshire Association*, LXI, p. 211. [3] J. J. Alexander, *Dartmouth M.P.s.*
[4] *C.J.*, 9 March, 1641.
[5] See also Chapter V for the East Anglian merchants. [6] See above, p. 44.

poor attenders in the House, and were secluded. Coventry was represented by John Barker, draper, and Simon Norton, dyer, who died in 1641 and was succeeded by another of his trade, William Jesson. Several pieces of evidence combine to make it likely that Norton would have been a Royalist, had he lived; one of his sons was squire of the body to Charles and captain of a troop of horse in his army, while another son was made a baronet in 1661 and represented Coventry in 1685, the year that saw the most Tory of Parliaments. Barker was on the Purge lists, but was readmitted, while there is no trace of Jesson's having sat between 1648 and his death in 1651. Colonel Barker was a much more active and aggressive politician. King's Lynn elected the Mayors of 1638 and 1639, Thomas Toll and John Perceval, who had both become freemen by apprenticeship. The Worcester members were clothiers: John Nash was secluded in 1648; John Cowcher, who was seventy-nine in 1640 and so the oldest member of the House with the exception of Sir Francis Knollys the elder, was repeatedly excused attendance, and may never have taken his seat at all.

Whatever the opportunities offered by the successive stages of the Revolution, our local merchants did not in general use them for the founding of great estates. The names of their descendants are usually absent not only from the Peerages but from the *Landed Gentry* and the lists of later Parliaments. Nothing more is heard of the families of Snow, Waddon, Exton, Ferris, or Matthew. Robert Walker's son was also an Alderman of Exeter and represented it in the last years of the Cavalier Parliament, but his successors did not continue the political tradition. If Robert Trelawney had any sons they remained in obscurity.

The merchant Recruiters did not fare much better. A few, such as Robert Blake the Cromwellian Admiral, who was a merchant in Bridgwater between his graduation at Oxford and his election for the town, rose to wealth and fame in the interregnum; a few more, such as Richard Ellison, merchant of Newcastle, and its member from 1645 to 1648, prospered after the Restoration. But the majority were and remained obscure men whose brief appearance at Westminster was associated with no lasting material benefit to themselves or their successors. Indeed the impression from this single Parliament, for what it is worth, is that though landed fortunes were being supplemented or repaired through trade they were less easily founded. None of the merchant members can match such figures of the previous generation as Lionel Cranfield or Baptist Hicks who rose in a lifetime from shopkeeping to vast estates and a higher peerage. There were of course merchants who enjoyed a period of opulence through their purchases at the great sales of land between 1650 and 1654. Edmund Harvey[1] (Great Bedwin 1646-53), citizen and mercer of London (or, according to Walker, 'a poor silkman') bought the lands of the Bishop of London and established himself in the episcopal palace. Much of the money he invested came from his gains as Colonel of Horse during the war. Gregory Clement (Fowey 1648-52) began his acquisitions with Irish lands in 1646, and went on to the more tempting offers of Deans' and Chapters' lands. These gains were wiped out at the Restoration, and there is little evidence of our merchants sharing in what proved to be the much sounder investments—the estates of Royalists who were forced to sell or mortgage privately. Thomas Pury probably acquired Minsterworth in this way, but his son sold it again; Thomas Boone[2] (Dartmouth 1646-53), a merchant trading to Spain, added some sequestered lands to the estate he had already acquired before the war. Other instances could be given, but there is nothing to warrant the idea that large numbers of petty bourgeois sat in the House and used their military and political success to turn themselves into landed gentry.

On the other hand there were many of the landed gentry in Parliament who were willing to put a little of their time and capital into trading ventures at home and abroad. Providence Island and Saybrook, the Puritan colonising schemes which set out to combine profit-making with the provision of refuges from persecution, have been the subject of detailed studies.[3] Ten of

[1] *D.N.B.*   [2] J. J. Alexander, *Dartmouth M.P.s.*
[3] A. P. Newton, *The Colonising Activities of the English Puritans*. Lists of the M.P.s are in Hexter, *The Reign of King Pym*, pp. 77-81.

the members were among the 26 Providence Island subscribers, and 3 more among the original patentees of Saybrook. A third and eventually more successful venture in colonising was the Massachusetts Bay Company,[1] which as shown elsewhere had a remarkably close connection with the London and Dorset M.P.s. Its other subscribers included Sir William Brereton (Cheshire), Henry Darley (Northallerton), who was also concerned in both Providence Island and Saybrook, and Sir Robert Crane (Sudbury) who was alleged to have become a Royalist shortly before his death. Six other members involved in these enterprises died during the war; 7 of the survivors were secluded, and 6 sat in the Rump.

It would be impossible to list the members whose interests in trade, finance, or government contracts and concessions added to their revenues from land and put them on the wide and indeterminate margin of the merchant class. The Moores in Lancashire and the Barnardistons in Suffolk have already been mentioned. The ancient Kentish family of Twisden, one of whom was a Recruiter for Maidstone, was concerned in a wide variety of trade in London and local markets.[2] In Staffordshire the Royalist Biddulphs and the Parliamentarian Bowyers were among the families whose exploitation of the mineral resources of their estates led them to become part-time industrial entrepreneurs and traders. Ralph Sneyd of Keele, Royalist member for Stafford, was killed in the second Civil War, with his fine still partly unpaid, and many of his lands had to be sold; but after the Restoration the development by his brother of the coalfields on the remaining estate restored the family to prosperity. Activities of this kind are less readily traced than sales and acquisitions of land; and our information is not full enough to show convincingly how far they were associated with the Parliamentary rather than the Royalist side of the House. Among county families it is easier to find Parliamentarian than Royalist members who were exploiting local assets and opportunities.

---

[1] F. Rose Troup, *The Massachusetts Bay Company*. See also chapter VI below.
[2] J. R. Twisden, *The Family of Twysden and Twisden*. R. H. Tawney in *Ec. H.R.*, Vol. XI, p. 1.

More characteristic of the Royalists are the supplementary sources of income that could be picked up through connections at Court and in the capital. Jack Ashburnham (Hastings 1640-4), Groom of the Bedchamber and close friend of Charles, spent most of his life trying to revive the family fortunes which his father had ruined (through his 'good nature and frank disposition towards his friends' says his monument). In addition to land speculation and moneylending he joined with his brother in the project for a tapestry manufacture at Mortlake. Endymion Porter[1] (Droitwich) was another Royalist courtier and landowner who engaged in many projects. At one time or another he became collector of fines for the Star Chamber, Surveyor of Petty Customs in the Port of London, and a participant in the soap monopoly. He also lost on a drainage scheme in Lincolnshire and profited by Sir William Courten's association of East India traders. Sir John Trevor,[2] a Welshman who sat for Grampound throughout the Long Parliament and for Arundel and Steyning under the Protectorate, succeeded his father as part-owner with Bludder and the others of the Newcastle coal-farm. Three of his brothers had been M.P.s, one of them a judge who supported Ship Money and another a Surveyor of the Navy. But Sir John, after losing his place as Surveyor of Windsor Great Park, became an Independent and an advocate of the offer of the crown to Cromwell, to whom he was related through his son's marriage to Ruth Hampden. He was an extensive buyer of lands from the Treason Trustees, but had the good sense not to be a regicide and to become an early supporter of the Restoration. In 1668 the son became Secretary of State.

Many more names could be added, both of those who learned to enrich themselves before the war and of those who took advantage of the examples and opportunities that came their way during their membership of the Long Parliament. Perhaps it is men like these, with their manifold interests and their aptitude for tempering political theories with sound business instincts, who should be hailed as the true fathers of later generations of M.P.s.

[1] Dorothea Townsend, *Life and Letters of Endymion Porter*.   [2] *D.N.B.*

CHAPTER V

THE EASTERN ASSOCIATION

I

NORFOLK AND SUFFOLK: THE ORIGINAL MEMBERS

THE army of the Eastern Association played a leading part in the struggle against the King. It followed up its local successes by a decisive share in the Marston Moor campaign, and when the New Model Army came to be formed to clinch the victory of 1644 in the north and neutralise Essex's disaster in the west, the largest contribution in regiments came from the Eastern Counties.

In the counties of Norfolk, Suffolk, Essex, Huntingdon, Hertford, Cambridge, and Lincoln, which were eventually linked in the Eastern Association, there was general support for the Parliament, though everywhere there were Royalists, who in Cambridge University and Norfolk formed a relatively formidable dissident group. The proportion of Royalist and Parliamentarian M.P.s is not a trustworthy criterion of local feeling —Lynn for example sent two Parliamentarians but was held for the King, while Suffolk elected more Royalists than Norfolk— but it provides a useful indication. The 7 counties returned 64 members, a number increased to 69 by 2 promotions to the Lords and 3 deaths before the end of 1642. Of the 2 Peers, Capel joined the Royalists; Rich, though he became a neutral, was sentenced to a fine for joining the King at York and has therefore been counted as a Royalist. Of the 3 who died William Rainsborough, father of the Leveller leader, was a Parliamentary sympathiser, as was Sir John Jennings. The other member, Thomas Hussey, is more difficult to place, but his family connections make it very probable that he would have been a Royalist. Of the 69 all but 14 were Parliamentarians, and of the

64 still in the Commons in the summer of 1642 all but 11. Essex, after Rich's promotion to the Lords, was solidly for Parliament.

In our statistical information the Eastern Association shows much the same results as the other regions. The few Royalists were rather older than the average elsewhere: 7 of them were over forty and 7 under. The median age of the Parliamentarians was forty-seven—the same as that for the whole country. Half of the Royalists and half of the Parliamentarians had sat before. Of 6 Royalist survivors at the Restoration 3 sat again in the Commons and 1 in the Lords; of 22 Parliamentarian survivors there were 5 in the Commons and 1 Peer. All but 2 of the Royalists came from families with a previous parliamentary record, and all 14 had successors in later Parliaments. Of the 55 Parliamentarians 29 had predecessors in earlier Parliaments and 29 had successors in later ones; 22 of these were of families represented both earlier and later.

Perhaps the most striking feature of parliamentary representation in this region is the large number of members who were related to each other. With the exception of Huntingdonshire, which from being a preserve of the Cromwells had been transformed into something like a Montagu monopoly, every county can provide examples of the way in which political society consisted of a congeries of intersecting family circles. Sir Nathaniel Barnardiston, senior of the two Suffolk Knights of the Shire, was uncle, through his wife, of his colleague, Sir Philip Parker. Sir Nathaniel's mother was daughter of Sir Richard Knightley of Fawsley, Northamptonshire. By 1640 the Knightleys of the old branch, an important Puritan family, had died out, and the inheritance had gone to a cousin from the Staffordshire line. But the new Knightley had his eldest son in the House as member for Northampton, and it was to Fawsley that this son, Richard, invited Pym and other opposition leaders after the dissolution of the Short Parliament. Sir Nathaniel's eldest son, Thomas, was knighted in 1641 and was later Recruiter for Bury St. Edmunds. He married the daughter of Sir William Armine, Bt., M.P. for Grantham, who had sat in turn for Boston, Lincoln, and the county since 1621 and played a leading part in the Long Parliament until his death in 1651. Sir William Armine in his turn was brother-in-law of Thomas Lister, M.P. for Lincoln. His son and successor, Recruiter for Cumberland, married the daughter of Sir Robert Crane of Chilton, Suffolk, who was M.P. for Sudbury. On the death of this second Sir William the baronetcy became extinct, and the estates passed to his two daughters, one of whom was married to the son of Lord Belasyse, M.P. for Thirsk, while the other was married three times, first to Sir Thomas Wodehouse of Kimberley, Norfolk, grandson of Sir Thomas (Thetford), and then to Thomas, Lord Crewe of Stene, son of Thomas, M.P. for Brackley, and later 1st Lord Crewe, who in his turn was father-in-law of Edward Montagu, later 1st Earl of Sandwich, Recruiter for Huntingdonshire.

We have travelled a long way from Sir Nathaniel Barnardiston, but this instance may serve as one of many to illustrate the ramifications of parliamentary relationships. In future these relationships will usually be confined to the area of the Eastern Association. Sir Nathaniel's daughter married in 1648 Nathaniel Bacon, Recruiter for Cambridge University. Nathaniel and his brother Francis, Recruiter for Ipswich, were younger sons of Edward Bacon of Shrubland, Suffolk. Anthony Bedingfield (Dunwich) was their brother-in-law. Anthony's nephew, Philip, married the daughter of Sir John Potts of Mannington, M.P. for Norfolk.

Sir Philip Parker (Suffolk) was nephew of Sir Nathaniel Barnardiston and brother-in-law of John Gurdon (Ipswich). Sir Philip was also related at some distance to Sir Frederick Cornwallis (Eye), Sir Frederick's first cousin having married Sir Philip's aunt. Sir Charles Le Gros (Orford), married his daughter and heiress to the son of Richard Harman (Norwich). The heir of the younger Richard changed his name to Le Gros. Sir Charles Le Gros' mother was a cousin of Sir Frederick Cornwallis. Sir Roger North of Mildenhall (Eye) was nephew of the grandfather of Sir Dudley North (Cambridgeshire). Sir Edmund Moundeford (Norfolk) was distantly related to John Spelman (Recruiter for Castle Rising), and Spelman's son was given the Christian name Moundeford. Miles Corbet (Yarmouth) was great-uncle of Robert Brewster (Recruiter for Dunwich). The son of Richard Catelyn (Norwich) later married the niece of Anthony Bedingfield (Dunwich). Sir William Spring (Recruiter for Bury) died soon after he was forty; his son married the daughter of Sir Dudley North (Cambridgeshire) and a daughter married the son of Sir John Palgrave (Recruiter for Norfolk). This is not an exhaustive list, but it contains the names of half the original members and Recruiters for constituencies in Norfolk and Suffolk, while ignoring the names of families like the Lestranges which did not send a member to the Long Parliament but provided links of relationship between families which did.

In Lincolnshire a similar picture could be painted if the reader could endure a repetition, but even a brief outline will amply support the evidence from Norfolk and Suffolk. Sir Anthony Irby (Boston), was brother-in-law of Sir Christopher Wray (Grimsby), and uncle of William Wray, Sir Christopher's son and successor in the Grimsby seat. Sir John Wray, half-brother of Sir Christopher, sat for the county. The other Knight of the Shire, Sir Edward Ayscough, was related to Thomas Grantham (Lincoln) and to Thomas Hatcher (Stamford). Thomas Lister (Recruiter for Lincoln) was son-in-law of Sir William Armine (Grantham) who has been mentioned before. The Wrays and Armines had parliamentary connections outside the county, as had William Ellis (Boston), Gervase Holles (Grimsby), and Henry Pelham (Grantham), whose uncle became M.P. for Hull in 1641. This list includes two-thirds of the members for Lincolnshire.

Something has been said in the introductory chapter of the problems which are investigated in this study. Stress has been laid on the difficulty of propounding general solutions for a number of cases which are essentially individual and usually complex. Yet a survey of the family background and parliamentary history of members is enlightening. The Eastern Association is particularly useful from this point of view as a good deal of information can be obtained from reliable county

histories of Norfolk, Suffolk, Essex, Hertfordshire, and Huntingdonshire.[1] Let us study the members for Suffolk and Norfolk and then turn to those from the other three counties named
and those from Cambridgeshire to see whether they confirm
the impressions gained from the first two.

Suffolk County

Sir Nathaniel Barnardiston, M.P. for the County of Suffolk,
came of an old Suffolk family, situated at Kedington since 1347
beyond doubt. Statements that he was the thirteenth in descent
from the twelfth century and was the twenty-third knight of
that name are to be treated with reserve, but it is quite clear that
the Barnardistons were one of the oldest county families in
Suffolk. In Lincolnshire they enjoyed even greater antiquity. A
Barnardiston of Great Cotes was Knight of the Shire for Lincoln
in 1357, and six generations later a Sir Thomas Barnardiston
was Sheriff of Norfolk and Suffolk in 1511 and of Lincolnshire
in 1513. They added to their lands in the reign of Edward VI
and also acquired a Puritan tradition—Sir Nathaniel's grandfather was educated at Geneva under Calvin. Sir Nathaniel's
father was Sheriff of Suffolk a few years before his son's birth in
1588. In 1618 Nathaniel was knighted. In 1619 he succeeded his
grandfather in estates which were said to be producing nearly
£4,000 a year—a very large income for a landowning commoner at that time. He became Sheriff and then M.P., first
for Sudbury in 1625 and 1626, then for the county in 1628
and in the Short and Long Parliaments. This was the usual *cursus
honorum* for a man seeking distinction in county politics: Sheriff,
Burgess and then Knight of the Shire; but even considerable
prestige did not usually carry with it long retention of the
coveted county seat. His marriage to the daughter of a former
Lord Mayor of London brought him wealth and a City connection. He was somewhat above the average age of members

[1] F. Blomefield, *Topographical History of Norfolk* (2nd edn. 1805-9). W. A.
Copinger, *The County of Suffolk* (1904-5) ; P. Morant, *The History and Antiquities of Essex* (1768); H. Chauncy, *Historical Antiquities of Hertfordshire* (2nd
ed. 1826); R. Clutterbuck, *History and Antiquities of Hertfordshire* (1815-27).

of the Long Parliament and took no active part in the war, though he was a convinced Puritan and in close touch with the Parliamentary leaders. He was not secluded at Pride's Purge, but retired from Parliament in 1649 because of the breakdown of his health. Whether this was the reason or a pretext we do not know, but he died in 1653. His eldest son Thomas, knighted in 1641, was Recruiter for Bury St. Edmunds. He was secluded in 1648, but represented the county in 1654, 1656, and 1659. In 1661 he was elected for Sudbury on a double return and unseated. He was created a baronet 'for the antiquity of the family and the virtues of his ancestors'. He died in 1669. His brother, Sir Samuel of Brightwell, also made a baronet, was a prominent Whig City politician and, as deputy-governor of the East India Company, played a leading part in the famous case of *Skinner* v. *The East India Company*. He was Knight of the Shire for Suffolk in nine parliaments between 1673 and 1701. Four more of Sir Nathaniel's sons were prominent oriental merchants, Nathaniel, the son-in-law of Nathaniel Bacon, being the agent of the Levant Company at Smyrna from 1649 to 1650. Sir Thomas's son and namesake, the second baronet, sat in every parliament from 1685 till his death in 1699, first for Grimsby and later for Sudbury. His sitting for Grimsby in 1685 and 1689 is to be explained by the extinction of the male line of the Armines (a powerful Lincolnshire family, as we have already seen), in 1683, when the family estates were shared between two heiresses, one of whom was Sir Thomas's mother. Sir Samuel's son sat for Ipswich in 1698.

After the turn of the century the parliamentary history of the Barnardistons ends. The last baronet died in 1750. The history of the Barnardistons is a terrible warning to those who persist in dividing the landed from the mercantile interest, particularly in a county where the cloth trade was the most important mercantile activity. It may also serve to illustrate the weaknesses of that singularly inept term, 'the new middle class', which is still sometimes used to conjure away by magic inconvenient problems with no obvious answer. There was nothing 'new' about the Barnardistons, although their rise to prominence in the seventeenth century symbolised the frequent alliance between land, trade, and Puritanism. From the time of Sir Nathaniel's imprisonment in 1627 for refusing to carry out his work as commissioner for the forced loan in Suffolk to Sir Samuel's interference with Charles II's policy, the Barnardistons represented the great Presbyterian interest, sometimes with the King, but more often against him.[1]

The Parkers of Erwarton were an important county family, but unlike the Barnardistons never intruded on national politics. They had become established at Erwarton in the reign of Edward VI by the second marriage of Henry Parker, Lord Morley, to the heiress of Philip Calthorpe. Sir Philip, born of this marriage, married a daughter of Sir John Goodwin of Buckinghamshire. The Sir Philip who represented Suffolk in the Long Parliament was thus related through his grandfather to the leading political family of Buckinghamshire, which became involved in the Stuart's first parliamentary controversy, the case of *Goodwin* v. *Fortescue*,[2] and provided the senior Knight of the Shire to accompany John Hampden in 1640. The first Sir Philip, Sheriff in 1580, named his son Calthorpe after the family to which he owed Erwarton. Sir Calthorpe, brother-in-law of Sir Nathaniel Barnardiston through his marriage to the daughter of Sir Stephen Soame, Lord Mayor of London, sat for Suffolk in 1601. In the same year or the year before, Philip was born. He was knighted in 1624 and became Sheriff in 1637. He was elected to the Short and Long Parliaments, but did not play a particularly conspicuous part. He was secluded in 1648 and never sat in another parliament. He died in 1675. His son, who had been made a baronet, sat for Harwich in 1679 and 1681 and for Sandwich in 1685. Another Parker sat for Harwich later, from 1715 to 1734, but there was no representation of the family in Suffolk after the Long Parliament. The Parkers continued to own Erwarton until 1740 and Thorington Hall until 1699.[3]

[1] *D.N.B. Harleian Society*, I, p. 89. G.E.C. *Baronetage*. Copinger, *Suffolk*, V, p. 256. [2] See Appendix II.
[3] Metcalfe, *Visitation of Suffolk*, p. 155. Copinger, *Suffolk*, VI, p. 37. Page, *Suffolk*, p. 4 is inaccurate.

Norfolk County

Neither of the county members for Norfolk came of families of such high local standing as the Barnardistons and the Parkers. The senior Knight of the Shire, John Potts of Mannington, inherited that estate from his mother, who died in 1642. His father, also John, was of Lincoln's Inn and married Anne, the daughter and coheiress of John Dodge of Mannington. The elder John Potts only received arms in 1583, and his marriage provides an example of what was perhaps the commonest method of entering the ranks of the landed gentry. His death in 1598 left his son, a minor, at the mercy of the Court of Wards, which forced on him a marriage with the daughter of a Court favourite. She brought with her a small fortune, but the marriage none the less seems to have been regarded as disparaging. After her death John married again and so became the stepfather of the Recruiter for Castle Rising, John Spelman. In 1641 he was created a baronet, but, like many of the numerous creations of that year, sided against the King. He seems from his conduct on the sequestration committee to have been a man of moderate views and behaviour in religious as well as political matters. He was secluded in 1648 and in 1660 played a more prominent part in affairs, being a member of the Council of State from February to April and of the deputation which brought the King home. One of his sons became Governor of Windsor Castle. Sir John sat in the Convention for Yarmouth, but neither he nor any other of his family ever afterwards secured representation in the House. He died in 1673, probably in his late eighties. His son succeeded him. In 1732 the baronetcy became extinct.[1]

The rise of the Potts family, with its connection with the law (John's brother Charles was a Bencher of the Middle Temple and married the daughter of a London merchant), and its accumulation of a small number of manors and advowsons is typical enough in county history, but Knights of the Shire were ordinarily taken from rather more distinguished men or more old-established families.

[1] *Harleian Society*, LXXXVI, p. 169. Blomefield, *Norfolk*, II, p. 464. G.E.C. *Baronetage*.

If John Potts provides an example of a new family in the making, his colleague, Sir Edmund Moundeford of Feltwell, shows us the end of a very old, though not particularly eminent, county family. The Moundefords had owned land in the county since the fourteenth century. The member's father, also Sir Edmund of Feltwell, had been a barrister and had been knighted in 1603, seven years after the birth of his son. His mother belonged to a more important family, the Gawdys of Claxton. He represented Thetford in 1628 and the county in the Short Parliament. He was married but without children and, having no successor, sold Feltwell in 1642 to a syndicate of 12, including the Thetford members, Wodehouse and Gawdy. In the following year he died.[1]

Although they had antiquity, the Moundefords hardly seem to have had the status appropriate to Knights of the Shire. The elder Sir Edmund had, it is true, married well, and he may have prospered sufficiently at the Bar to push the family fortunes. His alliance with the Gawdys would certainly have been useful, for they were a most eminent legal family. Yet the impression remains after a survey of the county representation before and after 1640 that the choice in 1640 was exceptional. Both of the Recruiters, as we shall see later, were men with more powerful county connections.

The Ports

Aldeburgh and Ipswich in Suffolk and King's Lynn and Yarmouth in Norfolk were all ports of some importance. Mr. Nef has brought out clearly the importance of the rivalry between the East Anglian ports, which meant to maintain a practical monopoly of the Newcastle coal-trade with London, and the Newcastle merchants, who wished to break it.[2] At Aldeburgh we see the importance of shipping interests. The members were Alexander Bence, merchant of Aldeburgh, and William Rainsborough, father of the Recruiter for Droitwich. Rainsborough, who was fifty-three in 1640, was one of the most experienced seamen in the King's service and was often consulted on matters

---

[1] *Harleian Society*, XXXII, p. 201. Blomefield, *Norfolk*, II, pp. 182, 193.
[2] J. U. Nef, *Rise of the British Coal Industry*, II, p. 27 etc.

of naval administration. He was not a Suffolk man—he lived at Wapping—but he was an old colleague of Bence at Trinity House.

Alexander Bence came of the leading merchant family of Aldeburgh. His uncle and great-uncle had both sat for the borough; his father, also Alexander, was Bailiff of Aldeburgh six times; and an older brother, John, who was Bailiff four times, represented the borough in 1624. This John, also a merchant, bought a good deal of land in Suffolk before his death in 1635. He founded the county family of Bence of Thorington Hall, and one of his sons established himself at Heveningham. Another elder brother of Alexander, Robert, was a citizen and salter of London. Alexander himself first represented Aldeburgh in the Long Parliament; he was secluded in 1648, but was chosen for Suffolk in 1654. He was a grocer of London and became an Alderman in 1653, but was soon discharged on the plea of insufficiency of estate. From 1659 to 1660 he was Master of Trinity House. His eldest son, Sir Alexander, moved to Dublin, but another son, John, also grocer of London and Alderman in 1664, sat for Aldeburgh in 1659 and again from 1669 till his death in 1686 with the exception of the first Parliament of 1679. This John's only daughter and heiress married the Earl of Westmorland. Another John, great-nephew of Alexander and Squire Bence, sat for Dunwich in 1691 and 1694, and for Ipswich in 1705 and 1708. Alexander's younger brother, Squire, so-called not because of any social pretensions, but because his mother was daughter of Thomas Squire, merchant, succeeded Rainsborough on his death in 1642 as M.P. for Aldeburgh. He had already sat with him in the Short Parliament. He, too, was a merchant. He was born in 1597 and died in 1648.[1]

William Cage, senior member for Ipswich, had the longest parliamentary record in East Anglia, apart from Sir Thomas Jermyn and Sir Robert Crane, and was also the oldest M.P. from this region with the exception of the former and, possibly,

---

[1] *D.N.B. Mariner's Mirror*, XXXI, p. 178. Burke, *Landed Gentry* (2). Copinger, *Suffolk*, II, p. 166. *Harleian Visitations*, XCII, p. 19. Beaven, *Aldermen of London*, I, p. 222; II, p. 82.

also of Sir Thomas Cheeke of Pirgo, M.P. for Harwich. He was essentially a local figure, portman and seven times Bailiff of Ipswich, and son of a Bailiff. He was born in 1573 or 1574 and represented Ipswich continuously from 1621. He died in 1645 and left his country house in Burstall to his only daughter's son. His estate was considered to be about £300 a year.[1]

His colleague, John Gurdon, son of Brampton Gurdon of Assington, Suffolk, and Letton, Norfolk, was a country gentleman. Brampton's grandfather, John, came from Essex and bought the estate of Assington in Suffolk from Sir Miles Corbet, grandfather of the member for Yarmouth in 1640. He became Sheriff of Suffolk and died in 1577. His son, also John, married Amy, daughter and heiress of William Brampton of Letton in Norfolk, and so obtained the manor of Letton. He, too, was Sheriff of Suffolk and also sat once for Sudbury in 1571. His son, Brampton, succeeded him in 1623, sat for Sudbury in 1621 and became Sheriff in 1629. Brampton married twice. His eldest son, John, who succeeded him at Assington in 1649, was born in 1595 or 1596. He sat for Ipswich in the Short and Long Parliaments and supported the Army party, though he refused to act at the King's trial. He was elected to the Council of State in 1650. In 1654 he sat for Suffolk and in the Convention for Sudbury. He died in 1679. His son and grandson each sat once for Sudbury. Though the Gurdons were not destined to become a great parliamentary family, they were securely based in Suffolk, and were still a county family in 1900.

John's father, Brampton Gurdon, left the Letton estates to his offspring by his second marriage. John's half-brother, Brampton, born in 1606, became a cavalry colonel on the Parliamentary side. He was Recruiter for Sudbury, but does not seem to have played a prominent part in the House. He died in 1649 and was succeeded by his son, also named Brampton.[2]

King's Lynn remained loyal to the King, but both of its members took the side of Parliament. Thomas Toll and John

[1] Page, *Suffolk*, p. 11. Bacon, *Annals of Ipswich*, p. 443.
[2] *D.N.B.* Burke, *Landed Gentry* (2, 4, 5). *Harleian Society*, LXI, p. 158. Copinger, *Suffolk*, I, p. 18.

Perceval were local merchants, neither of whom played a large part in the House, though Thomas Toll sat until the expulsion of the Rump in 1653. Toll was the eldest son of the rector of Wells and was apprenticed to a linendraper. He married the daughter of a Mayor and Alderman of Lynn and himself became Mayor in 1639 and again in 1646, when a safe man was needed to take control over a Royalist town. He died in 1654. His son was Mayor of Lynn in the following year and represented it in 1659. It seems likely that it was the son who was not approved as a freeman of Norwich in 1639. A John Toll died in 1672, when acting as Sheriff of Norwich. The clerical connection probably continued, as a number of Tolls appear among the local clergy in the sixteenth and seventeenth centuries. One of them resigned his Norwich rectory in 1624, and another was curate of Lynn in 1657.[1] John Perceval, described like Toll as 'gent.' in the election return, was also a freeman by apprenticeship and a merchant. He was Mayor in 1630 and again in 1638, when the Mayor had died in office. He may have been related to John, rector of Great Snoring in 1574 and of Stiffkey in 1600, but no proof has been found of this. He died in 1644.[2]

Yarmouth showed obstinacy in 1640 by refusing to elect Sir John Suckling to please the King or Sir Henry Marten to please the Earl of Northumberland. Instead the borough elected its Recorder, Miles Corbet, and Edward Owner, one of the Aldermen. Miles Corbet, Recorder of Yarmouth and of Lynn, was second son of Sir Thomas Corbet of Sprowston. The Corbets had been at Sprowston from 1545, the founder of the family being a lawyer. Miles was related to the Wodehouses of Kimberley through his great-aunt's marriage to the grandfather of Thomas, M.P. for Thetford, while the Corbet and Spelman families were remotely connected by the father of the Recruiter for Castle Rising having as his stepmother a lady who then married Miles Corbet's grandfather, Sir Miles, as her third husband. Miles Corbet's father and grandfather were both Sheriffs of Norfolk, and his brother, Sir John Corbet, Bt., was

[1] *Norfolk Record Society*, V, p. 223. *Lynn Freemen*, pp. 140, 155, 157, 159.
[2] *Lynn Freemen*, pp. 135, 150, 155.

Knight of the Shire in 1624 and Burgess for Yarmouth in 1625 and 1626. He himself represented Yarmouth in 1628 and the Short Parliament. He was a regicide and gained the office of Clerk of the Court of Wards during the Civil War and of Registrar in the Court of Chancery in 1648 in place of an impeached member. From 1650 to 1660 he was in Ireland, where he became Chief Baron of the Exchequer in 1655. Though an embittered partisan he seems to have been an honest one. Ludlow, not the most easily satisfied of men, paid tribute to his integrity, and he claimed in his dying speech to have spent his estate in the service of Parliament and never to have bought King's or Bishops' lands. He was elected for Yarmouth in 1660 on a double return, but the election was annulled. His execution after his flight to Holland was the result of Downing's treachery. His nephew, the 3rd Baronet, was a devoted Royalist and had to sell Sprowston. The baronetcy, which was created in 1623, became extinct on this nephew's death in 1661.[1]

Edward Owner, though a person of much less national importance, seems also to have been a difficult man and a man of great weight in the town, where he was vigorously and successfully engaged for many years in various improving and philanthropic projects. When he was first Bailiff of Yarmouth in 1634, he caused a dispute by refusing to allow the Bailiffs of the Cinque Ports to sit with those of Yarmouth, as had been the custom. He was a wealthy merchant and leader of the Presbyterian party in Yarmouth, which he had already represented in 1621, 1625, and the Short Parliament. He was not secluded, so far as is known, in 1648, but he was by this time seventy-two and there is no trace of further participation by him in parliamentary business before his death in 1650. Owner was essentially a local politician, a freeman by birth, son of a Yarmouth merchant and sea-captain, and himself a Yarmouth grocer. Such local notables, when as in this case men of powerful character, were in no way to be ignored.[2]

---

[1] *D.N.B. Harleian Society*, XXXII, p. 84. Blomefield, *Norfolk*, pp. 458-9.

[2] Manship, *Yarmouth*, pp. 348-9. *Palmer's Continuation of Manship*, pp. 101, 307. *Yarmouth Freemen*, p. 49.

Norwich

More important, of course, than any of these ports was Norwich, probably the second largest city in the country. Richard Harman and Richard Catelyn were declared elected, another indenture returning Harman and Alderman Thomas Toolie, M.P. for Norwich in the Short Parliament, being removed from the file by order of the House. The Harmans seem to have been worsted weavers at Norwich in the sixteenth century. Richard, son of Edmund Harman of Norwich, was a freeman merchant by 1613. He was a hosier and married a Norwich Alderman's daughter, by whom he had two sons; after her death he married the widow of a former Sheriff of Norwich. By 1633 he was an Alderman, and in 1639 he was Mayor: he had also been Sheriff in 1626. In the Short Parliament he had sat for Castle Rising. He died in 1646. His second son, Thomas, was, like his father, a merchant, but the eldest son, Richard, had been prepared for the ranks of the landed gentry by education at Cambridge and Gray's Inn and the purchase of the estate of Woodalling. He was married to the daughter of Sir Charles Le Gros, M P. for Orford since 1626. The Le Gros family of Crostwick, Norfolk, was a very old one; they had been at Crostwick since 1362 and may have been Norfolk landowners in the twelfth century. Sir Charles had been Sheriff of the county. He died at the age of sixty in 1656. Richard Harman died two years later before he was forty, but, the male line of the Le Gros being extinct by 1671, his children took the name of Le Gros and so assumed the identity of one of the oldest county families in Norfolk.[1]

The Catelyns of Kirby Cane, Norfolk, were originally a Suffolk family. The great-grandfather of the Richard who sat in the Long Parliament was Sheriff of Norwich in 1531 and later became an Alderman. The grandfather was a Serjeant-at-Law, autumn reader at Lincoln's Inn, and Steward of Norwich in 1555. Thomas Catelyn, father of Richard, was the second son and inherited the estate of Kirby Cane. Richard was born in 1582 or 1583 and succeeded his father by 1636. He seems, though there

[1] *Harleian Society*, XCI, p. 98. Blomefield, *Norfolk*, VI, p. 243. Millican, *Freemen of Norwich*, pp. 86, 87, 104.

is some disagreement on the point, to have first married the daughter of a judge of King's Bench and later to have married a daughter of Sir Henry Neville of Billingbeare, thus becoming the brother-in-law of Henry Neville, M.P. for Abingdon in 1650, who was one of Harrington's Republican group. He joined the Royalists and according to Le Neve was killed at Newbury. This, apart from his being rather old for active service, seems improbable, as he was petitioning the Committee for Compounding in November 1645 and only came before a more august, but, it is to be hoped, less exacting tribunal in 1662. His son, Sir Neville of Kirby Cane and Wingfield Castle, Suffolk, was Knight of the Shire for Norfolk in the first parliament of 1679, when he successfully opposed the Whigs, and sat for Norwich in 1685 and in the Convention. On his death in 1702 the male line became extinct. It is possible that the Catelyns were represented in Parliament once before 1640. A George Catelyn sat for Rochester in 1572; the unusual name makes relationship probable, but none has been traced.[1]

Castle Rising and Thetford

Sir John Holland, Bt., of Quiddenham, M.P. for Castle Rising, was the longest lived of all the members of the Long Parliament, spanning the whole century from 1602 to 1701. The Hollands were a fairly new and prospering family; they first appeared at Quiddenham in 1572, when the manor was bought by the member's grandfather, and claimed descent from the Lincolnshire Hollands. The purchase of Quiddenham was followed by a number of other purchases: the Hollands were clearly growing in power and influence. Sir Thomas, Sir John's father, married the daughter of Sir Thomas Knyvett. Sir John himself married an heiress from Denbighshire who was the widow of Lord Sandys, while his daughter married the eldest son of Sir Thomas Garrard, Bt., of Norfolk. His grandson and successor married the younger daughter and heiress of the last Earl of Yarmouth and became Comptroller of the Household to

[1] *Norfolk Record Society*, IV, p. 49. *Harleian Society*, VIII, p. 161. Blomefield, *Norfolk*, VIII, pp. 31-2.

Queen Anne in 1709. He was a leading Whig, and his words as one of the conductors of the Sacheverell impeachment are quoted by Burke in his 'Appeal from the New to the Old Whigs'.

Sir Thomas Holland, Sir John's father, had sat for Thetford in 1621 and for the county in 1624. Sir John, who had been created a baronet in 1629, first sat for the county in the Short Parliament, but had to content himself with Castle Rising in the Long Parliament. He was secluded in 1648, sat for Castle Rising again in the Convention and represented Aldeburgh in the Cavalier Parliament. His grandson, who has been mentioned above, sat for the county in William's last parliament and in the first three of Anne. In 1729 the baronetcy became extinct.[1]

Holland's colleague was Sir Robert Hatton, uncle of Sir Christopher Hatton, who elected to sit for Higham Ferrers instead of Castle Rising. Sir Christopher, whose position as Steward of Higham Ferrers may account for his securing the seat there, was one of Henrietta Maria's candidates, most of whom failed to secure election. Sir Robert's elder brother, Sir Christopher, father of the M.P. for Higham Ferrers, had inherited the lands of Lord Chancellor Hatton, the founder of the family's fortunes. Their father was John Hatton of Stanton, Cambridgeshire, and their mother the daughter of Robert Shute, Baron of the Exchequer and later Justice of Common Pleas. The Hattons through their Court connections had a very varied and extensive parliamentary history. The first Christopher was Knight of the Shire for Northamptonshire three times before becoming Lord Chancellor. The Sir Christopher who inherited his estates sat for Buckingham in 1601, Bedfordshire in 1604, and Huntingdon in 1614. He died in 1619. His son sat for Peterborough in the last parliament of James and the first of Charles, for Clitheroe in 1626 and for Higham Ferrers in the Long Parliament. In 1626 he had been made a Knight of the Bath like his father, at the age of twenty-one. He was a Royalist and in 1643 was rewarded for his services by being created Baron Hatton of Kirby. He returned to England in 1656 after discontinuing his visits to the King to avoid sequestration of his estates.

[1] Blomefield, *Norfolk*, I, p. 341.

In 1662 he became first a Privy Councillor and then Governor of Guernsey. He married the coheiress of Sir Charles Montagu of Boughton, Northamptonshire, and so secured alliance with another powerful and more lasting parliamentary dynasty. His son, Christopher, sat for Northampton in 1663 and succeeded his father in the peerage in 1670. This peerage became extinct in 1762.

Sir Robert may have had a share in the manor of Northwold, but he was not a Norfolk man, and Castle Rising in 1640 marked the family's only parliamentary incursion into Norfolk. He was approaching sixty at the time of his election to the Long Parliament and had sat for Queenborough in 1614 and for Sandwich in the next 3 parliaments, in the last of which he had also been elected for Stafford. He took the Royalist side and died before the Restoration. His younger brother, Thomas, began his parliamentary career as M.P. for Corfe Castle in 1621; this constituency had already been represented by Sir William Hatton in 1586 and 1588. He went on to Malmesbury in 1624 and 1625, and represented Stamford in 1628 and the Short Parliament. Sir Thomas did not sit in the House of Commons again, but in 1641 he was created baronet of Long Stanton in Cambridgeshire, the home of his father. He died in 1658, aged seventy-five; his son was Knight of the Shire for Cambridge in 1674. Thus the Hattons in their hundred years of parliamentary history represented constituencies in nine counties, but their strength undoubtedly lay in Northamptonshire and in Stamford, which lay almost on the border. At the same time they illustrate the difference between the mass of gentry who sat in the Commons and the few great Court families with wide-scattered estates and useful connections in many counties.[1]

Of less importance, but considerable prestige in the county, were the Wodehouses of Kimberley. Sir Philip, the father of Sir Thomas, M.P. for Thetford in the Long Parliament, was one of the baronets of the first creation in 1611 and married his son to the daughter of Lord Hunsdon. The Wodehouses are said

[1] D.N.B. G.E.C. *Baronetage* and *Peerage*. Wotton, *Baronetage* II, p. 182. Blomefield, *Norfolk*, II, p. 212.

to have had their first connection with Thetford through reward for services at Agincourt. They had owned Kimberley since the fourteenth century. Sir Thomas Wodehouse of Kimberley had been Sheriff of Norfolk in 1553 and 1563, and had been Burgess for Yarmouth in 1558 and 1559. A representative of another branch of the house had been Sheriff in 1584 and Knight of the Shire in 1572 and 1588. Sir Roger of Kimberley married a Corbet of Sprowston; their son, Philip, member for Castle Rising in 1586, was Sheriff in 1594 and became one of Essex's Cadiz knights. He was made a Deputy-Lieutenant of Norfolk and his son Thomas became Gentleman of the Chamber to Henry, Prince of Wales. Thomas succeeded his father as 2nd baronet in 1623, and in 1625 acted as Sheriff. He was fifty-six or fifty-seven at the outbreak of the Civil War, and there is no evidence of his serving in the Parliamentary forces. He chose to apply for readmission to the House some time after Pride's Purge though he seems to have played no active part in the Rump. He died in 1656. His son, Philip, who succeeded him, sat for the county in 1654 and 1656 and for Thetford in the Convention. He died in 1681, having outlived by ten years his eldest son, Sir Thomas, who was created baronet in his own right and married the daughter and coheiress of the last Armine of Osgodby, the powerful Lincolnshire family which provided an original member for Grantham and a Recruiter for Cumberland in the Long Parliament. Their son, Sir John, 2nd baronet of the later creation and 4th of the first, sat for Thetford in 1695, 1701, and 1705, and for the county in 1710. The Wodehouses continued to prosper and in 1797 became Barons, in 1866 Earls.[1]

The Gawdys also rose to local prominence in the sixteenth century, and their parliamentary history is more conspicuous, though they had less distinguished Court connections. The great-grandfather of Framlingham, the member for Thetford in the Long Parliament, sat for King's Lynn in 1547 and for Norwich in 1553 and 1558. One of his brothers was Chief Justice of Common Pleas and he himself was made a judge of

[1] *Norfolk Record Society*, V, p. 240. *Harleian Society*, XXXII, p. 322. Blomefield, *Norfolk*, II, pp. 543 seq.

King's Bench. He married twice; his eldest son by his second marriage, Sir Henry of Claxton, sat for the county in 1597 and 1601 after being Sheriff in 1592, and his second son, Sir Clipsby, sat for Dunwich in 1597. By his first wife, daughter and coheiress of John Bassingbourne, he had a son, Bassingbourne, who was Sheriff in 1578. His estate was at West Harling. Bassingbourne's son, Sir Bassingbourne, was also Sheriff twice, and sat for Eye once, Thetford twice, and the county before his death in 1606. His brother, Philip, also sat once for Eye and twice for Thetford, then for Sudbury and for Dunwich. Sir Bassingbourne's first wife had been the heiress of Sir Charles Framlingham of Crow's Hall, Suffolk, and his eldest son was named after that family. Framlingham, who was born in 1589, sat for Thetford in almost every parliament from 1614 until his death in 1654. It is claimed in the *D.N.B.* that he sat throughout the Long Parliament, but this is unlikely as there is no trace of him on committees after Pride's Purge. He has left an account of the proceedings in 1641 and 1642. Gawdy had been Sheriff of the county in 1627 and later became Deputy-Lieutenant. His son, William, by Lettice, coheiress of Sir Robert Knollys, was made a baronet in 1663. He sat for Thetford in the Cavalier Parliament, and a nephew, the 2nd baronet, sat for Eye in 4 parliaments between 1678 and 1685. The baronetcy became extinct in 1723.[1]

The Gawdys have the longest and most impressive parliamentary record of the Norfolk and Suffolk members and may rank as one of the great parliamentary families of England in the seventeenth century. Unlike the Howards and the Hattons and other great Court families they were confined to two adjacent counties instead of seeking election at a variety of widely-separated constituencies.

Bury St. Edmunds

The Jermyns ran the Gawdys close as a parliamentary family, but they became a Court family too and represented a number of constituencies outside Suffolk. They had been at Rushbrooke

[1] *D.N.B. Harleian Society,* XXXII, p. 126. Blomefield, *Norfolk,* I, p. 305 seq.

for more than 300 years in 1640. Already an eminent county family, they gained in power and wealth at the Dissolution, when Sir Thomas bought many of the manors belonging to the great abbey of Bury St. Edmunds for £13,000. Incidentally, his ability to pay this sum shows the position held by his family in the county. His son, Sir Ambrose, was Sheriff of Norfolk and Suffolk in 1558 and again in 1572. Sir Ambrose's son, Sir Robert, was Sheriff of Suffolk in 1579 and sat for the county in 1584 and 1586, and for East Looe in 1588: another Jermyn sat for Sudbury in the same year. Sir Robert died in 1614, leaving as his heir a son of forty-two, Sir Thomas, who was a Knight of the Bath, but who never assumed the duty of Sheriff, a usual, though not an invariable precursor to the county seat. Perhaps his religion was the reason for this. In 1614 he was Knight of the Shire (he was also elected for Andover), and from 1621 onwards sat for Bury St. Edmunds in every parliament till his death in 1645. In 1640 he was appointed Lord-Lieutenant of Suffolk and in 1641 he became Comptroller of the Household. His son, Thomas, who sat with him for Bury in the Long Parliament, had been in the House in all of King Charles's parliaments, but for a different constituency on each occasion, first Leicester, then Lancaster, then Clitheroe, then Corfe Castle. Henry, a younger son of the elder Thomas, had also sat for Corfe Castle in the Short Parliament, and for Bodmin and Liverpool in the first three parliaments of the reign. This was the more famous brother, Henrietta Maria's favourite, who was raised to the peerage in 1643. Thomas died at fifty-eight the year before the Restoration. His son, another Thomas, sat as a Tory for Bury in all the Exclusion Parliaments and succeeded his uncle in the peerage in 1684. The male line became extinct in 1708 with the death of the 3rd Baron. The property would have been divided among five sisters, but the husband of one of them, Sir Robert Davers, bought the others out. Davers was a wealthy Barbados planter. He was Sheriff of Suffolk in 1684, but seems to have spent his year of office attending to his business in Barbados. He was M.P. for Bury from 1689 to 1701 and from 1703 to 1705, and then sat as Knight of the Shire from 1705 till his death in 1722. His grandson repeated this performance by succeeding him at Bury in 1722 and sitting for the county in the next three parliaments—so much prestige does the Rushbrooke estate seem to have acquired in county politics by that time.[1]

Dunwich

One of the members for Dunwich was a Royalist—rather unexpectedly, for he was a son of Chief Justice Coke. Coke's relations with his family were of such a kind that it would not have been surprising if one of his sons had raised the banner of the Great Mogul to spite his father, but, none the less, there is perhaps room for something more than cynical amusement in the reflection that two Bacon lawyers (though nephews, not sons of the Lord Chancellor) should have appeared in the Long Parliament as Recruiters after Sir Edward Coke's son had been disabled. Henry's elder brother, John, of Holkham, however, M.P. for Lynn in 1625 and 1626, sided with the Parliament and was Sheriff of Norfolk in 1644. His eldest surviving brother, Sir Robert, had also sat in the House of Commons for Fowey in 1624 and for Gloucester in the Short Parliament, and his younger brother, Clement, of Longford in Derbyshire, sat in the House from his twentieth year till his death nine years later. His grandson, the 2nd baronet of Longford, was county member for Derby in 1685. Henry himself had an estate at Thorington which had been bought for him by his father in 1593, two years after his birth. He first sat for Wycombe in 1624, 1625, and 1626, and then for Dunwich in 1628 and the Short and Long Parliaments. He died in 1661, but his son, Richard, sat for Dunwich in the Cavalier Parliament until his death in 1669. A nephew of Henry sat for Lynn in 1670. Richard's great-grandson became Earl of Leicester in 1744.

Before leaving the Cokes it may be of interest to see a list of the constituencies represented by the family, or, to be more accurate, for which they secured election, in just over a century —Aldeburgh, Norfolk, Liskeard, Buckinghamshire, Coventry,

[1] G.E.C. *Peerage*. Page, *Suffolk*, p. 739. Metcalfe, *Visitation of Suffolk*, pp. 197 seq. Copinger, *Suffolk*, VI, pp. 329 seq.

Fowey, Gloucester, Lynn, Wycombe, Dunwich, Clitheroe, Hedon, Aylesbury, Derbyshire. But such an example is the exception, not the rule.[1]

Anthony Bedingfield, the other member for Dunwich, came of a family with many branches in both Norfolk and Suffolk. Perhaps the most distinguished were the Bedingfields of Oxburgh, Norfolk, who profited greatly by the Dissolution, but who none the less remained loyal to the old faith and were one of the most important Catholic families in the Eastern counties. Anthony belonged to the Bedingfields of Bedingfield, who had been at Fleming's Hall from before 1300 and had also settled at Ditchingham, Norfolk, in the sixteenth century. They became lords of the manor of Hedenham in 1569 and were still so in the middle of the eighteenth century. Thomas Bedingfield, Anthony's father, sat for Eye in 1586. In 1611 he bought the manor of Darsham in Suffolk. In 1636 he died, leaving three sons, Philip, Thomas, and Anthony. Anthony was the youngest and became a mercer of London and an Alderman in 1650, but was discharged on account of his being an M.P. He sat for Dunwich in the Short and Long Parliaments until Pride's Purge, and died in 1652. About three years before he had bought the manor of Swartshall in Gislingham and given it to his brother Thomas, who in his turn gave it to Philip, when he bought Darsham from him in 1655. Swartshall remained with Philip's family until the late eighteenth century. Before inheriting Darsham in 1636, Philip had already inherited in 1621 the estate of Ditchingham in Norfolk, which had gone to a younger branch and was now devised to him by his father's cousin, Sir Philip, who died without issue.

Philip's brother, Sir Thomas, as he became, sat for Dunwich in 1621 and 1626 and for Suffolk in 1654; Philip represented Norfolk in the same parliament. Sir Thomas was a Serjeant-at-Law until 1648, when he was a judge of Common Pleas for about two months before refusing to continue. He was restored to his serjeanty at the Restoration, but died in 1661. Philip, who

[1] Copinger, *Suffolk*, II, p. 165. C. W. James, *Chief Justice Coke and his Family*.

had married the sister of Nathaniel Bacon, Recruiter for Cambridge University, and of Francis, Recruiter for Ipswich, had already died in the previous year. Philip's eldest son, Thomas, died without issue in the same year as Sir Thomas, but his second son, Philip, who married the daughter of Sir John Potts (M.P. for Norfolk), carried on the line. The Bedingfields of Ditchingham and Darsham, who had sat in a Commonwealth parliament, were not represented in the House after 1660, but a nephew of the three Bedingfield brothers sat for Dunwich in the Convention and for Aldeburgh in 1685 before becoming Chief Justice to James II. This Sir Henry of Halesworth was son of John Bedingfield of Halesworth, who had predeceased his father, Thomas, and whose line achieved not only legal distinction after the Restoration, for a brother of the Chief Justice became Lord Mayor.

Anthony Bedingfield, as has been already remarked, provides yet another example of the very close connection between land and trade. The youngest son of an old family, he seized his opportunity, as did other merchants, in the crisis of the Civil War. He seems to have assisted his elder brother, who was a landed gentleman, and it is interesting to observe the eminence of two other branches of the family in the legal profession. Anthony seems to have had no children, but the landed wealth of the Bedingfields of Darsham and Halesworth, founded on success at the Bar, illustrates appropriately the comparative stability that often seems to have characterised legal as opposed to mercantile fortunes, though it is not difficult to find in abundance old and prosperous families of mercantile origin.[1]

Eye

Such a family was that of Sir Frederick Cornwallis, Bt., M.P. for Eye, a Royalist. The Cornwallises of Broome Hall, Suffolk, were, though an old family, not so old as the Bedingfields, but, unlike the Bedingfields, they had played a part in national

---

[1] *Harleian Society*, LXXXV. *Norfolk Record Society*, IV. Burke, *Commoners*, III, p. 508. Beaven, *Aldermen of London*, I, p. 317; II, p. 74. Copinger, *Suffolk*, III, p. 270; IV, p. 20.

affairs. The founder of the Cornwallis fortunes was Sheriff of London in 1378. He died in 1384, and his son joined the ranks of the landed gentry in the usual way by marrying the heiress to Ling Hall, Broome. In the sixteenth century the family rose to prominence; Sir John, son of a Knight of the Bath, was Steward of the Household to Prince Edward, and his son, Sir Thomas, was a trusted adviser of Mary, Treasurer of Calais and Comptroller of her Household. He was Sheriff of Norfolk and Suffolk in 1553 and sat for Gatton once and for the county twice; though he lost his political importance on Elizabeth's accession, he lived on in prosperity until 1604. Sir Thomas's younger son, Sir Charles, achieved success as a diplomat. He sat for Norfolk in 1604 and became Treasurer to the Prince of Wales in 1610; his son married the daughter of Sir Philip Parker, grandfather of the M.P. for Suffolk, and their son, also Sir Charles, sat for Eye in the Convention and again in 1662. Sir Thomas's eldest son was Sir William, member for Lostwithiel in 1597 and for Orford in 1614. His son by his first marriage, Thomas, sat for Horsham in 1621 and for Suffolk in 1625. On his death in 1626 the succession passed to Frederick, born of Sir William's second marriage and at that time sixteen years old. The next year he was created baronet. He sat for Eye in both Short and Long Parliaments and rendered conspicuous service in the wars, for which, and for his adherence to Charles II, he was raised to the peerage in 1661. He had sat for Ipswich in the Convention. In 1662 he died, and at the time of his death his son and successor was sitting for Eye. The 2nd Baron also died young in 1673, when his son was only eighteen, but his grandson sat for Eye at the age of twenty before succeeding to the peerage three years later. In short, the Cornwallis heir seems to have had no difficulty in securing a seat at Eye, but the marked lack of longevity in the family in the seventeenth century (Sir Thomas had lived to eighty-six in the sixteenth century) made previous service in the Commons short or impossible. Sir Frederick had been a leading Royalist and a Straffordian, and had followed the King into exile, but his great-grandson in 1695 was a Whig, a significant and, of course, by no means uncommon change of allegiance amongst the great landed families. The Cornwallis line continued until 1852.[1]

The other member for Eye was Sir Roger North of Mildenhall, the head of a younger branch of the more famous Norths of Kirtling. The founder of the North family, as of the Cornwallises, was a London merchant, but he lived more than a hundred years later. He died in 1509, leaving a son, Edward, who was Clerk of the Council of the City of London and then Clerk of Parliament from 1531 to 1540. In 1533 he bought Kirtling, and from 1540 to 1543 he was Sheriff of the Counties of Cambridge and Huntingdon. In 1554 he was raised to the peerage, an example of fortune in trade consolidated in the service of the Crown—the surest way to power and prosperity in both its legal and administrative branches. His successor, Roger, was Knight of the Shire for Cambridge three times before entering the House of Lords, and was Lord-Lieutenant of Cambridge in the Armada year. His wife, a daughter of Lord Rich, was the widow of Sir Henry Dudley; his eldest son was Knight of the Shire three times and predeceased him. Dudley, 3rd Baron North, grandson of the 2nd Baron and son of the heiress of Dr. Dale, Master of Requests, was only eighteen when he succeeded to the peerage. He was Lord-Lieutenant of Cambridge for the Parliament in 1642 and died after the Restoration at the age of eighty-four. His son, Sir Dudley, sat for Horsham in 1628 and for Cambridgeshire in the Short and Long Parliaments. Like his father, who had opposed Charles in the Lords as early as 1626, the younger Dudley sided with Parliament. He had fought in the Palatinate in 1620. In 1648 he was secluded; in 1660 he was defeated in the county election, but sat for the borough of Cambridge. He did not try for election to the Cavalier Parliament, succeeded his father in 1666 and died in 1677 aged seventy-five. His wife was a cousin of the Earl of Manchester who commanded the troops of the Eastern Association. His eldest son became 1st Baron Grey of Rolleston in 1673, and his grandson, the 6th Baron North and 2nd Baron

---

[1] Metcalfe, *Visitation of Suffolk*, pp. 21 seq. Collins, *Peerage*, II, pp. 537 seq. Copinger, *Suffolk*, III, pp. 236 seq.

Grey, became a leading Jacobite and died childless in exile. Dudley's second son, Sir Francis, M.P. for King's Lynn, became first Solicitor-General and then Attorney-General. He then became Chief Justice of Common Pleas in 1674, Lord Keeper in 1682 and Baron Guilford in 1683 two years before his early death at forty-eight. His eldest son became Lord-Lieutenant of Essex, and his grandson, after sitting for Banbury, became 3rd Baron Guilford and then 1st Earl. The Norths despite their antecedents were keen Tories from the time of Sir Francis, and the famous Lord North is thus partly responsible for the persistent historical legend that George III set about reviving the Tory party. Our Sir Dudley North had another son, also Sir Dudley, who was a mercer of London and became Sheriff and Alderman. He was a leading Turkey merchant and sat in the House for Banbury; his son, also Dudley, sat for Thetford in three parliaments and for Orford in two.

The Norths of Kirtling have been dealt with at some length, but the digression from Suffolk has been justified by the striking illustration they afford of that close connection between the land, the law and trade, the triangle which forms the framework of any study of English society in the sixteenth and seventeenth centuries. There is, perhaps, risk of tedium in repetition of this point, but this connection is still not always understood. Irresponsible theories, sufficiently disproved, it is true, by the exercise of political sense, but supported by a distressingly naïve approach towards economic forces, are still popular with many because of their attractive simplicity. Investigation of the personnel of the House of Commons supports the lessons of common sense, but there will still be those who believe that all merchants belonged to one party, the Whigs. Belief is after all easier and more comfortable than thought.

The Norths of Mildenhall were descended from Sir Henry, younger son of Roger, 2nd Baron North. Sir Henry received some of the monastic property bought by his father and acquired by successive purchases a fair estate in the parish of Mildenhall where he had settled. He also owned the adjacent property of Wickhambrooke. Our member, his son, Sir Roger, was born in 1577, succeeded his father in 1620 and thenceforward sat for Eye in every parliament up to his death in 1651 except for that of 1624, in which he was Knight of the Shire. He was never Sheriff, though his father was acting in the year of his death. His mother had been coheiress of one of the Knyvetts; Sir Roger, by marrying the coheiress of Sir John Gilbert, added Great Finborow to his estate, but this was sold again by his son in 1656. Sir Roger applied for readmission to the House after Pride's Purge, but seems to have taken no active part in the proceedings of the Rump; it is hardly surprising that he should not have done so, as he was by now over seventy. His son sat for the county in 1656, the Convention, and the Cavalier Parliament until his death in 1671, having been created baronet at the Restoration. Copinger, an excellent, indeed invaluable source where the transmission of land is concerned, is not impeccable in his political history, and gives us a charming picture here of the Norths as a loyalist family. Especially delightful is the account of Henry, Sir Roger's son, whose loyal meditations in his library are described, but whose election to the parliament of 1656 is omitted. Copinger has, of course, accepted the family's own account of its embarrassing connections at this time, but in his words we can see the development of conventional attachments instead of loyalties. Perhaps this is the inevitable consequence of civil war, but it marks a considerable decline in the moral standards of the gentry and forecasts sentimental Jacobitism and that form of allegiance to Church and King which carried great satisfaction at little cost to the Tory gentleman whose views enabled him to pursue his prejudices and persecute his opponents without much advantage to either his religious faith or his monarch.

Sir Henry North's son sat for the county in 1685 and died in 1695 when the male line became extinct. He had a sister, Thomasine, who married a son of Sir John Holland of Quiddenham, M.P. for Castle Rising. The estate went to Sir Roger's granddaughter, wife of William Hanmer, father of Sir Thomas Hanmer, Speaker of the House of Commons and leader of the Hanoverian Tories. Sir Roger was father-in-law of the member for Helston, Sidney Godolphin, one of the most attractive of the younger Royalists.[1]

Orford

Sir Charles Le Gros, M.P. for Orford, has already been mentioned in connection with the Harman family who assumed the name of Le Gros when the male line of this very old family became extinct within twenty years of Sir Charles's death in 1656. Sir Charles married one of the Knyvetts of Ashwellthorpe, thus becoming distantly related to Sir Roger North through his mother. Sir Charles's mother was the daughter of Sir Charles Cornwallis of Beeston, who was mentioned in dealing with the family history of his nephew, Sir Frederick Cornwallis, M.P. for Eye. Sir Charles Le Gros had sat for Orford in every parliament from 1626.[2]

His colleague, Sir William Playters, Bt., of Sotterley, belonged to a fifteenth century family. Sotterley had been forfeited by the Sotterley family about 1471, in the course of the Wars of the Roses, and had been given to Thomas Playters, Esq., a Yorkist, of Thorndon. By the time of his son William's death in 1512 the Playters had acquired several manors in Suffolk. William's grandson, Thomas, married a daughter of Sir John Jermyn of Rushbrooke; the Jermyns at that time had not yet reached their full strength, but the price Sir Thomas Jermyn was able to pay later for his abbey lands shows that they must have been of great consideration in the county. Another Thomas, grandson of the last, was the first of the Playters to reach knighthood; two years later in 1605 he became Sheriff of Suffolk, but he never sat in the House of Commons. He became a baronet in 1623 and died in 1638 aged seventy-three or seventy-four, when his son and successor, Sir William, was forty-eight. Sir William sat in the Long Parliament for the first and only time. He was a J.P. and of the quorum, Deputy-Lieutenant of the county, Vice-Admiral (at this time, of course,

[1] Collins, *Peerage*, IV, pp. 454 seq. Copinger, *Suffolk*, IV, p. 178.

[2] *Harleian Society*, XXXII, p. 86. *Norfolk Record Society*, IV, pp. 119-20. Blomefield, *Norfolk*, XI, pp. 10-11.

a post involving no active naval duties), and a colonel of foot, but he fell out with the army and in 1650 was in danger of sequestration as a delinquent. His wife's account on his tombstone with its references to the rebellious parliament and his consequent loss of office would make one think him a Royalist like his son, but he was not. Sir William was the only member of his family to sit in the House of Commons, and he does not seem to have been an influential figure there. His son, Thomas, a Royalist colonel of cuirassiers and later commander of a fleet of six ships for Don John, died before his father in 1651. Sir William died in 1668 and was succeeded by his half-brother, Lionel, who bought his estates and whose line continued till 1852, though Sotterley was sold by the 5th baronet between 1722 and 1730.[1]

Sudbury

Sir Simonds D'Ewes, the antiquarian and Parliamentary diarist, sat for Sudbury. He appears to have had some qualms of conscience about this, as well he might, for he was Sheriff of Suffolk at the time and it was plainly illegal for the Sheriff to allow himself to be returned for a constituency within his own county. However, as the great Sir Edward Coke had sinned even more flagrantly in this respect, D'Ewes was in good legal company. Sir Edward, indeed, though allowed the privileges and title of Knight of the Shire, had not been allowed to sit in the House.

The D'Ewes family seems to have been Flemish in origin; Sir Simonds, whose antiquarian proclivities sometimes led him into strange but convenient discoveries, decided that they were descended from the lords of Kessel in Gelderland. Adrian D'Ewes settled in England some time in the early 1500s; his son, Gerard, was a citizen and stationer of London, who six years before his death in 1593 bought the estate of Gaines in Essex. His son, Paul, was an official, one of the six clerks in Chancery. He

[1] G.E.C. *Baronetage*. Metcalfe, *Visitation of Suffolk*, pp. 56, 158. Page, *Suffolk*, pp. 364-5. *Genealogist*, New Series, I, pp. 45 seq., 169 seq., 243 seq. Copinger, *Suffolk*, II, pp. 176 seq.

alienated Gaines in the year of his father's death and bought the manor of Stowlangtoft in Suffolk which remained the family seat. His son, Simonds, was born in 1602 and retired on the threshold, as we are told, of a brilliant career in 1626. He had been called to the Bar at the Middle Temple in 1623, but was an antiquarian rather than a barrister with a large practice. He was knighted in the year of his retirement, succeeded his father in 1630 and sat in the House for the first time in the Long Parliament. In 1641 he was created a baronet. D'Ewes was not a very effective political figure, but he enjoyed great prestige as a scholar and became important through his capacity for cloaking illegal action on the part of the House with the respectability of precedent. His most striking intervention in politics was his astonishing discovery after the King's withdrawal to the north that Parliament had in the past issued ordinances having the force of law without receiving the King's consent; the truth was, of course, precisely the reverse, the King having on many occasions issued ordinances outside Parliament. D'Ewes' character, so far as we know it, suggests that this convenient error was the result of muddle headedness rather than deliberate distortion of the truth, but the incident of the Sudbury election leaves more than a trace of suspicion that he may, like so many of his Puritan fellows, have possessed in a highly exaggerated form the human feeling that legal and moral right must properly lie where he would like them to be. D'Ewes belonged to the Presbyterian party and was secluded at Pride's Purge. He retired to his estate and died two years later.

D'Ewes made two excellent bargains in the marriage market. (If he had established his facts with the same care as an antiquarian, he would have earned his reputation for scholarship.) He first married the heiress of the late Sir William Clopton of Lutons Hall, Suffolk, from whom he obtained a large estate contiguous to his father's property, on the strength of which he was able to retire from the Bar. After her death he married Elizabeth, the daughter and coheiress of Sir Henry Willoughby, Bt., of Risely, Derbyshire, who survived him and married Sir

John Wray of Glentworth, son of the Sir John who was M.P. for Lincolnshire, and himself chosen for the county in 1654. Sir Simonds' son, Sir Willoughby, and grandson, Sir Simonds, did not sit in the House, but followed the family tradition, established by Paul, of successful marriages: the younger Sir Simonds married Delariviere, daughter and coheiress of the last of the Jermyns of Rushbrooke. This fortunate and prudent family, in which love and interest seem never to have widely diverged, was admirably suited to the social conditions of the seventeenth century, but its last representative, Sir Jermyn, the 4th baronet, died unmarried in 1731. It would be interesting to know whether he died a bachelor in reaction from the family tradition or in despair of an heiress who would match the achievements of his ancestors.[1]

Sir Robert Crane of Stonham and Chilton, colleague of Sir Simonds D'Ewes at Sudbury, came of a very sound old county family. Metcalfe's *Visitations of Suffolk* gives six generations of Cranes before the Visitation of 1561, and there is no doubt that they were at Chilton from about 1436 when it was obtained by marriage, and that they had been at Stonham from a very early date. The great-grandfather of our member married the daughter of Sir Thomas Jermyn of Rushbrooke, which again established a very remote relationship between the Cranes and the Playters. Sir Robert Crane was the only member of his family to enter the House of Commons, but his period of service there was long. He sat for Sudbury in every parliament from 1614 onwards except for the two occasions on which he was elected Knight of the Shire. He was born in 1584 or 1585, was the first of his family to receive knighthood, in 1605, became a baronet in 1626 (in which year he sat for the county) and Sheriff in 1632. His connection with the Massachusetts Bay Company has been remarked in the first chapter, but no confirmation has been found of the statement that he changed sides shortly before his death in 1643. He was not disabled, nor were his successors mulcted by the Committee for Compounding on

[1] *D.N.B.* G.E.C. *Baronetage.* Page, *Suffolk*, pp. 805-6. Copinger, *Suffolk*, I, pp. 366 seq. Morant, *Essex*, I, p. 108.

account of his activities, so that a change of allegiance seems unlikely, unless it were a mental one unaccompanied by visible consequences. Members of the House were treated normally with extra severity rather than with lenience when they were convicted of delinquency.[1]

On the death of Sir Robert Crane in 1643 the male line became extinct. He had first married the daughter of Sir Henry Hobart, Chief Justice of Common Pleas, and was thus brother-in-law of the Recruiter for Norfolk. He had no children by this marriage, but by his second wife he had four daughters who shared his estate. They all married well, an indication, like Sir Robert's parliamentary career, of the family's prosperity under his leadership. The eldest, Mary, married Sir Ralph Hare, Bt.; the third, Susan, Sir Edward Walpole, K.B.; the fourth, Katherine, Edmund Bacon, nephew of Sir Robert Bacon, Bt.; and the second, Jane, married first Sir William Armine, Bt.— Recruiter for Cumberland and son of the M.P. for Grantham— and afterwards became the second wife of John, Lord Belasyse. The Armines, as mentioned above, were a prominent Lincolnshire family. Both father and son were Rumpers, the father being a particularly active member both of Parliamentary committees and of the Council of State. The Belasyses, on the other hand, were one of the great Yorkshire Catholic families, and John, M.P. for Thirsk in the Long Parliament and an active Royalist like his elder brother, the Knight of the Shire for Yorkshire, had been in the Tower for some years before his marriage to Armine's widow as the victim of Titus Oates, who had designated him as the intended, though very improbable, leader of the Catholic army. Henry, the eldest son of Lord Belasyse by his first wife, married Sir William Armine's daughter, and the considerable Armine estates were divided on the death of Sir William between Sir Henry Belasyse and Sir Thomas Barnardiston, Recruiter for Bury St. Edmunds and husband of Sir William's other daughter. Here was indeed a strange juxtaposition of fortunes and opinions; but it resulted from that

[1] Metcalfe, *Visitation of Suffolk*, pp. 22 seq. Page, *Suffolk*, pp. 931-2. G.E.C. *Baronetage*. Copinger, *Suffolk*, I, pp. 71 seq., II, pp. 291, 363.

mixture of foresight and gambling which characterised the dynastic game of chance in a society where land was at once the most secure of possessions and the gauge of social prestige. Political rivalries and alliances were often a part of the game, and political power one of the prizes; but the loyalties and enmities of politics were often overturned in the manoeuvres that led to dynastic success.

II

NORFOLK AND SUFFOLK: THE RECRUITERS

The Recruiters for the two counties were not, on the whole, of a different social standing from the original members. In a number of constituencies the Recruiter came from a more distinguished family than the member he replaced. Six of the twelve Recruiters belonged to families represented in parliament both before 1640 and after 1660; two others had predecessors of their direct line in earlier Parliaments, and two had successors in later ones. One would not perhaps have expected Maurice Barrowe (Eye) or Robert Brewster (Dunwich) in a normal House; but they were both men of substance belonging to the lesser gentry, and some members of lower social position than theirs can be found in the original Parliament. As elsewhere the Recruiters were a noticeably younger group—more so in Norfolk and Suffolk than in the rest of the Eastern Counties. Half the original members for the two counties were born in 1590 or earlier, but only one of the 12 Recruiters was born as early as 1590. Though only one of the original members was born as late as 1605, five of the Recruiters were born then or later. The youngest, Sir Thomas Barnardiston, was born about 1618.

Norfolk County

We saw that the original Norfolk Knights of the Shire came of families of secondary importance in the county, and without representation in earlier or later parliaments. One of them, Sir Edmund Moundeford, died in 1643, and in December 1645 Sir John Hobart, Bt., was elected in his place. Sir John was a man of greater wealth and social distinction in the county than either of the original Knights of the Shire, although his family, despite possessing land in the county for over 150 years, was a new one in the sense that its prominence in Norfolk was recent. His father, Sir Henry Hobart, Bt., was the second son of a family of modest significance. He was a lawyer of considerable talent and rose to be Chief Justice of Common Pleas. Before his elevation to the Bench he sat for St. Ives, Yarmouth and Norwich, where he was twice Sheriff and then Steward. His legal ability is sufficiently shown by his terrible hammering of Coke's arguments when, as Attorney-General, he had to oppose the Chief Justice's singular and sudden discovery that the powers of the Court of High Commission were not and never had been what they had commonly been assumed by lawyers to be. Hobart, who had already disappointed Bacon's ambitions by succeeding Coke as Attorney-General, succeeded Coke again as Chief Justice of Common Pleas on his being kicked upstairs to the technically higher but much less lucrative Court of King's Bench. Two years earlier he figured as 9th in precedence of the new order of baronets. The office of Attorney-General was extremely rich in its perquisites and opportunities, and few merchants could rival the revenue of the Chief Justice of Common Pleas. He ranked in seventeenth century society as a millionaire, and his profits were not speculative like the merchant's. When most law, too, was land-law, a lawyer had the advantage in securing his wealth—he was for one thing likely to be in some ways a better business man where land was concerned (though, of course, very many successful merchants were of the landed gentry), and he knew his way through the shoals of common law that lay in wait for the purchaser and might involve him in expensive litigation, if not in an actual defect in title.

Sir Henry was a great purchaser of land. The family estate of Plumstead had come to the Hobarts through James Hobart, a successful lawyer who had lived in the last sixty years of the fifteenth century. The family was supposed to have belonged originally to Tye, Essex, and then to Suffolk, but its history before James's time is obscure. Many instances are to be found in Blomefield's *Norfolk* of Sir Henry's extensive purchases and often also of sales. He died in 1625 and was succeeded by our member, Sir John, 2nd baronet of Blickling, brother-in-law of Sir Robert Crane, M.P. for Sudbury. He had already sat for Cambridge in 1621, Lostwithiel in 1624 and Brackley in 1626 when he was elected to the House as Recruiter for Norfolk in 1645. He had also acted as Sheriff in 1633. He died in 1647 aged fifty-four. He was married twice, first to a daughter of the Earl of Leicester and then to a daughter of the Earl of Bridgewater (the great Lord Chancellor Ellesmere), but had no children. He was succeeded by his nephew, John, son of Sir Miles Hobart, M.P. for Marlow in 1628: this Sir John, son-in-law of John Hampden, acted as Sheriff in 1666 and was M.P. for the county in 1654, 1656, 1659, 1673, and in all three Exclusion Parliaments. The next two generations of Hobarts also sat for the county, though not continuously. They also secured election to King's Lynn, Thetford and some west-country constituencies. The 5th baronet was raised to the peerage in 1728, and the Hobarts became Earls of Buckinghamshire a little later.

The Hobarts provide an admirable example of the extent and stability of the great legal fortunes. The family was first established by one lawyer and then, over a hundred years later, brought into prominence by a man who as Attorney to the Court of Wards, Attorney-General and Chief Justice of Common Pleas enjoyed the plums of the legal profession. He and his son both showed energy and discrimination in their constant enterprises in the land market and this tradition was followed by their descendants. By 1660 the family's position was too secure to be shaken. One of the Hobart brothers had been a keen Royalist, but the family as a whole had sided with Parliament. The reigning baronet had been elected to all the Interregnum parliaments except Barebones', but he was not elected in 1660 or 1661. The check, however, was merely temporary. In 1673 he came in at a by-election for Norfolk and continued to represent the county till his death. By the time of the Hanoverian accession the family was ready for a final recognition of its eminence in the county and, through the county, in national affairs. That recognition came in 1728, and in the Cabinet crises of the generation preceding the Reform Bill the Earl of Buckinghamshire is sometimes to be found exerting an obstructive influence in proportion to his social importance rather than to his talents.[1]

On Sir John Hobart's death Sir John Palgrave, Bt., was elected Knight of the Shire. The Palgraves were not a family of comparable distinction to the Hobarts, but they had been at Northwood Berningham since the early sixteenth century. They claimed to have owned the manor of Little Palgrave from the time of Henry V, but such claims are only too common. They may indeed have been a very old family, but the fifteenth century is as far back as they can be traced with certainty. The grandfather of Sir John had been a Bencher of the Middle Temple and his father, Sir Augustine, was also a barrister. The Palgraves were not a parliamentary family; Sir Augustine was Sheriff in 1617, and his grandson was again Sheriff in 1691, but Sir John was the only Palgrave to sit in the House, unless, as is quite possible, for he had several brothers, he was uncle or great-uncle to the John Palgrave who sat for Norwich in 1703 and had his election disallowed in 1705. In 1641 he was created a baronet two years after succeeding his father; in 1645 he was a Commissioner of the New Model; in 1647 he was elected to the Long Parliament, but was secluded at Pride's Purge in the next year. One of Sir John's sisters married the son of Sir William Playters, M.P. for Orford: his eldest son and successor married as his second wife the daughter of the late Sir William Spring, Recruiter for Bury St. Edmunds. Sir John sat for Yarmouth in the Convention until his election was voided. He died in 1672 aged sixty-seven; his son, Sir Augustine, became a Gentleman of the Privy Chamber, and his son died unmarried in 1732, when the baronetcy became extinct.[2]

[1] G.E.C. *Baronetage. Harleian Society*, XXXII, p. 166. *Norfolk Record Society*, IV, p. 101. Blomefield, *Norfolk*, VI, pp. 395 seq.

[2] G.E.C. *Baronetage. Norfolk Record Society*, V, p. 154. Blomefield, *Norfolk*, VIII, pp. 94-5.

Ipswich and King's Lynn

The Recruiters for the important towns, far from showing any decline in social position compared with the original members, on balance showed the reverse. At Ipswich Francis Bacon, a barrister, replaced William Cage; his elder brother, Nathaniel, likewise a barrister and Bencher of Gray's Inn in 1640, was Recruiter for Cambridge University. Nathaniel (also Recorder of Bury) became Recorder of Ipswich in 1643 and may very well have helped his younger brother to gain this seat. This is not, however, by any means necessarily the case as the large estate of Shrubland owned by their eldest brother until 1637 and then by their nephew is situated very near Ipswich and might easily appear a suitable place from which to select a gentleman with legal training as member. Edward Bacon, father of Francis and Nathaniel, was son of Lord Keeper Bacon; he obtained Shrubland by marrying the heiress of its owner, Thomas Little. Edward sat for Yarmouth, Tavistock, Weymouth, and the County of Suffolk before becoming Sheriff in 1601. His eldest brother had sat for Beverley and then for Suffolk and had been Sheriff first of Suffolk and then of Norfolk; and another elder brother, Nathaniel, had sat for Tavistock, Lynn, and the county of Norfolk. Better-known are his two half-brothers, Anthony, who was Essex's adviser on foreign affairs and M.P. for Wallingford and Oxford, and Francis, who sat for constituencies in many counties and was Sheriff of Norfolk before becoming Lord Chancellor.

The parliamentary history of the Bacons is very full, but not very long. The stream was already drying up at the accession of James I. After the disgrace of the Lord Chancellor, Sir Edmund, 2nd baronet of Redgrave, sat for the County of Norfolk in 1625, but there is no further representation of the family until 1645. It would be hard to find a more active parliamentary family in the last thirty years of the sixteenth century; in 1611 the head of the Bacon house became senior baronet of England—as he still is—but a generation later, though they were a numerous family, their parliamentary influence was gone except for the brief interlude of the Civil Wars and Interregnum.

Nathaniel seems to have played a more important part than Francis. Both applied for readmission after Pride's Purge, but do not appear to have made much use of their resumed right to sit in the Commons. Both sat in the parliaments of 1654, 1656, and 1659 for the same constituencies as in 1645. Both were Masters of Requests, and Francis was also a Suffolk J.P. Nathaniel sometimes acted as an intermediary between Cromwell and the Council of State when there were disagreements. Both the brothers sat for Ipswich in the Convention; Nathaniel died in the course of the Parliament aged sixty-six or sixty-seven, and Francis died three years later aged sixty-three. The Bacons continued at Shrubland till the late eighteenth century.[1]

King's Lynn had stayed loyal to the King, though its M.P.s were both Parliamentarians. It chose as Recruiter, after the death of Perceval, Edmund Hudson, woollen draper and Alderman. Hudson had been Mayor in 1643, and the House pronounced him incapable to sit because of his part in a riot which took place in Lynn that year. It seems probable that Lynn was, in fact, presuming to choose a Royalist.

After the execution of the King and the abolition of the House of Lords three peers decided to signalise their adherence to the new order by gaining seats in the Commons. Lord Howard of Escrick, M.P. for Carlisle, was afterwards expelled for taking bribes, a rather remarkable achievement when the standards of venality in the Rump are remembered. The Earl of Pembroke and Montgomery, M.P. for Berkshire, was perhaps the most respectable of this unsavoury trio. The Earl of Salisbury decided to do King's Lynn the dubious honour of representing it. He was the only son of Robert Cecil, a statesman whom history has treated more kindly than he deserves, for it was under his selfish and unimaginative leadership that the problems facing Elizabeth in her declining years and James in his unfamiliar kingdom were neglected or mishandled. A great deal of the corruption and discouragement of these years must be debited to the influence of this cold, conservative *nouveau riche* with his intuitive hatred

[1] *D.N.B.* Metcalfe, *Visitation of Suffolk*, pp. 109 seq. Copinger, *Suffolk*, II, p. 244.

of genius and his devious zeal in undermining it. Firmly he kept himself between the King and his people, so that all government should be carried on through him or not at all. He wished his son to succeed him in office, but even the nepotism of the seventeenth century was not equal to such a choice, and Robert realised the impossibility of training him for such responsibility. William succeeded his father as 2nd Earl of Salisbury in the year of his majority. He became Lord-Lieutenant of Hertfordshire in the same year, and in 1624 he received the Garter. In 1642 he became Lord-Lieutenant of Dorset for the Parliament, and he took part in the Assembly of Divines in 1643. Few of the most influential peers were active on the side of Parliament, and those who were were prized accordingly. In 1646 Salisbury was one of the Commissioners of the Great Seal; in December of the previous year Parliament had voted him a Marquessate for his services. In February 1649 he was elected a member of the first Council of State, but he was not re-elected. He sat for Hertfordshire in the 1654 and 1656 parliaments and survived the Restoration, by which time he was approaching seventy. In 1663 he was made High Steward of St. Albans; in 1668 he died. His eldest son, Charles, Viscount Cranborne, sat for Hertford in the Short and Long Parliaments and predeceased him in 1660: another son sat for Old Sarum in the Long Parliament and again in the Convention. His grandson, James, was elected to the Cavalier Parliament for Hertfordshire at a by-election, but shortly afterwards succeeded him in the earldom. Another Cecil of this branch sat for Wootton Bassett in 1708, but the Hertfordshire Cecils figure in the House hardly at all after the Restoration. The Earl of Salisbury's venture in 1649 was their only incursion into Norfolk or Suffolk; the first Robert Cecil had sat for Westminster first and then for Hertfordshire, where, of course, their influence was strongest.[1]

Norwich

The two Recruiters for Norwich played a more important part in politics than their predecessors. Thomas Atkins was a

[1] G.E.C. *Peerage*. Warrand, *Hertfordshire Families* (*V.C.H.*), pp. 109 seq.

merchant and Alderman of both Norwich and London. In 1627 he became Sheriff of Norwich; in 1637 he was Sheriff of London. He was elected for Norwich in the Short Parliament, but was not chosen again in October 1640. By trade he was a mercer of London and grocer of Norwich, and became Master of the Mercers in 1644. From 1644 to 1645 he was Lord Mayor of London; he took a prominent part in City military politics, being Colonel of the Red Regiment from 1642 to about 1645. Though he refused to attend the King's trial, he supported the Army against the Presbyterians in the City and remained one of the most prominent London politicians during both Rump and Protectorate. He was knighted by Cromwell in 1657. In 1659 he again sat for Norwich, but after the Restoration he soon sank into obscurity; it was now the turn of the former Major-General Richard Browne and the Presbyterian majority to lord it. Atkins was President of Christ's Hospital from 1660 to 1661, but in the latter year he was removed from his aldermanry. He must by this time have been old, and nothing more is known of him. There is no trace of his having had either ancestors or descendants of any great significance.[1]

His colleague, Erasmus Earle, who came into the House over a year later than Atkins to replace Harman, was an eminent barrister. In 1639 he was a Reader at Lincoln's Inn, and from 1635 to 1641 he was a Bencher. In 1644 he became secretary to the English commissioners at Uxbridge, in 1647 he entered the House and in 1648 he was made Serjeant-at-Law and Steward of Norwich, of which he was also from 1649 to 1653 Recorder. In December 1653 he was made one of the counsel to the state. At the Restoration, in his seventieth year, he again became a Serjeant-at-Law and his large income enabled him to resume the building up of his Norfolk estates. He had already acquired Heydon from Sir Roger Townshend in 1643 and the manor of Stenton in the same year; in 1662 he bought the manor of Cawston for £3,250 from the nephew and successor of Sir John Hobart, Recruiter for Norfolk. Earle's son set the seal on

[1] Beaven, *Aldermen of London*, II, pp. 64, 180. Millican, *Freemen of Norwich*, pp. 86, 87, 104.

5

this process by serving as Sheriff, in 1654, it is true, when the holding of this office hardly carried its usual prestige. Expenses of war and fines gave opportunities to a prosperous partisan lawyer, who could gain rather than lose by the conflict. The acceleration of changes in ownership of land reacted also to the benefit of the lawyers, who drew a large part of their profits from matters concerning land. The complication and uncertainty of the law touching title was also a source of litigation, one of the favourite hobbies of the seventeenth century gentleman and one chiefly rewarding to the lawyers.[1]

The smaller Boroughs

All the Recruiters for the smaller constituencies were country gentlemen of more or less importance. John Spelman of Narburgh, Recruiter for Castle Rising, belonged to a branch of that family which had never been represented in Parliament. His grandfather's cousin, Sir Henry Spelman, the antiquarian, had sat for Castle Rising twice and for Worcester once, and Sir Henry's son had also sat for Worcester, but this was a distant relationship: these Spelmans were Royalist and the younger, though the more distinguished and prosperous, branch of the family. Both branches were descended from Sir John Spelman, judge of King's Bench, but the Spelmans of Narburgh were the offspring of his eldest son, the great-grandfather of our member, John Spelman. The Spelmans were lords of Bekerton in the fourteenth century. Narburgh had originally been bought by Henry Spelman, Recorder of Norwich and father of the judge, Sir John Spelman, in the second half of the fifteenth century. John Spelman, elder brother of Clement, Recorder of Nottingham, was step-son of Sir John Potts, the county member, by his second wife. Spelman's son, who succeeded him on his death at fifty-seven in 1663, was named Moundeford, presumably after the other original county member, Moundeford of Feltwell, who died in 1643. No relationship, however, has been traced between the two families except for the very remote one that the sister of John Spelman's great-grandfather was

1 D.N.B. Blomefield, *Norfolk*, VI, pp. 243 seq., 259.

grandmother of Sir Edmund Moundeford. Possibly, but no evidence can be adduced for this suggestion, Sir Edmund acted as godfather to Moundeford Spelman. What is quite certain is that nobody would inflict such a name on a child without cause, so that it seems in any case clear that John Spelman was closely connected with both the original county members. John's father, Sir Clement, had been Sheriff in 1598, an office filled a little later by Sir Henry Spelman of Congham, of the other branch. John Spelman was secluded in 1648 and sat once more for Castle Rising in the Convention. Here the parliamentary history of the Spelmans of Narburgh ends. The family's connection with Narburgh, which began in the late fifteenth century, continued into the eighteenth century. They had also acquired other manors in the sixteenth century.[1]

One of the Recruiters for Bury St. Edmunds, Sir Thomas Barnardiston, has already been dealt with; his father was Knight of the Shire for Suffolk. His colleague was Sir William Spring, Bt., of Pakenham. The Springs had been at Pakenham since the Dissolution, when it had been granted to Sir John of Lavenham, grandson of Thomas, a wealthy clothier of Lavenham in the late fifteenth century. Sir John's son, Sir William, had married a widowed daughter of Sir Ambrose Jermyn of Rushbrooke and had become Sheriff of Suffolk in 1578 and 1596. His son only survived him by two years, but his grandson, father of our member, was Sheriff in 1621, county member in 1624 and 1628 and M.P. for Bury in 1625. He died in 1638. His son was Sheriff in 1641 and was created a baronet in the same year; he was elected for Bury in 1645 and for the county in 1654, in which year he died. His eldest son William, the 2nd baronet, married the daughter of Sir Dudley North, M.P. for Cambridgeshire; he became Sheriff, and county member in all three Exclusion Parliaments and died in 1684 aged forty-two. His daughter married Francis Drake, M.P. for Amersham, and his son, the 3rd baronet, married one of the coheiresses of Lord Jermyn of Rushbrooke: the Jermyn inheritance seems

[1] *Norfolk Record Society*, V, p. 205. Blomefield, *Norfolk*, II, p. 279 ; VI, pp. 151 seq.

to have acted as a sort of rallying cry for a number of our parliamentary families. The baronetcy became extinct in 1769.[1]

The Springs were clearly a family of considerable local importance. This could not be said of the Brewsters, who, as has been remarked earlier, were solid, substantial folk of the lesser gentry, but not of the usual stuff of which members were made, especially perhaps in East Anglia. It was one thing for a town like King's Lynn to elect local worthies who were lower in the social scale and perhaps no wealthier, though this last is unlikely. (William Cage, however, of Ipswich was supposed to be poorer than Brewster.) It was quite another for a constituency like Dunwich to elect someone of as little local standing as Brewster. Examples can, however, be found here and there in other regions.

The Brewsters had been at Wrentham since 1576, when it had been purchased by Humphrey Brewster. Robert Brewster, the elder (Copinger has proved it was the elder Robert, not, as is usually alleged, the younger, who was the Recruiter for Dunwich), was Humphrey's grandson; he was forty-six when elected, and brother-in-law of Miles Corbet, M.P. for Yarmouth. The Corbets of Sprowston were a sound family, and Robert's marriage showed that the Brewsters of Wrentham were rising in the world. In fact, Robert's land purchases sent up the family's income from land from £700 to £1,000. One of his sisters-in-law was the daughter of Thomas Atkins, Recruiter for Norwich and Lord Mayor of London. What was in reality happening was that the Brewsters by their enthusiastic championing of the Independent cause and, later, of Cromwell at the very time when men of older and more powerful families were tending deliberately towards caution, were able to assume in the county a leadership which would in normal times have been quite outside their reach. Robert sat in the Rump, in 1654, 1656, and 1659. His brother Francis sat for Suffolk in Barebones' Parliament, and his son Francis for Dunwich in 1656. At the Restoration their brief importance vanished, but the Brewsters retained their

[1] Metcalfe, *Visitation of Suffolk*, pp. 22 seq., Page, *Suffolk*, pp. 728 seq. Copinger, *Suffolk*, I, p. 75; VI, pp. 304 seq.

lands until 1797. Robert died in 1663 and his son, Francis, in 1677 aged fifty-four. In the Exclusion Parliaments Dunwich was represented by Sir Philip Skippon, Bt., descendant of the Parliamentary general, who came of a good Norfolk family: Sir Philip was the widower of Francis Brewster's daughter.[1]

Maurice Barrowe of Barningham, Recruiter for Eye, also came of an undistinguished family of the lesser gentry, but one which was prospering and steadily accumulating property. His grandfather, a Norfolk man, had married a Suffolk coheiress, and came to own a good deal of property in Suffolk. Five Suffolk manors were in the hands of the Barrowe family in 1543 ; so they became landowners a generation earlier than the Brewsters. Maurice's father, William, was described as being of Westhorp, one of the manors obtained in 1543. Maurice, who was born in 1596 or 1597, bought Barningham, where he took up his residence in 1628, fifteen years after his father's death. He had been to Cambridge and Gray's Inn, and had married a co-heiress. But his parliamentary career was brief and undistinguished: he was elected in 1645 and secluded in 1648, and does not seem to have returned with the Secluded Members in 1660. He died childless in 1666 and the estates went to a cousin.[2]

Norfolk and Suffolk, like any other counties that could have been selected for this full biographical examination, can in part be taken as samples of the region as a whole and are also in part unique. Repetition of the process for the other counties would be unbearably tedious; but we can survey some of them more briefly to see how far they confirm what has already been shown.

III

THE OTHER COUNTIES

Cambridgeshire

With only the County Town and the University to add to the seats for the shire, Cambridgeshire did not offer its gentry much scope in politics. The University sent to the Long

---

[1] *Harleian Society*, LXXXVI, p. 253. Copinger, *Suffolk*, II, p. 212.

[2] *Harleian Society*, LXI, p. 208. Copinger, *Suffolk*, I, pp. 174, 276.

Parliament its Reader in Civil Law and the secretary to its Chancellor Lord Holland.[1] One of the county members, Sir Dudley North, has already been described. One of the borough members, John Lowry, was a chandler by trade and a lesser notable of the town. He became an Alderman in 1641 and Mayor in 1644, served as a colonel in the Parliamentary forces, and sat in the Rump. He was able to send his son to Eton and to the local University; but after John's death in 1669 the Lowrys returned to their original obscurity.[2]

The other two original members provide stories of distinguished ancestry and of the danger of extravagance. Thomas Chichele of Wimpole was descended from a brother of Archbishop Chichele who was Sheriff and Alderman of London, and the family had been at Wimpole from the fifteenth century. Thomas was a Royalist and compounded for a heavy fine; he sat for the county again in the Cavalier Parliament and for the Borough of Cambridge in every parliament thereafter until his retirement from politics after the Convention of 1689. He was the only member of the Eastern Association group to join the handful of survivors of the Long Parliament in that of 1689. He was knighted and became a Privy Councillor in 1670; he was also for a time Master-General of the Ordnance. Pepys says that he lived extravagantly in London—in any case he sold Wimpole in 1686, thirteen years before his death in 1699. In an interesting chapter in the Victoria County History of Cambridge it is suggested that Wimpole was one of a small group of estates which established a claim to periodic possession of the county seat. It is certainly true that Chicheles sat for the county at intervals for 200 years and that the Harleys who owned Wimpole from 1720 did so in the eighteenth century.[3]

Lowry's colleague for the borough was Oliver Cromwell. His own career is fairly well known, but a few words on the subject of his family may perhaps be allowed. Sir Richard Cromwell, born Williams, who assumed the name of his uncle,

---

[1] D.N.B.   [2] Blomefield, *Collectanea Cantabrigiensia*, p. 80.
[3] D.N.B. *Harleian Society*, XLI, p. 33. *V.C.H. Cambridgeshire*, II, p. 411.

the famous Thomas Cromwell, was granted at the Dissolution Hinchingbrooke, Ramsay, St. Neots and other monastic estates. These enormous possessions gave the Cromwells dominance in the small county of Huntingdon—a dominance they maintained until the sale of Hinchingbrooke to the Montagus in 1627. The list of Cromwell Sheriffs and Cromwell M.P.s would be long and tedious, but it includes Oliver's father as M.P. for Huntingdon once. Sir Oliver of Hinchingbrooke, grandson of Sir Richard, exhausted his estate by extravagance more than twenty years before the end of his life. He and his family were ardent Royalists in a part of the country where Royalism was rare and liable to be disastrous. Robert, his brother, who lived in a much smaller way, was Burgess for Huntingdon once and a J.P. Oliver lived under the shadow of the senior branch—his uncle, Sir Oliver, was ruining himself in great style and was a friend of King James, whom he often entertained at great expense. In 1627 the crash came. Oliver had never been on good or close terms with his uncle. He, too, was having financial difficulties, and, after sitting for Huntingdon in the parliament of 1628, he sold up and moved to St. Ives and then to Cambridgeshire. The wealth of the Cromwell family, established by its great relative and by a marriage with the daughter of a Lord Mayor, had been mainly transmitted to the senior line and was there squandered. The Cromwells were prolific, and the younger branches were straitened, though most of Sir Oliver's brothers did better for themselves than Robert. Oliver Cromwell in 1640 belonged in substance to the lesser gentry, though his family antecedents were much more distinguished than his own position.[1]

We shall not try to explore here the great network of Oliver's relations in the House; but there is no need to look far for one of them. Francis Russell, Recruiter for the county, was brother-in-law of Chichele, the Royalist he replaced, and became father-in-law of Henry Cromwell. He was made a colonel in the Parliamentary army, though not in the New Model, and was Governor of Ely, Lichfield and, later, of the Channel Islands.

[1] *V.C.H. Hunts.* II, pp. 357-8.

He was probably a little under thirty when he was elected; he was secluded in 1648, but was later re-admitted to the House, though he seems to have played a very small part in its proceedings. He sat for the county again in 1654 and 1656, and was put into the Cromwellian House of Lords in 1657. The Cromwellian connection was reinforced by his son and successor's marriage to Elizabeth, widow of the son of the Earl of Warwick. Francis, who had succeeded his father at Chippenham as 2nd baronet in 1654, died in 1664. One of his brothers, Gerard, sat for the county in 1679; another brother, Sir William, of Bury St. Edmunds, was noted for his loyalty to the King in the Civil War.[1]

Huntingdonshire

The County and Borough of Huntingdon have already been remarked as practically a Montagu monopoly, with the exception of the senior Knight of the Shire, Valentine Walton, brother-in-law of Oliver Cromwell and head of a very old though not particularly eminent or wealthy family. Incidentally, Walton's difficulty in securing part of his patrimony throws a rather surprising light on the lawlessness which could still flourish near to London in the time of James I. It certainly looks from the tale of the Sheriff's unsuccessful attempt to enter a house defended by armed friends of the usurper, Throckmorton, as though Star Chamber was more necessary for the enforcement of ordinary law and order than has sometimes been supposed. The Waltons were never elected to Parliament before or after 1640. Valentine Walton was a colonel in the Eastern Association and Governor of Lynn. He was a regicide and a member of every Council of State until the dismissal of the Rump, but despite his relationship with Cromwell his republicanism made him hostile to the Protectorate. He thus failed to secure election to the 1659 Parliament. At the Restoration he was excepted from the Act of Indemnity and fled to Germany, where he probably died in 1661. He lost both the estate from the Queen's dowry which he had purchased and the paternal

[1] G.E.C. *Baronetage*. Wotton, *Baronetage*, II, p. 138.

estates at Great Staughton which had been in the hands of the
Waltons since 1406.[1]

The other Knight of the Shire was Sir Sidney Montagu, sixth
son of the judge, Sir Edward Montagu of Boughton Castle,
founder of the fortunes of that great parliamentary family. He
had himself become a barrister and after being Groom of the
Bedchamber to James I was Master of Requests to Charles I. He
bought land extensively in the '20s and '30s, his greatest purchase
being Hinchingbrooke in 1627. Sir Sidney refused to engage
himself against the Royalists and was expelled the House and imprisoned in 1642. He died two years later, when he was approaching seventy. Otherwise the Montagus in their various branches
were for the Parliament. Sir Sidney's eldest son, the admiral who
was made Earl of Sandwich at the Restoration, succeeded him
as Recruiter for the county. He was a colonel in his cousin Manchester's army and then in the New Model; but he resigned and
apparently took no part in the second Civil War. He was secluded in 1648, but after the expulsion of the Rump he became
a member of the Council of State, and in 1656 General-at-Sea.

George Montagu, member for Huntingdon, was half-brother
of the General and one of the youngest members of the House,
being only sixteen or seventeen. His distinction consists in being
grandfather of the Lord Halifax of the Whig Junto. His colleague and cousin, Edward Montagu, was twenty-three when he
succeeded to the barony of Boughton in 1644.[2] His promotion
to the Lords resulted in the election as Recruiter of Abraham
Burrell, who seems to have been a Montagu nominee. He was
second son of a wealthy grocer of London who had bought the
estate of Dowsley, Lincolnshire, which went to his eldest son,
Sir John. The Dowsley branch was Royalist. Abraham Burrell
obtained the manor of Medloe, Huntingdonshire, in 1641; he
had already acquired the manor of Chertsey through his wife.
Unlike the Montagus, who were all secluded, he was an active
Rumper. He died in 1657, and his property went to his four
daughters.[3]

[1] D.N.B.   V.C.H. Hunts. II, pp. 357-8.
[2] V.C.H. Hunts. pp. 24 seq., 62-6.   [3] V.C.H. Hunts, II, pp. 28, 319.

Hertfordshire

The members for Hertfordshire and its boroughs of Hertford and St. Albans provide some good specimens of the Tudor sources of the wealth of seventeenth-century families. Arthur Capel of Little Hadham, the senior Knight of the Shire, was descended from a merchant, Sir William Capel, who had been Lord Mayor of London and had bought Hadham in 1505. The Capels had prospered in the county, and had sat in the House of Commons. Arthur was created a Peer in 1641. An early opponent of the Court, he was converted into a Royalist leader and was executed in 1649 for his part in the second Civil War. His mother was a sister of Sir Sidney Montagu. His son Arthur was made Earl of Essex at the Restoration and played a leading part in politics, but was destroyed by his alliance with the Whigs. Another son, Henry, sat in many parliaments before being called to the Lords.[1]

Sir Thomas Dacres of La Mote, Cheshunt, who succeeded Capel in 1641, was one of the many members who derived their wealth both from the City and from Crown offices: Cheshunt was granted in 1538 to George Dacres, son of a Master of Requests and grandson of an Alderman of London. Sir Thomas was secluded at Pride's Purge and sat again in the Convention of 1660 for Higham Ferrers. He died in 1668, when he was about eighty years old. As his son Thomas (Recruiter for Callington) died before him, he was succeeded by his grandson Robert, who sold the property to the Earl of Salisbury.[2]

Sir William Lytton of Knebworth was son of a county member, Sir Rowland, who had been Captain of the Band of Gentleman Pensioners to Queen Elizabeth. The Lyttons were considerable landowners and had been at Knebworth since 1492. Sir William had sat for the county twice before 1640, and four generations of Lyttons held the office of Sheriff; but after Sir William's death in 1660 their parliamentary history ceased. His son and successor sat for the county in 1656, 1659, and in the

[1] G.E.C. *Peerage*. Collins, *Peerage*, III, p. 474. *V.C.H. Herts.* IV, p. 52. Warrand, *Hertfordshire Families (V.C.H.)*, pp. 77 seq. Chauncy, *Hertfordshire*, I, pp. 306 seq.
[2] *V C.H. Herts.* III, p. 453. Chauncy, *Hertfordshire*, I, p. 585.

Convention, but Sir William himself did not return to the House after Pride's Purge.[1]

Sir Thomas Fanshawe, K.B., of Ware Park, member for Hertford, came of an official family, which enjoyed the hereditary office of Remembrancer of the Exchequer. His grandfather, Thomas Fanshawe of Fanshawe Gate, Derbyshire, had inherited this office from his uncle, who held it under Mary and Elizabeth, and had bought Ware Park in the 1570s from the Countess of Huntingdon. Thomas and his son, Sir Henry, had sat in Parliament, but not for Hertfordshire constituencies. Our member was born in 1596 and succeeded his father Sir Henry in 1611. He sat for Hertford in 1624 and 1625 and became a prominent Royalist, being Deputy-Lieutenant in the King's interest in 1641. His goods were sold in 1643, and although he managed to compound for some of his estates he was almost ruined, and was heavily in debt at his death in 1665. Three years later Ware was sold by his son and heir—to a man who became M.P. for Hertford in 1672. The son also inherited the Irish Viscounty of Dromore which had been given to his father in 1661 for his record of loyalty, for Fanshawe had been one of the Royalist exiles. A brother sat for Cambridge University in the Cavalier Parliament, while the Viscount and his eldest son sat for the County and Borough of Hertford respectively. Another son, Sir Charles, sat for Mitchell in 1689 as a Tory and was expelled the House for refusing to take the oath to William and Mary. The Thomas who originally purchased Ware married again, and from this second marriage were descended the Fanshawes of Jenkins, Essex, one of whom, Thomas, was Royalist M.P. for Lancaster, for which his uncle had previously sat. Lancaster, like other towns in the Duchy, was particularly susceptible to government influence at elections, though this influence had greatly declined by 1640. Thomas Fanshawe of Jenkins was nephew of Sir Christopher Hatton, Royalist M.P. for Higham Ferrers, and great-nephew of Sir Robert Hatton, Royalist M.P. for Castle Rising.[2]

---

[1] *V.C.H. Herts.* III, pp. 115 seq. Chauncy, *Hertfordshire*, II, pp. 95 seq., 103.

[2] *D.N.B. G.E.C. Peerage. V.C.H. Herts.* III, pp. 387 seq. Chauncy, *Hertfordshire*, I, pp. 406 seq.

Fanshawe's colleague at Hertford, Viscount Cranborne, has already been mentioned. For St. Albans sat Sir John Jennings, K.B., and Edward Wingate. The founder of the Jennings family was a Middlesex man, in all probability a merchant, who bought the manor of Churchill, Somerset, in 1563: a few years later Sandridge, Hertfordshire, came to the Jenningses by marriage. It had belonged to the Abbots of St. Albans, but had been granted to the Rowlets at the Dissolution. Sir John Jennings was great-grandson of the founder of the family; he succeeded his father, who seems to have died a lunatic, in 1609, became Sheriff of Hertfordshire in 1626 and two years later M.P. for St. Albans. He died in 1642 and was succeeded in Parliament as well as in his property by his son, Richard, father of Sarah, later Duchess of Marlborough. Richard was only twenty-three in 1642 and, as he was captured by the Royalists and imprisoned for some time, it is not surprising that he made very little mark in Parliament. He was secluded in 1648, but played a much more prominent part in 1660 when the secluded members returned. He sat for St. Albans in 1659 and in both the Convention and the Cavalier Parliament and died in 1668. His father had been a man of some standing, as his K.B. proves, and the Jennings interest was dominant at St. Albans. One of Sir John's daughters married a Turkey merchant called Hill—hence the relationship between Sarah Churchill and Abigail Hill, Queen Anne's favourite. The Jennings family, though not an old one, was older than the Churchills, who owed their eminence first to Sir Winston Churchill, a country gentleman who turned himself into a successful Court politician of the young Royalist school under Charles II, and then to his daughter Arabella, who became the Duke of York's mistress and mother of the brilliant Marshal Berwick. The present Sir Winston Churchill, in his *Life and Times of the Duke of Marlborough* (amongst its many other merits the most valuable work on party history in the reign of Anne), rather ingeniously—and possibly quite accidentally—conveys the impression that Robert Harley was an upstart in politics, whereas a study of parliamentary history would show that it was the Churchills, much more than the Harleys, who were newcomers.[1]

The other member for St. Albans, Edward Wingate, was a man of much less standing than Sir John Jennings. He was the second son of Edward Wingate, gent., of Harlington, Bedfordshire, and obtained through his wife the manor of Holmes, or Cannons in Shenley, Hertfordshire; he sold this estate in 1656. The Wingates remained at Lockleys till 1715, when the manor was sold. Edward was secluded in 1648; he was a captain of militia and a J.P. for many years, and in Charles II's time a commissioner of excise. He was nearing eighty when he died in 1685. The Wingates were a new family and, it seems, one of only moderate prestige in the county; they did not succeed in settling themselves as substantial landowners. Edward, however, through his daughter Mary, wife of Sir Jerome Smithson, Bt., was a remote ancestor of the family who became Dukes of Northumberland in the mid-eighteenth century.[2]

The only Recruiter for a Hertfordshire constituency was William Leman of Northaw, a woollen draper of London, and later member of the Fishmongers' Company. His father lived at Beccles, Suffolk, and the son owed his fortune to his uncle, Sir John Leman, Lord Mayor of London in 1616. Sir John, who had been Prime Warden of the Fishmongers in 1605 and was President of Christ's Hospital, left most of his estate to his nephew in 1632; this estate was valued at £4,000 a year and included the manor of Warboys, Huntingdonshire, bought from Sir Oliver Cromwell, and lands in Framlingham and other parts of Suffolk. William bought the estate of Northaw in the year that he inherited his fortune, and became Sheriff of Hertfordshire in 1635 and of Huntingdonshire in 1641, before being elected as Recruiter for the Borough of Hertford. A keen Rumper, he was on the Council of State in 1651, and he also became joint treasurer of war with Backwell. He sat for Hertford again in 1659 and prospered at the Restoration, becoming a baronet before his death in 1667. He gave £100 in Charles II's

[1] V.C.H. Herts. II, p. 433. Chauncy, Hertfordshire, II, pp. 399 seq.
[2] V.C.H. Herts. III, p. 167. Chauncy, Hertfordshire, II, p. 31.

reign to discharge the debts of Hertford Corporation. His son, Sir William, was Sheriff in 1676 and M.P. for Hertford in 1690.[1]

Essex

Families who owed their prominence to merchants and lawyers two or three generations away had often by the seventeenth century taken some trouble to disguise the fact. In Essex the Knights of the Shire were both holders of hereditary titles— Robert Lord Rich, K.B., and Sir William Masham, Bt. The Riches proclaimed themselves a fourteenth-century county family, but were really descended from the prosperous Sheriff of London in 1441 who established an Essex county family (to which Sir Robert Rich, Master of Chancery in 1620 and M.P. belonged), and a younger branch which included Richard Rich, Lord Chancellor and Baron, from whom our member was descended. Richard Rich earned the distinction of being remembered as perhaps the meanest and most tortuous of the many vicious ministers of Henry VIII's reign. The Riches were a great parliamentary family. Robert was to succeed his father as Earl of Warwick, and his uncle was the first Earl of Holland. Many constituencies sent a Rich to Parliament in the seventeenth century—the East Anglian ones were Harwich, Maldon, and Dunwich. Robert was called to the Lords in 1641 at the age of thirty; he joined the King at York, but like a number of Peers never actually bore arms for him, and he had his fine remitted on the petition of his father the Lord Admiral. He died in 1659, a year after succeeding to the earldom. His son had married one of Cromwell's daughters.[2]

Sir William Masham of High Lever, brother-in-law of Sir Thomas Barrington (M.P. for Colchester) was grandson of a Sheriff and Alderman of London. The family claimed to be of Masham, near Richmond in Yorkshire, until the time of Henry VI, when Sir John settled in Suffolk. This may have been so, but it is more probable that the story owes its origin to the

---

[1] G.E.C. *Baronetage. V.C.H. Herts.* II, pp. 358-9. Chauncy, *Hertfordshire,* II, p. 385. Beaven, *Aldermen of London,* II, pp. 82, 185.

[2] G.E.C. *Peerage. Harleian Society,* XIII, p. 278. Morant, *Essex,* II, p. 101.

accident of the name. Sir William's father was seated at Otes in Essex in the late sixteenth century and purchased High Lever between 1603 and 1610. Sir William was created a baronet in 1621 before he was thirty; he sat for Maldon in 1624, 1625 and 1626, and for Colchester in the Short Parliament. He was an active member, and though he refused to act in the King's trial, was on the Council of State from 1649 to 1652. He sat for Essex in 1654 and died soon after; his son was Recruiter for Shrewsbury and his grandson sat for the county seven times after 1688. His great-grandson, husband of Abigail Hill and M.P., was raised to the peerage in 1711 as one of the Tory dozen created to overcome the small Whig majority. The male line of the Mashams became extinct in 1776.[1]

Sir Martin Lumley, created baronet in the year of his election, succeeded Rich. His father of the same name was Lord Mayor of London, Master Draper, and President of Christ's Hospital. He bought the family estate of Bradfield Magna in 1608. His wife was daughter of a citizen and upholsterer of London, and his son, the younger Sir Martin, took as his second wife the daughter of a London Alderman. This Sir Martin succeeded his father in 1634 and sat in the House of Commons after serving as Sheriff in 1639: it was the family's only appearance in the House. He was secluded at Pride's Purge and died in 1651. He was a Presbyterian and on a number of important committees between 1643 and 1646. The Lumleys seem to have been descended from a Genoese, Domenico Lomellini, Gentleman of the Privy Chamber to Henry VIII; his son, James, an eminent merchant, died in 1592, and James's son was the elder Sir Martin. The Lumley estates were sold in 1715; the baronetcy became extinct in 1771.[2]

Harbottle Grimston, M.P. for Colchester, was son of Sir Harbottle Grimston, Bt., M.P. for Harwich. The Grimstons were an old family of moderate estate, of which the older branch belonged to Yorkshire, while the founder of the younger and more important branch had moved to Suffolk in the early

[1] G.E.C. *Peerage* and *Baronetage*. Morant, *Essex*, I, p. 141.
[2] G.E.C. *Baronetage*. Kimber and Johnson, *Baronetage*, I, p. 348. Morant, *Essex*, II, pp. 519–20.

fifteenth century. His son, ambassador to Bergen, was of
Rishangles and Ipswich. The grandfather of Sir Harbottle, Sir
Edward, married the daughter of an Ipswich merchant; his son
bought Bradfield from the Waldegraves, who had been granted
Church lands in Essex by Elizabeth. Sir Harbottle, son of a
Lavenham heiress, was born in 1578; in 1612 he was created a
baronet, and in 1614 he sat for Harwich and from 1626 con-
tinuously for the county until he returned to Harwich in the
Long Parliament. His grandfather had sat for Ipswich and
Orford, his father for Eye and his eldest son for Harwich. He
was imprisoned in 1627 for refusing to pay a forced loan; in the
Long Parliament he was far above the average age of
members and died in 1648 aged seventy. His second and eldest
surviving son, likewise Harbottle, was a barrister and became
Recorder of Colchester, for which he sat in the Short and Long
Parliaments and every parliament between 1660 and 1681, having
previously represented Harwich in 1628. He was an active but
moderate Parliamentarian of the Presbyterian wing; Parliamentary
Deputy-Lieutenant for Essex in June 1642 on the assurance that
there was to be no war on the King, he later opposed the Army
as commissioner for disbanding and had his house plundered.
He was imprisoned at Pride's Purge and excluded as member
for Essex in 1656. On the return of the secluded members he
was elected to the Council of State; he was Speaker of the Convention and on the commission for trying the regicides. In
November 1660 he was made Master of the Rolls; rumour
supposed that he had paid Clarendon £8,000 for the office, but
rumour in Charles II's reign, especially where Clarendon was
concerned, has less than its usual slight validity. In 1664 Sir
Harbottle became Chief Steward of St. Albans, for which his son
sat seven times before his death in 1700. Sir Harbottle the
younger opposed the attempt to relax the penal laws and the
King's rejection of the Commons' choice of Speaker. He died in
1685 aged eighty-two and was succeeded by his son, on whose
death the male line became extinct.[1] Sir Harbottle had married

[1] *D.N.B.*   G.E.C.   *Baronetage.*   Warrand, *Hertfordshire Families* (V.C.H.),
p. 173. Morant, *Essex*, I, pp. 464-5.

as his first wife the daughter of Sir George Croke, judge first of Common Pleas and then of King's Bench, the only judge to decide for Hampden on the main point at issue instead of on a technicality—a decision which significantly enough did not prevent one of the Crokes from joining the Royalists as M.P. for Wendover, though the family was not completely united in support of the King. This daughter had a life interest in the estate of Gorhambury; her husband bought the reversion of the estate and made it his principal seat. On the failure of the Grimston line it went to the Luckyns, who will shortly be described.

Sir Thomas Barrington, Bt., of Barrington Hall, M.P. for Colchester, came of a very old family, which claimed to have been at Barrington Hall since about 1200; a Barrington was Sheriff of Hertfordshire and Essex in 1197, and a later Barrington was Sheriff in 1451. Clavering was also added to the Barrington estates in 1553 by the restoration of blood to Sir Thomas Barrington's wife, daughter of Henry Pole, Lord Montague who was executed for treason. Sir Thomas had been married before to Alice, daughter of Sir Henry Parker, Lord Morley, ancestor of the Suffolk Knight of the Shire. Sir Thomas was Sheriff of Hertfordshire and Essex in 1562 and of Essex alone in 1580; he belonged to one of the families that prospered in those days of difficulty and opportunity for the landowner, and Sir Francis, heir of Sir Thomas, succeeded to a greatly increased estate. Sir Francis was one of the original creation of baronets in 1611 and sat for the county in every parliament between 1601 and 1628, in which year he died. Sir Thomas, the 2nd baronet, had already sat for Newtown in the Isle of Wight since 1621 and succeeded his father as county member in the Short Parliament; he died in 1644 before he was fifty. He was cousin through his mother of Oliver Cromwell; he was brother-in-law of Sir William Lytton, M.P. for Hertfordshire, of Sir William Masham, M.P. for Essex, and of Sir Gilbert Gerard, Bt., M.P. for Middlesex. He was a close associate, both in Essex politics and in commercial and colonising enterprises, of the Lord Lieutenant of the County, the Earl of Warwick. With the Earl he became a friend of Pym, and a leader of the Puritan organisation in the East. His brother had sat with him for Newtown in 1628, and his son sat for the same constituency in the Long Parliament, the Convention, and the Cavalier Parliament; he was secluded in 1648, being a Presbyterian like his father, who was a lay assessor in the Assembly of Divines in 1643. His great-grandson, Sir Charles, sat for the county seven times under William and Anne. The Barringtons continued as a great parliamentary family, as any student of eighteenth century history will know, and their sixteen appearances as Knights of the Shire exceeds by a long way the record of any other of our Eastern Association families. The Barrington baronetcy became extinct in 1833.[1]

Sir Thomas Cheeke of Pirgo, M.P. for Harwich, belonged to a family which claimed to have been established at Motston, Isle of Wight, since the time of Richard II. Its prominence, however, dated from Sir John Cheeke, K.G., Professor of Greek at Cambridge, preceptor of Edward VI and Secretary of State. His son, Henry, was Secretary to the Council of the North and brother-in-law of its President, the Earl of Sussex; he sat in the House of Commons three times before his death. His son, our Sir Thomas, bought the estate of Pirgo from Lord Grey of Groby early in James I's reign: he sat for Yarmouth (Isle of Wight) in 1614 (another Thomas Cheeke sat there in 1604), for Boston in 1621, Essex in 1624, Berealston in 1625, Maldon in 1628, and Harwich in the Short and Long Parliaments. Through his second marriage he was uncle to Lord Rich, M.P. for Essex. He was one of the oldest members in the Eastern Association group, and must have been eighty-five or over at his death in 1659. He was succeeded first by his son, Robert, and then by another son, Thomas, Lieutenant of the Tower and colonel in the time of Charles II and James II. There was no further representation of the family in the House, and the male line became extinct in 1707.[2]

The Long Parliament resembled all parliaments in being a very mixed assembly. Moreover, opportunities and temptations

[1] G.E.C. *Baronetage*. Kimber and Johnson, *Baronetage*, I, p. 39. Morant, *Essex*, I, pp. 464-5.
[2] Morant, *Essex*, I, p. 61.

were more present than usual, and members more likely to reveal the possibilities of their characters to a later generation. Among the many scoundrels in the House it would be hard to find two members for a constituency more unattractive than the members for Maldon. This may, in fact, be no coincidence, as Sir Henry Mildmay, by far the more unsavoury of the two, was Chief Steward of the borough and may have been able to help find a seat for the other, Sir John Clotworthy, whose election, according to Clarendon, was contrived by 'some powerful persons'.

The Mildmays were an Essex landowning family from the fifteenth century, but only reached wealth and prominence through the skill of Thomas Mildmay, auditor of the Court of Augmentations, who was able, not surprisingly, to ensure that his own family was one of the chief gainers by the dissolution of the monasteries. He had a large family, and his share of the plunder provided for the endowment of numerous branches of it. By the time of James I's accession there were no less than nine families of Mildmay in Essex, all with large estates. The youngest son of Thomas, Sir Walter, of Apthorpe, Northamptonshire, was Chancellor of the Exchequer to Queen Elizabeth; he sat for Maldon, Peterborough, and from 1557 to 1589 for Northamptonshire. The second son, Humphrey, of Danbury, Essex, married the daughter of Henry Capel of Hadham, great-grandfather of the member for Hertfordshire, who was thus a distant cousin of Sir Henry Mildmay. Humphrey died in 1613. His third son, Sir Henry, became Master of the Jewel House, an important office under James I, in 1620 and entered Parliament in the next year; the Long Parliament marked his sixth appearance there, and always except once he had sat for Maldon. He was given the estate of Wanstead by the King and became Deputy-Lieutenant for Essex. In 1630 he was on the committee of compounding for knighthood and a collector of the fine. He opposed Strafford's attainder, but Sir John Clotworthy's choice of constituency leaves some doubt as to his sincerity, especially as he went over to the Parliamentary party in September 1641, when many honest men were leaving it. He was regarded as an important acquisition, and it is possible from the rest of his career, though it cannot be proved, that he was putting up his price. He was an extremely wealthy man and chosen on this account as hostage to the Scots in December 1646, but he was able to get in July 1649 a parliamentary order to repay him from the sales of cathedral lands £2,000 with interest which he had lent to the King. He was present at the King's trial, but did not sign the sentence. He was on the Council of State from 1649 to 1652 and seems to have been a Republican, for he signed the protest of the excluded members in 1656, though he remained Keeper of Greenwich Park from 1654 to 1660. At the Restoration he was degraded and imprisoned for life; he died probably in 1664. Most of his vast wealth went to the Crown; Wanstead House, which he had bought from Buckingham in 1619, being given to the Duke of York. Henry Mildmay of Baddow Parva sat for the county in the Exclusion Parliaments and the first two of William III's reign, but no close relative of Sir Henry was likely to have the land or the influence to sit again in a Stuart House of Commons. Sir Henry was found at the Restoration to have peculated on an enormous scale as Master of the Jewel House; he was, in fact, the worst type of rapacious scoundrel.[1]

Sir John Clotworthy, described somewhat misleadingly as of St. Andrews, Holborn, in the writ, was one of the leading land-grabbers of the Ulster plantation. The Clotworthys were a Devonshire family, removed to Antrim, of which Sir John's father had been Sheriff; Sir John was M.P. for Co. Antrim in 1634 and a great opponent of Strafford's attempt to assert royal control over Ireland. He was brought over to England in 1640 to help Strafford's English enemies crush him in the new parliament; he sat for Bossiney in the Short and for Maldon (he was elected for two constituencies to prevent accidental miscarriage of plans) in the Long Parliament. He was the spokesman of the Irish Presbyterians and extremely active against the Catholics. In Strafford's time he had represented the interests of those who held land under the charter of the London corporation; he now

[1] *D.N.B.* Morant, *Essex*, I, p. 30; II, p. 29.

became a leading City politician and in 1647 was one of the 11 Presbyterian members impeached and forced to withdraw by the Army. He was disabled in January 1648, but readmitted in June; after Pride's Purge he was kept under arrest for three years and took little part in public affairs until the Restoration, when he did very well out of the Irish land settlement and was raised to the Irish peerage as Viscount Massereene. He had no male issue and was allowed to transmit the title to his son-in-law, Skeffington, son of the Recruiter for Staffordshire, on his death in 1665. From the time of his succession to his father in 1630 Sir John Clotworthy was a successful man despite serious temporary setbacks. He and Sir Henry Mildmay represent the worst of the Presbyterians and the Rumpers respectively; Sir Henry triumphed in the short run, but Sir John in the long.[1]

There were two Recruiters for Essex, John Sayer for Colchester and Capel Luckyn for Harwich. The Sayers seem to have been an old family settled at Birch as early as the reign of Edward II, but there is no proof of land in their possession until 1411, when they were at Aldham and Great Tey. They settled at Colchester, where they became wealthy and of high standing in the corporation. John Sayer, Alderman of Colchester, died in 1509; his grandson, George, Alderman and several times Bailiff, bought Bourchiers Hall from the Marquess of Northampton in 1574 and also possessed various other estates in Stanway, Copford, Loxden and elsewhere at his death in 1577. George's great-grandson was the Recruiter, who succeeded his father in 1630 when forty-one years of age. He was brother-in-law of a son of Sir Thomas Jermyn, M.P. for Bury St. Edmunds. He died in 1658.[2]

The Luckyns had a less distinguished past but a more distinguished future. Capel's grandfather was a yeoman farmer of Baddow Magna, who had accumulated land in 10 parishes in Essex; his son, William, made a large fortune out of a saltpetre company and bought a baronetcy and the estate of Little Waltham. He married a daughter of Sir Gamaliel Capel, the head of the Essex branch of the Capels; his son, named Capel

---

[1] *D.N.B. G.E.C. Peerage.*   [2] Morant, *Essex*, II, pp. 194, 199–200.

after his mother's family, was born in 1622. His career in the Long Parliament was short—elected in April 1648, he was secluded in December, but he sat for Harwich again in the Convention and in the Cavalier Parliament after a by-election in 1664. Sir William died in 1661 aged sixty-six and Capel in 1679. He may have been related to Robert Luckyn, M.P. for Cambridge in 1624, as the name is unusual, but no connection has been traced. Capel was son-in-law of Sir Harbottle Grimston the younger of Gorhambury and grandson through his mother of the judge, Sir George Croke; he was succeeded by his son, William. His grandson, who assumed the name of Grimston at the time he succeeded to the estates of his great-uncle, Samuel Grimston (Grimston's grandchild being passed over in his favour), and so to the estate of Gorhambury, was M.P. for St. Albans from 1710 till 1722 and again in 1727, and in 1719 was raised to the Irish peerage with the title of Viscount Grimston. In 1737 he joined the estates of the Luckyns to the estates of the Grimstons when he succeeded his elder brother, the 4th baronet, who was cup-bearer to Anne and George I. In 1815 the family was raised to the English peerage as Earls of Verulam.[1]

The impression given by the members from these counties could be confirmed by a study of those from Lincolnshire. There too we should find a few important parliamentary families, like the Wrays and the Irbys, and others of less significance. For the Eastern Association, perhaps even more than for the rest of the country, the parliamentary history of the seventeenth century can only be written in terms of families, and of local rather than national affairs. In Norfolk and Suffolk especially, but in the other counties too, there is a marked scarcity of members of our Parliament who played a conspicuous part in national politics. None of the boroughs fell normally under the control of the Court or of one of the great families outside the region. Carpet-baggers were completely absent—unless Clotworthy may be considered as a rather exceptional one. Nor did the prestige of its army bring any outstanding military men to find seats in the

[1] G.E.C. *Baronetage*. Warrand, *Hertfordshire Families* (V.C.H.), pp. 171 seq. Morant, *Essex*, II, p. 177.

region at the later elections. One of the few Royalists—Arthur Capel—was prominent in the war; but in Presbyterian leaders, active Rumpers, and Counsellors of State the Eastern Association did not send in proportion to its numbers. There is one obvious exception; but Cromwell was not a man to attract the support of many of the older members, and the favours he showed to his relations did not extend to his neighbours. His emergence as a leader of the extremists may indeed have helped to drive the strong Puritan element among members from the Eastern Association into hostility hidden under the guise of indifference.

CHAPTER VI

THE SOUTH-WEST

I

THE SIX COUNTIES

THE Counties of Cornwall, Devon, Somerset, Dorset, Wiltshire, and Gloucestershire are in area about fifteen per cent. of England and Wales. In the Long Parliament they had 150 seats —not quite thirty per cent. of the total of 507. It was an area neither as remote from new economic influences as the north, nor as much under the domination of London as the south-east; it included strongly Royalist and strongly Puritan districts; and it provides specimens of all the main categories into which boroughs and their representatives could be divided.

As a result of the original elections and the settlement of disputes arising from them 148 members established their right to sit for the six counties. (Those whose return was disputed and afterwards quashed are not included in any of the figures given here.) In addition 15 new members entered at by-elections before the outbreak of war, making a total of 163 to be examined. On the method of classification already defined there were 82 Royalists and 78 Parliamentarians. Three members, John Upton, Thomas Wise, and Miles Fleetwood, died in 1641 and have not been allocated to either side. On the Parliamentary side 36 of these members were secluded or ceased to sit at Pride's Purge—excluding those who were afterwards allowed to resume their seats. 19 had died before the Purge, and 23 sat in the Rump.

The vacancies caused by deaths, elevation to the peerage, and the departure of the Royalists were filled between 1645 and 1648 by 88 new members. Four of these died before Pride's Purge; 51 were secluded; 33 sat in the Rump. 11 of the original south-western members and 20 of the Recruiters returned in

February 1660. The proportions of Royalists and of 'Presbyterians' secluded in 1648 are thus rather higher than in the Parliament as a whole.

Distribution of these groups among the six counties varied widely. Cornwall with 44 seats was predominantly Royalist; only 17 of its original members sat during the war, and only 3 after 1648. Wiltshire, which with 34 seats had the next largest representation of the English counties, was a Puritan region and had 23 members on the Parliamentary side; 9 of them survived Pride's Purge. Of the 26 Devonshire members first elected 13 were Parliamentarians (but of the other 13 Russell was Royalist for only a few months, Wise died in 1641 and was replaced by a supporter of the Parliament, and Trelawney claimed to have been disabled by mistake). Dorset with 20 seats had 12 Parliamentarians; Gloucestershire with 10 seats had 4; Somerset with 16 seats had only 5.

In this region of close equality of numbers between the two sides their equality in some of our tests of social status is striking. There were, it is true, 7 Peers and sons of Peers on the Royalist side and only 2 on that of the Parliament; but there were 7 Royalist baronets and 6 Parliamentary; 18 Royalist knights and 17 Parliamentary. 8 Royalists and 9 Parliamentarians had been Sheriffs (occasionally in order to prevent them from sitting in the House); 6 Royalists and 5 Parliamentarians had been Mayors or Aldermen; 4 on each side were Recorders. Holders of crown offices and sinecures were also represented in both groups. Edward Herbert, former Attorney-General to the Queen, became a Royalist. So did Francis Windebank, the Secretary of State and friend of Catholics and Monopolists. But Miles Fleetwood, Receiver of the Court of Wards and Liveries, showed no sign of favouring the King; and Benjamin Rudyard, Surveyor of the same court, became—after a career unhampered by political consistency—an active Parliamentarian. The elder Vane had held many household offices, and Oliver St. John accepted in 1641 the lucrative post of Attorney-General. 40 Royalists and 37 Parliamentarians had been educated at Universities. Oxford had almost a monopoly in the south-west. Only

11 of its M.P.s had been to Cambridge, and most of these were either complete outsiders, like Samuel Browne of Bedfordshire, or men with close family connections further east. The link between Exeter College and the counties of Devon and Cornwall was strong enough for well over half of their Oxonian members to have been there. 42 Royalists and 48 Parliamentarians had been to one of the Inns of Court; 11 Royalists and 16 Parliamentarians were barristers.

The 'Royalist Party', as pointed out in Chapter I, was a phenomenon that appeared rapidly a very short time before the war. In the south-west many of those who led the landed families in support of the King had already established themselves as leaders of the resistance to the 'illegal' acts of his ministers. In Devon Sir Thomas Heale had refused the forced loan and been a witness against Strafford. In Cornwall with a few exceptions (such as John Mohun and Richard Edgecumbe) the principal landowners had followed Eliot and Bevil Grenville in opposing the loans and ship-money. John Dutton in Gloucestershire had also refused to pay ship-money; so had Sir Francis Seymour in Wiltshire. Edward Kyrton of Somerset had been active in preparing the impeachment of Buckingham. George Digby of Dorset was on the committee to draw up the impeachment of Strafford. All these eventually joined the Royalist nucleus that began to appear among the landed families as the implications of opposition became more apparent. Grenville announced his conversion at the outbreak of the Bishops' War; Digby opposed the third reading of the Attainder Bill; Kyrton was also a Straffordian, and in all 13 of the south-western members appeared on the list of these 'betrayers of their country' that was posted in Old Palace Yard. By the time of the outbreak of war the Royalist gentry in each county knew their leaders, and knew each other. The military organisation of the King's supporters was preceded by the rudiments of a political organisation which was only possible because in each county landowners great and not so great were so closely associated.

When we look at the other extreme—the Independents—no such local basis of unity can be found among the M.P.s. Political

Independency in its various forms was established at the centre, in a Parliament and an Army whose members had had many years in which to develop new friendships and associations. In some counties—of which Yorkshire is outstanding—the Independent members had as much in common with each other as the earlier groups. But in the south-west, where their numbers were comparatively small, it is apparent that they were a very motley collection. Devonshire's 5 Rumpers were Philip Skippon, a military outsider; Thomas Boone, a local new-rich landowner who became a diplomat; Lawrence Whitaker, Secretary to the Master of the Rolls and Clerk to the Privy Council; Christopher Martyn gent., from an obscure branch of a county family; and Oliver St. John. The only connection of the great Cromwellian lawyer-statesman with Totnes was that he had been employed by the Russells. The Rumpers from the rest of the region were hardly less diverse.

Though the six counties had the usual common features each of them had a clear character of its own. Gloucestershire had practically only three boroughs, since Bristol elections were a purely City affair. (Gloucester also returned one Alderman for the Long Parliament but it did not always do so.) The Berkeleys, though none of them sat in the Long Parliament, were the greatest electoral power, and had sponsored John Dutton for his county seat. The Tracys were also without a seat, and their rivals the Stephenses had two. In Somerset seven boroughs, all of them open to pressure from the landed families, gave scope for wider manoeuvres. The Poulett and Paulet connection had a strong claim on a county seat; other families usually had a link with particular boroughs—the Pophams with Minehead, Bath, and Bridgwater, the Portmans with Taunton, the Berkeleys and the Phelips or Phillipps family of Montacute with Ilchester —but all shared in the general distribution. Digbys from Dorset and Hungerfords from Wiltshire sometimes trespassed across the border. Dorset and its coastal towns where the county families and urban candidates jostled together is the subject of fuller treatment later. Devonshire too had ports whose elections were controlled locally, and at the other extreme the borough

of Tavistock where, after many outsiders had sat for earlier
Stuart Parliaments, the Russells now began to keep one seat
exclusively for themselves. But the enfranchisement in 1640 of
Okehampton, Honiton, and Ashburton gave plenty of room
for the Pooles, Youngs, Fowells, and their kind.

Cornwall and Wiltshire had not much in common except
their large number of boroughs. Cornwall had already, in the
elections to the Short Parliament, given an emphatic snub to the
election managers of the Duchy. They had tried then to have
one of their nominees returned for each borough, and 15 of their
16 candidates had been rejected. In the October elections there
were fewer Duchy candidates, and none of them was successful.
William Coryton, Vice-Warden of the Stannaries, who had
formerly been a close associate of Eliot and Pym, was now the
chief agent for the Court. He was returned himself for Grampound and Launceston but was refused admission by the House
when he was found guilty of falsifying the returns for Bossinney.
After the outbreak of war he 'became sensible of his errors' in
supporting the King, and took the Oath and Covenant.[1] Another
Duchy official, Thomas Gewen, also joined the Parliamentary
side and was elected as a Recruiter.

Marriage connections explain the presence among the Cornish members of James Campbell of Essex who married (in
1638) the daughter of John Lord Mohun and sat for the borough
of Grampound; and of Sir John Trevor of Trevallyn, Flint-
shire, who succeeded Coryton in the other Grampound seat
and whose mother was a Trevanion. Grampound for the past
ninety years had been a hunting-ground for several south-
western families—Mohun himself represented it in 1624—and it
was now coming more closely under the control of the Trevanions. Another Cornish borough which found its members
of the Long Parliament outside the county was Callington,
enfranchised under Elizabeth. It had formerly belonged to the
Poulett family, but passed by marriage to Sir Henry Rolle,
whose family held one of the seats in all the parliaments of

---

[1] M. Coate, *Cornwall in the Civil War*, pp. 20-24. *D'Ewes' Journal* (ed.
Notestein), pp. 35, 118, 352.

James I and the earlier ones of Charles I. One of them, John Rolle (M.P. for Callington in 1626 and 1628 and for Truro in the Short and Long Parliaments) was a London merchant and had been engaged in a lengthy law-suit concerning the seizure of his goods by the customs authorities for his refusal to pay tunnage and poundage. Another London merchant, Sir Arthur Ingram, was chosen to represent Callington in 1640. Among other offices he held (for life) the post of Comptroller of Customs in the Port of London, which may or may not have helped him to sit for Rolle's borough. The Fiennes and Dacres families, who shared Callington in 1646 were related by marriage to the Rolles, and it may have been through them that a complete outsider, George Fane, son of the Earl of Westmorland, had the other seat in 1640. The Arundells had a habit of putting in lawyers for their borough of Mitchell, and there was nothing exceptional in the election of two barristers of Lincoln's Inn in 1640. The Bullers, who usually kept Saltash to themselves and their relations, gave one of its seats to Edward Hyde. Benjamin Valentine, who sat for the Eliot borough of St. Germans, had been one of Sir John Eliot's colleagues in the early resistance to the crown, and had suffered long imprisonment. The other Cornish boroughs went to a local group typical in everything except its numbers.

At the election of the Recruiters most of the normal borough influences in Cornwall were naturally out of action. 30 new members were elected, and only 12 of them were Cornishmen. Marriages and military importance helped. Colonel Feilder married the sister of Sir John Trevor, and sat for St. Ives; Lionel Copley, Commissary-General, was chosen for Bossinney. The members for Callington were Edward Lord Clinton (son of the 4th Earl of Lincoln) and Thomas Dacres of Cheshunt. Clinton had three sisters, married respectively to a Trefusis, a Boscawen and a Rolle; the Dacres family had married a Rolle and a Carew in the reign of Elizabeth. For Fowey the new members were two Plymouth merchants, Nicholas Gould and Gregory Clement. Clement was later a regicide and a speculator in confiscated lands. But he wrote to the disabled Royalist member, Jonathan Rashleigh, asking for his help in being elected in his place, and signing himself 'your very loving friend'.[1] Rashleigh was the brother-in-law of Clement's cousin, and owed him money. One of the Recruiters for Lostwithiel, John Maynard, had relations in Cornwall; the other was the son of Denzil Holles. Perhaps the most unexpected of them is Charles Carr, later 2nd Earl of Ancram, member for Mitchell in 1647. His father Robert was Keeper of the Privy Purse to Charles I; he had a grant of the profits of the impost on starch, but died in debt. Charles was secluded in 1648 and returned in 1660, to become a prominent member of the Court Party. Newport in 1648 had two famous names—William Prynne and Alexander Pym, son of John. Both came from Somerset, but Pym's brother-in-law Sir Francis Drake owned the manor of Werrington in Newport and had formerly sat for the borough himself. Five Cornish boroughs gave seats to lawyers from outside the county; and another complete stranger was the member for St. Mawes, William Priestley, a Hertfordshire squire who married the widow of Thomas Dacres.

Wiltshire shared with some Welsh counties the doubtful blessing of being a main centre of the Pembroke electoral system.[2] Its influence was shown not merely in the presence of a Royalist and a Recruiter from the Herbert family, but in the admission of outsiders like the Earl of Pembroke's friend the elder Vane, his 'supple creature' Michael Oldsworth, and Benjamin Rudyard who helped in his election activities. But again there was ample scope for the county families too—Ludlows, Bayntons, Hungerfords and the rest—as well as for newer and lesser gentry. A few Londoners and a few clothiers not yet in the landed class were also able to take advantage of the abundance of boroughs.

We attempted for the south-western members a tentative numerical analysis of the 'age' of the landed families. For this purpose the families of members who held lands in the area

---

[1] M. Coate, *Cornwall in the Civil War*, pp. 245-8.
[2] See the article on the Pembrokes' electoral influence by V. A. Rowe in *English Historical Review*, Vol. L.

were divided into three categories. The first consists of those whose ancestors held the same sort of status before that speeding up of land transference of which the dissolution of the monasteries may be taken as the decisive point. In the second group are those whose families had previously been lords of manors but had conspicuously added to their possessions in the sixteenth and seventeenth centuries. It includes representatives of the 'Tudor Nobility' and the branches of medieval families founded by younger sons who acquired estates in the south-west after the dissolution. In the third group are the families that first emerged from obscurity in the same period. The figures, based of course on fallible evidence and judgment, are as follows: in the first group 11 Parliamentarians and 20 Royalists; in the second 18 Parliamentarians and 19 Royalists; in the third 22 Parliamentarians and 14 Royalists. Among the Recruiters, though there are rather more who are not classed as landed at all, there is certainly no greater proportion of 'new' men than among the original Parliamentary members: 11 had estates of mainly medieval origin, 15 were of medieval families who had extended their possessions more recently, and 15 had acquired them mainly since the dissolution. The one conspicuous difference between the Recruiters and the rest was in the higher proportion who came from landed families outside the south-western area. There were 19 of these, including some who can also be counted as lawyers or professional soldiers.

The greatest single difficulty in arriving at these approximate and subjective estimates is the definition of a 'medieval' family. Quite apart from the pedigree-fakers, and the claims, based on a single recorded knight of a similar name, to have been 'seated in the county since the Conquest', it is hard to lay down what constitutes family continuity on the same estate. Descent of a manor in an unbroken line from father to eldest son very rarely lasts for more than a couple of centuries. Where owners of the same name continue longer they almost always do so hazardously, through nephews and cousins and heiresses who marry within the family. Later, when it becomes the accepted custom blandly to adopt a surname, with or without a hyphen, on acquiring the estate that goes with it, the complexities grow greater still. It is arguable that when it is the behaviour, outlook, and status of a man that concerns us, then if he persuades himself and others that his estate was bestowed on his direct ancestor by a grateful William the Conqueror, for our purposes it was so. But for the figures quoted above we have in general accepted only reasonably detailed and coherent accounts of a family's tenurial history, from the county histories, the genealogical works, and the few tolerable parish and family histories.

By following family records down to about 1750 it is possible to see, very roughly, what happened to the estates of the landed south-western M.P.s as a whole in the century after the Committee for Compounding was at work and the Commonwealth land-sales taking place. Our results—again subject to a wide margin of possible error or difference of judgment—show that 31 Royalists and 24 Parliamentarians had descendants living on the same estates, that the estates (or a major part of them) of 10 Royalists and 4 Parliamentarians had been sold, and that 20 other Royalists and 26 other Parliamentarians had no direct descendants surviving. Failure of heirs seems, therefore, here as elsewhere, to be the commonest cause of transference of lands from one family to another.

II

FAMILIES AND FORTUNES

Without risking any further statistics, we can give examples of some of the men on whose family histories the calculations quoted above were based. In this section a few families from five of the counties are selected; in the next the County of Dorset is treated more fully.

Medieval families

Outstanding among the 'medieval' families ruined in the seventeenth century are the Hungerfords.[1] They had held lands

[1] R. C. Hoare, *Hungerfordiana*. Burke, *Vicissitudes of Families*, 1st series. D.N.B. G.E.C. *Peerage*.

in Wiltshire since the eleventh century, and had represented it in Parliament since the fourteenth. Sir Thomas, M.P. between 1351 and 1393, who bought Heytesbury, was the first Speaker of the House of Commons to be officially so called. But the family had bad luck in their political allegiances. Robert, the third Baron, was executed in 1464 as a Lancastrian, and his son in 1469 as a supporter of Warwick. In 1540 Sir Walter Hungerford was executed, charged among other things with supporting the Pilgrimage of Grace. Their divided allegiance in the Civil War led to no immediate disaster. In the seventeenth century there were two main branches: the Hungerfords of Farleigh Castle (two of whom had sat for Wiltshire) and the Hungerfords of Down Ampney, on the border of Wiltshire and Gloucestershire, and of Black Bourton, Oxfordshire. Three brothers of this branch sat in the Long Parliament—the sons of Sir Anthony of Black Bourton. Their father had sat for Wiltshire boroughs, their grandfather for Gloucestershire.

Sir Edward, the eldest, represented Chippenham in the Long Parliament and had previously sat for the county and the Boroughs of Wootton Bassett, Cricklade, and Bath. He had succeeded to Down Ampney in 1627. His mother, Sir Anthony's first wife, was Lucy, daughter and coheiress of Sir Walter Hungerford of Farleigh and widow of Sir John St. John. Sir Edward was a member of the County and many Parliamentary Committees, and was secluded at Pride's Purge. His half-brother Henry was a Recruiter for Great Bedwin. He too was secluded, but he returned in the second Protectorate Parliament. The other brother, Anthony, eldest son of Sir Anthony's second wife, sat for a third Wiltshire borough, Malmesbury. For 'deserting the Parliament' and sitting at Oxford he was disabled and imprisoned in the Tower in 1644. In 1646 he received his pardon on payment of £2,532, and Black Bourton, which he had inherited, was discharged from sequestration. In 1653 he inherited the estates of the Farleigh branch: his son Edward held at the Restoration about thirty manors in Wiltshire and neighbouring counties. Edward sat in the Convention and Cavalier Parliaments, and in most of the later ones down to 1705. On him,

6

'the spendthrift', Burke places all the blame for the collapse of the family fortunes; and he thanks nature for producing such improvident heirs, by whom 'the balance of society is kept even and the general harmony restored'. Sir Edward sold Farleigh to the Bayntons, and eventually parted with all the other estates too. He was removed from his lieutenancy for opposition to the Court, and tried to live on the profits of a market hall erected on the site of Hungerford House at Charing Cross. In the end that was sold too (to its architect Wren) and Sir Edward died as one of the 'Poor Knights of Windsor'.

The Arundells [1] of Cornwall had a background very similar to that of the Hungerfords; but unlike them they survived in their estates well into the eighteenth century. Of their two chief Cornish seats Lanherne was acquired by marriage to an heiress under Edward I and Trerice in the same way under Edward III. In the sixteenth century they bought Wardour Castle from Fulke Greville, and other manors in Somerset and Dorset. The first Arundell in Parliament sat for Cornwall in 1340. Throughout the sixteenth century they were representing the county and many of its boroughs, and marrying into the other county families—Edgecumbe, Bevill, Carew, Grenville. In the Long Parliament John Arundell of Trerice, second son of another John who had sat in nearly every Parliament from 1597 until the Short Parliament, was member for Bodmin. His brother Richard, the most enthusiastic Royalist of the family, sat for Lostwithiel. The fine for the Trerice Arundells was fixed at £10,000. The estates were sequestered and let for £400 a year, after which they were discharged on payment of £2,000. It was a large but not a ruinous penalty. Richard, who had been involved in the 'Sealed Knot' conspiracy under the Protectorate, entered Parliament again in 1662 and two years later was raised to the peerage. His heir John sat for Truro in 1666, and the male line continued until 1750.

The Lanherne and Wardour branches had no representative

[1] *D.N.B.* (article on the family). G.E.C. *Peerage*. Burke, *Peerage*. C. S. Gilbert, *Historical Survey*, I, pp. 470, 537 ; II, p. 3.

in the Long Parliament, but they too were Royalists who prospered after the Restoration. Two other Cornish Arundells however had borough seats and kept them until 1648. They were comparatively poor relations. Thomas (West Looe) was uncle of the Trerice Arundells. He was seated at Duloe, near his borough, until it was seized by the enemy. In 1647 his son was also returned for West Looe, as John Arundell, gent. Nothing more is heard of them after the Restoration.

The Cornish Royalists provide many instances of 'medieval' families who maintained their lands and developed their political influence. Some complained frequently of debt, but managed to preserve their principal estates; in others we can see where court or legal posts, the rewards of choosing a winning side, or the profits of matrimony, had augmented the revenue from rents and prevented the menace of growing mortgages and piecemeal sales. The Grenvilles of Stowe, the Trevanions of Caerhayes, the Godolphins of Godolphin, and the Edgecumbes of Mount Edgecumbe all had respectable medieval records. There was a Grenvyle in the Parliament of 1394, a Trevnignon in 1407, an Eggecombe in 1447.

The Grenvilles[1] had been at Stowe, in the extreme north of the county, since the eleventh century, and they held other manors at Bryn and Lanew. The estates were already described as 'encumbered' in 1636, on the death of Sir Bernard (M.P. for Bodmin in 1597). His son Sir Bevil, the leader of the Cornish Royalists and friend of Eliot and Sidney Godolphin, sold Lanew; and when he fell at Landsdowne his property was said to be swallowed up in debts. (It was of course expedient to say so when the fate of delinquents' estates was under discussion.) He had sat in all the Parliaments since 1621, for the county or the Borough of Launceston, and was an active opponent of the forced loan. When the Long Parliament met he was an uncompromising Royalist, and though he is not on the list of those who voted against the attainder of Strafford he is said to have urged others to do so. But neither debts nor sequestration

[1] D.N.B. G.E.C. Peerage (Bath). J. Edmondson, Genealogical Account of the Family of Grenville. Calendar of the Committee for Compounding, p. 2214.

proved fatal: the family remained at Stowe. Bevil's eldest son
John became first Earl of Bath; his younger son Bernard sat for
Liskeard in the Cavalier Parliament and later for four other
boroughs. Four Grenvilles of the next generation represented
boroughs in Cornwall and Devon. One of them, George, was
a Jacobite in 1715. By that time most of them were marrying
into the higher ranks of the peerage.

The Godolphins [1] claimed to have been at Godolphin, near
Helston, since the Conquest, though the name had been adopted
by heirs in the female line. Sir William Godolphin was 'a gentleman of great note' in the reign of Henry VIII, Warden of the
Stannaries and M.P. for Cornwall in several Parliaments. From
1586 there was hardly a Parliament in which a Godolphin did
not sit. Sir William's nephew Francis and Francis's two sons
Sir William and Sir Francis all became Knights of the Shire. In
the next generation the sons of the second Sir William—Sir
Francis and the poet Sidney—were members for Helston in the
Long Parliament, and their cousin William in the Short Parliament. Francis succeeded to the estates in 1613, and they were
released from sequestration when he surrendered the Scilly
Islands to Parliament. He represented Helston again in 1660 and
was knighted at the Coronation. His eldest son Sir William was
made a baronet in 1661 and was elected to the Cavalier Parliament for Helston in 1665. The second son Sidney had a more
spectacular career. He joined his brother as representative of
Helston in 1668, and was soon on his way to the top at Court.
He became Secretary of State for the South, First Lord of the
Treasury, and supporter of James II. But by 1690 he was a Lord
of the Treasury again, and in 1706 an Earl. Meanwhile his
nephew Francis and his cousin Sidney continued to represent
the electors of Helston.

Not that the Godolphins—or any of the Cornish families
except the Rashleighs—confined themselves to their family
borough. There was a constant interchange of seats arranged
by the heads of the county families for themselves and their
political dependents. ('A town or two will choose me if I will

[1] *D.N.B.* G.E.C. *Peerage* (Leeds). Burke, *Extinct Peerage*.

serve myself, but will not give me leave to put in another'[1] Sir
Bevil Grenville complained before the Long Parliament elections.) Godolphins sat for Lostwithiel, St. Ives, St. Germans,
St. Mawes, E. Looe and Tregony as well as Helston and the
county.

One of the greatest of the managerial families at seventeenth-
as well as eighteenth-century elections was the Edgecumbes,[2]
who had been seated at Mount Edgecumbe, on the peninsula
opposite Plymouth, since the thirteenth century. Sir Richard,
escheator of Cornwall and M.P. for the county under Edward
IV had abandoned the Yorkists and fought on the winning side
at Bosworth, to his great profit. 'His exertions must have been
of a very zealous and prominent nature to call forth such
munificent rewards' says Gilbert. His son Piers (M.P. for Cornwall in 1529) added to them by marriage, and Piers's son Richard
—the alternation of these names became a family tradition—
built the mansion at Mount Edgecumbe. The two members of
the family in the Long Parliament were sons of Sir Richard
(M.P. for Grampound and Bossiney) and grandsons of Peter
(M.P. for Totnes, Liskeard, Lostwithiel and the Counties of
Devon and Cornwall). Piers married the daughter of Sir John
Glanville; and his brother-in-law was chosen as the other member for Camelford. His son Sir Richard sat for Launceston in
the Cavalier Parliament in 1661, and Piers himself was elected
for the adjacent borough of Newport in 1662. Though a 'Mr.
Edgecumbe' appears on the list of Straffordians there was
nothing doctrinaire about their Royalism. Like so many of their
kind they had opposed the forced loan without going so far as
to suffer imprisonment for it, and they surrendered promptly to
Fairfax in 1646, in return for which he intervened to have half
their fines remitted. Richard Edgecumbe (M.P. for Cornwall in
1701 and for Plympton Earl from 1702 to 1742) received a
barony and his son George (his successor at Plympton Earl)
an earldom.

[1] M. Coate, *Cornwall in the Civil War*, p. 25.
[2] G.E.C. *Peerage* (Mount Edgecumbe). *D.N.B.* C. S. Gilbert, *Historical
Survey*, I, p. 444. D. Gilbert, *Parochial History*, III, pp. 103 *seq*.

The electoral powers of the Edgecumbes, who at various times shared or disputed with other families influence at Camelford, Fowey, Lostwithiel, Grampound, Launceston and Newport, could not be equalled by many. Nor could every family have its Lords of the Treasury and its earldom. But the political history of the Godolphins and Edgecumbes is only a more expensively ornamented specimen of a pattern that is common enough. The Trevanions[1] of Caerhayes had married into the Edgecumbe family, and at one time shared with them and the Eliots control of the Borough of Grampound. John Trevanion sat for Grampound in the Short Parliament and for Lostwithiel (where Edgecumbe influence predominated) in the Long. His father had represented the county and his grandfather Grampound. His son sat in the Cavalier Parliament for Grampound and later for Tregony where the family influence became strong. (Both Grampound and Tregony are within a few miles of Caerhayes.)

Tudor Nobility

Four distinguished families of the Tudor nobility had representatives among the south-western M.P.s. We shall not reproduce here the stories of the rise of the Cecils (who rejected the idea that they were descended from the Caecilii in Rome), or of the Herberts who were prominent in Wales in the fifteenth century, but owed their English fame to the Court of Henry VIII and monastic land. The Seymours[2] had a pedigree beginning with the familiar 'knight in William the Conqueror's army'. (He came from St. Mawr-sur-Loire.) In the thirteenth century they held two manors in Monmouthshire, and later marriages added land in Wiltshire and Somerset. The acquisitions at the time of their royal marriage were mainly in these two counties; they included the manors of Chippenham and Maiden Bradley. Berry Pomeroy, near Totnes, came from Sir

[1] C. S. Gilbert, *Historical Survey*, II, p. 304. D. Gilbert, *Parochial History*, III, pp. 203 *seq*. Vivian, *Visitation of Cornwall*, p. 501. *Harleian Society*, IX, p. 239.

[2] *D.N.B.* G.E.C. *Peerage*. A. A. Locke, *The Seymour Family*. St. Maur, *Annals of the Seymours*. Sanford and Townsend, *Great Governing Families*, II, p. 245.

Thomas Pomeroy—attainted for the rebellion of 1549. The estates of the Protector Somerset (who had increased his income from land from £2,400 to £7,400 per annum) were forfeited on his fall. They had been entailed on the issue of his second wife, Anne Stanhope, whose eldest surviving son was restored to his property and to the title of Earl of Hertford in 1559. It was his grandson Francis who, from 1640 until he was created Baron Seymour in 1641, sat for Marlborough (which he had represented in several earlier Parliaments). He had to mortgage some of the estates to pay his fine of £3,725; but his successors continued in Wiltshire. His son Charles sat for the county in the Cavalier Parliament, and his grandson Francis became 5th Duke of Somerset.

Sir Edward Seymour, Bt., of Berry Pomeroy, M.P. for Devonshire in the Short and Long Parliaments, was descended from the Protector's first wife. His grandfather had sat for Devon and his father for Devon, Lyme Regis, Totnes, and several Cornish boroughs. The Seymours had bought property in the adjoining borough of Totnes from the Edgecumbes, and shared electoral influence there with the Paulets. In 1655 their property in the borough was sold, but they continued to be chosen as its members from time to time. Sir Edward sat for it in the Cavalier Parliament and in all the other Parliaments of Charles II and James II until his death in 1688. His sons Edward and Henry and his grandson Edward also represented Totnes and other boroughs in Devon and Cornwall.

Russells [1] were established in Dorset by the fourteenth century, when three of them sat in Parliament for Melcombe Regis. In the fifteenth century Henry Russell of Weymouth, merchant, Bailiff, and M.P. held local offices under the Crown. John Russell, 1st Earl of Bedford, appeared at the Court of Henry VII as an interpreter. He rose rapidly in favour under Henry VIII and at the dissolution won one of the biggest prizes in the south-west, the lands of Tavistock Abbey. To this, in fulfilment of an alleged promise of Henry VIII, he added in 1547 the

---

[1] D.N.B. G.E.C: *Peerage*. G. Scott Thomson, *Family Background*, IV. J. H. Round, *Peerage and Family History*, II, pp. 350 *seq.*

manor and site of the Abbey of Woburn, and later part of the lands of Thorney Abbey. The first London property came from the lands of the attainted Duke of Somerset. Despite their great electoral influence there were not many Russells in the sixteenth century House of Commons. The 1st Earl and his son sat for Buckinghamshire. In the next generation three brothers represented Fowey, Northumberland, and Bridport. The 4th Earl had been member for Lyme Regis in 1610. His son William was the first to sit for the family borough of Tavistock, and after six months in the Long Parliament he succeeded to the earldom. The electors of Tavistock then chose his brother John Russell as Pym's new colleague.

William (who married the daughter of Robert Carr Earl of Somerset and Essex's divorced wife Frances Howard) was one of the few members who allowed his doubts about the merits of the struggle to interfere with his activities once it had begun. He fought on the side of the Parliament at Edgehill; then, when peace negotiations were in the air, he joined the King. But by the end of 1643 he gave up hope of peace and surrendered to Parliament. The sequestration of his estates was taken off and he was allowed to live undisturbed and occupy his time in promoting drainage schemes. At the Restoration he received a ceremonial pardon.

Courtiers and Office-holders

Several members of lower status than the Cecils were related, directly or more distantly, to high officers of the Tudor government. The ancestors of the Pouletts,[1] Paulets and Powletts were seated in Somerset by the fourteenth century, and there were branches of the family in Hampshire and Dorset. Sir William Paulet, 1st Marquess of Winchester, held his office of Lord Treasurer under Edward VI, Mary and Elizabeth ('by being a willow not an oak' he is reputed to have said). He spent some of the large fortune he accumulated on a great mansion at Basing, which his successors abandoned at the end of the century. The

[1] S. W. B. Harbin, *Somerset M.P.s*, p. 151. Collinson, *Somerset*, II, p. 166; III, p. 74. *Calendar of the Committee for Compounding*, p. 1051.

2nd Marquess married Lord Willoughby de Broke's daughter Elizabeth; the 3rd a Howard; the 4th a Cecil. Descendants of this branch represented Hampshire or its boroughs in the Cavalier and many later Parliaments.

The Somerset branch, the Pouletts, prospered less ostentatiously. Sir Hugh, cousin of the Lord Treasurer and M.P. for Somerset in 1572, was supervisor of the rents of Glastonbury Abbey at the dissolution. His son Sir Amias and his great-grandson Sir John also represented the county; and in 1627 Sir John became the first Baron Poulett. Until the war the family had been reputedly Puritans; but both the 1st Baron and his son John, of Hinton St. George and Court de Wick (M.P. for Somerset in 1640 and 2nd Baron in 1649) were active Royalists. The fine of the younger John was fixed at £9,400, but eventually 'out of respect to the Lord General' he was discharged when he had paid about £1,800. (His wife Catherine, widow of Oliver St. John, was daughter of Sir Horatio Vere, and Fairfax was married to her sister; but he intervened in many other cases to reduce the fines of Royalists who were prepared to be co-operative.) John, the 3rd Baron, sat for Somerset in the Cavalier Parliament until he succeeded to the title. He married a daughter of the 5th Earl of Pembroke, and their son John, 1st Earl Poulett, became First Lord of the Treasury in 1710. His descendants are still at Hinton St. George.

Undoubtedly the best way for a man of obscure origin to found a great landed family in the sixteenth century was to hold an office at Court and use it to take advantage of the market in real estate. If lands could be earned as a reward instead of bought, so much the better. Alternatively money from an heiress would help to buy them. The Thynnes [1] of Longleat may be picked out as a family that played this part well. They had a rather dubious medieval history under the name of Botevile. William, Clerk of the Kitchen and the Green Cloth under Henry VIII (and editor of Chaucer) got a place at Court for his nephew John, who became Steward to Somerset. The job cost

[1] *Topographer and Genealogist*, III, pp. 468 seq. Hoare, *Wiltshire*, I (ii), p. 60. Burke, *Peerage*.

him a year's imprisonment after his master's fall; but it enabled him in 1540 to buy the monastic estate of Longleat and later to build the great house there. He was not short of ready cash: for he married the sister and heiress of Sir Thomas Gresham. The Wiltshire member in the Long Parliament, Sir James Thynne, left no sons; but through his younger brother, member for Hindon in 1660, Longleat went to the line that became Viscounts Weymouth and Marquesses of Bath. (One of Sir James's nephews, 'Tom of Ten Thousand', found that catching heiresses, if a necessary duty of his class, could be a dangerous one. After he had married Lady Elizabeth Percy, heiress to the Northumberland estates, who at once ran away from him, he was murdered by a rival.) Besides the Thynnes the families of Seymour, Herbert, Baynton, Long, and Erle—all with representatives among the south-western members of the Long Parliament—are on the list [1] of purchasers of monastic land in Wiltshire.

Tudor Lawyers

The Portmans [2] of Orchard Portman were a medieval Somerset family whose progress had been assisted by a very common stimulant—a high legal post. They had been in Somerset for many generations when, in the fifteenth century, they acquired by marriage the estate near Taunton which later gave them a close connection with the borough. They had some Priory lands too. But it was only when Sir William Portman became Lord Chief Justice in 1554 that they reached the level on which county families merge into national ones. The Sir William who sat for Taunton in the Long Parliament was the only member of it to be a fifth baronet: his father was one of James's early creations, and his three brothers, two of them M.P.s, had successively died without heirs. His son did so too, and the estate went to a cousin, Henry Seymour, who became a Portman-Seymour and then a Portman, and sat in every Parliament from 1679 to 1710.

---

[1] *Wiltshire Archaeological Magazine*, XXVIII, p. 309.

[2] G.E.C. *Baronetage*. Burke, *Extinct Baronetage*. Collinson, *Somerset*, I, p. 62; III, pp. 274, 283. *Calendar of the Committee for Compounding*, p. 900.

Sir Hugh Pollard [1] (Berealston) owed his fortune to an ancestor, Sir Lewis, who became a Judge of the Common Pleas in 1515 and bought the estate at King's Nympton. Sir Hugh was a close associate of Hyde in the south-western counties, and a leading figure in both the military and the political organisation of the Royalists: ('he had a very particular influence on the Cornish and Devonshire men'). He was expelled from the House for his part in the Army Plot of 1641, and devoted himself to the preparation of military support for the King. But when, as Prince put it, he was 'able to yield distressed majesty no further service for the present', he submitted to the Parliament and 'spent the remainder of his fortunes in hospitality among his friends and neighbours'. At the Restoration he was rewarded with the post of Comptroller of the Household, a grant of £5,000, and the county seat in the Cavalier Parliament. Nevertheless he died in debt, and the estate was sold to his cousin Sir Arthur Northcote.

Tudor Migrants

Several of the parliamentary families belonged to a category common among seventeenth-century gentry: they were descendants of a younger son who had migrated under the Tudors to establish estates in a new county. The Digbys of Sherborne, Dorset, who will be described later, are one example. The Duttons [2] came into Gloucestershire through the purchase of monastic lands at another Sherborne. They claimed descent from a knight of the Conqueror who had acquired an estate in Cheshire from his kinsman Hugh Lupus. Thomas Dutton, who bought Sherborne in 1551, was a younger son. His son William became High Sheriff, and married the daughter of a Lord Mayor of London. Their son John gained the support of the Berkeleys in some keenly-contested elections, and sat for the county in

[1] *D.N.B.* G.E.C. *Baronetage.* Burke, *Extinct Baronetage.* Clarendon, *Life* (1827 edition), II, p. 209 (also quoted by Browning in *Transactions of the Royal Historical Society,* 1948). *Calendar of the Committee for Compounding,* p. 1287.

[2] Williams, *Gloucestershire M.P.s* G.E.C. *Peerage.* Burke, *Peerage, Extinct Baronetage.* Rudder, *Gloucestershire,* p. 649.

1624, 1625, and the Long Parliament. Until the last possible moment he was an active opponent of the Court: he had been in prison for refusing the forced loan, and in September 1642 he promised 10 or 20 horses for the Parliamentary army. But in 1644 he was disabled for raising forces against Gloucester. As Sherborne was so near to Oxford, he told the Committee for Compounding, 'he was compelled to adhere to the party there for the preservation of his house and estate'. And he did preserve it—though he had leave to sell lands to pay his fine of £3,434. His nephew Ralph, who inherited the estates, became a baronet in 1687. The male line was extinct in the eighteenth century: the later Barons Sherborne assumed the name of Dutton when they acquired the estates.

Merchant wealth

Among the 'new' families of the south-west merchant ancestry was not so normal a method of establishing estates as a few prominent examples sometimes lead us to suppose. We could cite the Smiths [1] of Somerset, descendants of an early Tudor Lord Mayor of Bristol; and the Rashleighs [2] of Fowey, a local ship-owning and trading family who transformed themselves by easy stages into a landed one. The first John Rashleigh was a Fowey merchant in the mid-sixteenth century; his son, who built the mansion at Menabilly and sat for the borough in 1588, was the father of Jonathan, member for Fowey in most of the Parliaments from 1614 to 1675. Jonathan bought other lands in Cornwall; but he maintained his interests, and his house, in the town. His descendants continued to sit for Fowey in an almost unbroken line until its disfranchisement in 1832. But there are considerably more merchants on the maternal than on the paternal side of the members' genealogies, and more still among younger sons and their fathers-in-law. The impression from this restricted evidence is that merchant wealth was less important in founding landed families than in infusing new

[1] Burke, *Extinct Baronetage*. Collinson, *Somerset*, II, p. 292.
[2] M. Coate, *Cornwall in the Civil War*, pp. 235 seq. E. W. Rashleigh, *Short History of Fowey. Calendar of the Committee for Compounding*, p. 1327.

economic strength after they were established. It is so common in families that survived that we begin to wonder whether a landed estate could last for more than a few generations without being subsidised through commercial or professional fortunes, or through the sale of new lands acquired by marriage. That is not a question we can attempt to answer here: it is as much as we can do to reckon the chances of survival of the estates of our members in the next hundred years.

With few exceptions the Royalist members had their estates sequestered and, unless their delinquency was exceptionally heinous, redeemed them by payment of their composition to the Treasurers of the Goldsmiths' Hall Committee. The calendars of the Committee's proceedings (besides being a source of information about Royalist estates for which there is unfortunately no parallel on the Parliamentary side) are full of the attempts of the victims to explain away their offence, to show that they were deeply in debt, or had only a life interest in estates that were said to be theirs, and to conceal the full extent of their possessions. The Committee can hardly have arrived at an estimate of the value of an estate accurate enough to be of much use to us; and the proportion of the fine varied according to the circumstances in which the delinquent submitted, and to his bargaining power later. Many of the south-western members surrendered under the Exeter Articles and paid only a tenth; others were fined a third or even a half. Of those fines that are recorded 5 were fixed at the maximum of £10,000, 4 at from £7,000 to £3,000, 18 at from £3,000 to £1,000, 15 at from £1,000 to £500, and 11 at less than £500. Many Royalists groaned loudly under these burdens and claimed to be ruined. ('Plundered and fined in Goldsmiths' Hall to my utter undoing', as Ralph Sydenham said.) Some certainly sold or mortgaged part of the estate to pay the fine, and this may sometimes have made all the difference between prosperity and a growing weight of debt that could crush its bearers in the second or third generation. But there is not much evidence of this happening among the M.P.s. Other manors or parcels of land may have been sold, and standards of extravagance reduced; estates on the verge of disaster may have been rescued by wealth from outside; but the Hungerfords and Pollards were the exceptions rather than the rule. The majority returned after the war to their principal seat, and remained there as long as the male line survived.[1]

The Parliamentary members who enriched themselves as a result of the war are also exceptional. A large part of the area was at one time or another under Royalist control, and the estates of rebels were seized. Eighteen of the members received the £4 weekly which the House voted to those whose estates were in the hands of the enemy. Others had lump sums in compensation for the losses incurred in the service of Parliament. William Strode got £500 when his house in Devon was plundered; Thomas Hodges had £1,000 out of the estate of the Earl of Worcester; Walter Long had £5,000 as compensation for his imprisonment in 1629. A few more did well in the land-market. Robert Reynolds, who became Solicitor-General in 1650, was a large purchaser of Bishops' lands. William Say, another barrister, held the lands of Lord Abergavenny, but as a regicide lost everything at the Restoration. John Dove of Salisbury kept some of his numerous acquisitions. But the colourful picture painted in the *Good Old Cause*, the *History of Independency* and other Royalist and Presbyterian pamphlets of members plundering the defeated enemy, holding lucrative offices, and retaining their Army commands contrary to the Self-Denying Ordinance applies only to a small minority.

If there are few instances among the M.P.s of old landed families being ruined, there are fewer still of new landed families being founded. It is difficult to find a single clear example in the south-west of a merchant, lawyer, town Alderman or country 'gent' who established a successful line on an estate acquired in the war period or the Interregnum. The impression is that, far from being a great opportunity for men to rise from nothing, the period was a less propitious one than that of the previous generation. But again it has to be remembered that M.P.s, even

[1] See the article by Joan Thirsk on sales of Royalist land in *Economic History Review*, 2nd series, Vol. V, No. 2.

if there were enough of them, are not a sample of any section of the community. Though the opportunities were greater for them, so were the risks. Perhaps the way to prosper was to stay at home, and not to meddle in Revolutions.

III

THE MEMBERS FROM DORSET

The County of Dorset was well represented in Parliament. It was not starved of seats like Cheshire and Derbyshire, nor had it a glut of pocket boroughs. Of its 20 members 8 were returned by ports—Lyme Regis, Poole, and the 'double borough' of Weymouth and Melcombe Regis. Eight more came from towns near the coast: Wareham and Corfe Castle, the small boroughs of the Isle of Purbeck; Bridport, where rope and sailcloth for the navy were made; and the County Town. The remaining borough, Shaftesbury, lay far off in the north of the county, nearer to Wiltshire and Somerset boroughs than to the other Dorset ones. Dorchester, Lyme Regis, Bridport, and Wareham were all represented in Parliaments of Edward I. Weymouth and Melcombe Regis, united by Elizabeth, appear as separate boroughs early in the fourteenth century; Poole first elected in 1362. Only Corfe Castle was a Tudor creation: it sent its first members to Elizabeth's third Parliament, through the influence of Sir Christopher Hatton to whom it had been granted by the Crown. Nevertheless the Tudor nobility played its electioneering games in Dorset as elsewhere. Paulets, Cecils, and Dudleys had at various times been involved; but the most important influence was that of the Russells [1] at Bridport, Lyme Regis, and Weymouth, which helped to establish a Puritan tradition in the county's representation. Under James I, though a Paulet and a Russell again appeared as Dorset members, local influence was clearly establishing itself to the exclusion of even west-country outsiders. Despite the connections that will be shown between families and particular boroughs, it was predominantly a county influence. Most of the landed houses that regularly sent

[1] See J. E. Neale, *The Elizabethan House of Commons*, pp. 197-200.

members divided their favours among several towns, and the county seats were not the preserve of any of them. The distribution of six boroughs among six families can be set out in a table.

	1588–1603	1604–29	1640–59	1660–1701
County	Rogers Trenchard Strangways	Napier Trenchard Strangways	Rogers Trenchard	Strangways
Bridport	Trenchard Napier		Strangways	Strangways
Corfe Castle		Napier	Bond	Napier
Dorchester	Trenchard Napier		Bond	Trenchard Bond Napier
Poole		Erle	Bond	Trenchard Strangways Napier
Wareham	Rogers	Trenchard Napier	Trenchard Bond Erle	Trenchard Erle
Weymouth & Melcombe Regis		Erle Napier	Erle Napier Strangways Bond Trenchard	Napier Strangways

Between November 1640 and April 1653 32 members took their seats for Dorset and its boroughs. Of those originally returned, 9 became Royalists and 11 Parliamentarians.[1] Seven of the Royalists were 'disabled to sit' between 1642 and 1644; Digby became a Peer in 1641 and was succeeded by a Parliamentarian, John Browne; Windebank's seat was declared vacant

[1] See Appendix V.

when he left the country, but his successor John Burlace was also a Royalist. One Parliamentary member, William Whitaker, died before 1648, and four—Green, Holles, and the Erles—were secluded at Pride's Purge. Richard Rose did not appear in the House after 1647, but the remaining six—Hill, Bond, Prideaux, Pyne, Browne, and John Trenchard—sat in the Rump. Hill, Pyne, and Trenchard returned in 1659. Nine new members were elected to fill vacancies existing in 1645.[1] One Recruiter, Starre, died in 1647 and was replaced by John Fry. Five—Ceeley, Chettel, Skutt, Allen, and John Bond—were secluded in 1648, and Thomas Trenchard does not appear to have sat after the Purge. Bingham and Sydenham survived it and returned in 1659.

Two of these members, Digby[2] and Holles,[3] achieved national fame and had interests extending far outside the county. These two sons of newly-created Earls offer tempting material for comparison. The Parliamentarian Holles was the descendant of a merchant; the Royalist Digby came of an old landed family. Holles was a staunch Presbyterian, Digby a convert to Rome. Holles married the daughter of a lawyer, Digby the daughter of a Russell. But it was Digby who inherited a monastic estate, who was on the committee that drew up the impeachment of Strafford, and whose father had been a victim of the displeasure of Buckingham; and it was Holles whom Charles I called his 'very old companion and bed-fellow', who tried to save Strafford—his brother-in-law—and later to impeach Cromwell.

The Digby family held the manor of Drystoke, Rutlandshire, in the fifteenth century. Under Henry VII they had received Coleshill, Warwickshire, and other 'extensive grants' as their reward for being on the winning side. Digbys represented Rutland and Warwickshire in several of the early Tudor Parliaments. They added still more to their possessions in the sixteenth

[1] See Appendix V.
[2] D.N.B. G.E.C. Peerage. Burke, Extinct Peerage. Hutchins, Dorset, IV, pp. 209 seq., 472–6. H. M. Digby, Sir Kenelm Digby and George Digby.
[3] D.N.B. Burke, Extinct Peerage. G.E.C. Peerage. Memoirs of Denzil Lord Holles (1649). Gervase Holles, Memorials (Camden Third Series, Vol. LV). A. C. Wood, 'The Holles Family,' Transactions of the Royal Historical Society, 1934.

century; and the accession of James, which hindered the rise of the Holleses, brought the Digbys to the height of their success. The new king 'took a fancy' to Sir John Digby and made him a Gentleman of the Privy Chamber and, in 1611, ambassador to Madrid. In 1616 he acquired the estate on the border of Dorset and Somerset that became the seat of his branch of the family. The monastic lands of Sherborne had been the property of Sir Walter Raleigh, and on his fall were granted to Robert Carr. When Somerset was also disgraced, Digby bought the estate for £10,000. (Raleigh's heirs continued to dispute the legality of the transfer, and when the Digbys in their turn forfeited Sherborne and the rest of their estates, one of their manors— Clevedon—was granted to Carew Raleigh.) Sir Kenelm Digby in 1634 compiled 'at a cost of £1,400' a genealogy which showed the family to be in possession of lands in Warwickshire, Staffordshire, Buckinghamshire, Leicestershire, Rutland, Kent, Norfolk, and Dorset.

Sir John had been successful enough in his earlier Spanish negotiations to be entrusted with the preliminaries of the renewed attempt at a marriage alliance in 1622—when he was made Earl of Bristol. But in the following year Charles and Buckingham both became his bitter enemies. Charles on his accession tried to prevent Digby from sitting in the Lords, and from 1626 to 1628 kept him under a charge of treason. By that time the new Earl of Clare, John Holles, had also joined the enemies of Buckingham.

The Holles family were less sure than the Digbys of their medieval origin. Holleses were Knights of the Shire in Norfolk and Cheshire in the fourteenth and fifteenth centuries; but Gervase Holles in the family Memorials refrained from inventing a pedigree to show his descent from them. 'Like the River Arethusa', he says, 'we have run some time underground until Sir William Holles the father (through God's blessing on his industry and providence) laid the foundation and groundwork for that greatness our family is now arrived at'.[1] Sir William, Warden of the Mercers' Company and Lord Mayor of London,

[1] Gervase Holles, *Memorials*, p. 12.

died in 1542, leaving his sons in possession of 7 manors in Lincolnshire, 8 in Derbyshire, and others in Staffordshire, Essex, Yorkshire, and Norfolk, besides land in London and Calais. But the elder line of his family lost the fortune he had founded. Sir Thomas Holles 'by his lavishness and improvidence was the ruin both of himself and his posterity'. His son William consumed what was left of the inheritance, and his great-grandson was at one time—so the story goes—turning a spit in the kitchen of the 1st Earl of Clare.

Sir William 'like a wise merchant had not adventured all his stock in one bottom'.[1] He left to his second son William 'very fair revenues' from lands in Nottinghamshire, Derbyshire, Lincolnshire, and London; and he married him to the coheiress of John Denzil of Cornwall. Sir William was seated at Houghton, Nottinghamshire, where, Gervase complains, his retinue was always, 'according to the magnificence of those days' far larger than was necessary. His eldest son Denzil inherited the Lincolnshire estates and enclosed them—'much to the benefit of him self and his tenants, for . . . he had this just care with him, to leave the commons very large; and . . . I never knew in the township any tenant that was not thriving'.[2] His wife was the daughter of the 1st Baron Sheffield and Anne Vere, and it was their eldest son John who advanced the family 'from the lesser to the greater nobility' with the title of Earl of Clare.

John Holles (M.P. for Nottinghamshire in 1604 and 1614) became a Gentleman Pensioner at the Elizabethan Court, and a warrior in the Netherlands, Hungary, and Ireland. But he was one of the Elizabethan courtiers who lost their places on the accession of James, and he returned to his midland estates. There, despite some expensive law-suits, he continued his father's successful management. Manors and rectories in Nottinghamshire and neighbouring counties were added to the possessions he had inherited, and he acquired also a good deal of property in the Drury Lane district. Gervase puts his annual revenue at £8,000. One of the purchases was the manor of Lower Loders

[1] Gervase Holles, *Memorials*, p. 37.
[2] Gervase Holles, *Memorials*, p. 62.

near Bridport where his second son Denzil went to live. Denzil by his marriage to the heiress of Sir Francis Ashley obtained the Priory House in Dorchester and an income of £1,200 a year. In 1610 John Holles was back at Court as Comptroller of the Household to the Prince of Wales. But he does not seem to have had many friends there: he was never on good terms with Buckingham for long, and Sir Edward Coke 'bore a particular spleen against him' and is blamed for his imprisonment in the Fleet. The fall of his friends Raleigh and Somerset, which gave Digby the Sherborne estate, damaged Holles's prospects still more. He was unsuccessful in several attempts to get a high office, which culminated in his trying to succeed Cranfield as Treasurer. But titles were now more easily won: Holles's barony cost him £10,000 and the earldom, in 1624, a further £5,000.

Both the Earls took part in the discussion of the Petition of Right in 1628 and neither committed himself decisively for or against it. But the Dorset electors who chose the sons George Digby and Denzil Holles in April and November 1640 knew them as firm opponents of the Court. Denzil had sat for Dorchester in the 1628 Parliament, where his fame as an opposition leader was established by the holding down of the Speaker. He had been in exile during the personal rule. Digby had not been a member before, but his father had emerged from comparative inactivity to become one of the leaders in the meeting of the Great Council, and George was soon prominent in the attacks on Charles's evil counsellors.

When the Long Parliament met, Digby's ideas had changed. He spent only seven months in the Commons before Charles rescued him from the wrath of his former allies by creating a new barony for him; and the leader of the attack on him was Denzil Holles, who prepared his impeachment. Holles's position as a Parliamentary leader was firmly established by the time he appeared as one of the five members sought out by Charles in January 1642. But he was soon identified with the right wing of the Parliament and was prominent in most of the peace moves down to the Treaty of Newport. In 1647 he was one of the eleven members impeached by the Army. He returned to the House in

1648, but after the failure of the last attempt at a settlement with the King he fled to France. Digby was there already, offering his services in the wars of the Fronde.

No great gulf separated the new nobility of Digby and Holles from the county gentlemen. Twelve of the Dorset members came from the county's highest landed families, most of which were already well known at Westminster. The Rogers [1] family held the adjacent manors of Bryanston and Blandford Forum early in the fifteenth century. At the beginning of Elizabeth's reign they had lands in several other parts of Dorset and in Berkshire—6,520 acres in all. Sir John Rogers (M.P. for Dorset in 1545) married the daughter of Under-Treasurer Weston. His sons Richard and Thomas and his grandson Sir John sat in many Parliaments for the county and the Borough of Wareham. Richard Rogers, member for Dorset in the Short Parliament and from November 1640 until he was 'disabled' in 1642, was the son of Sir John. At his death in 1645 the estates were taken over by his stepmother, and eventually discharged from sequestration in 1652. The only other consistent Royalists in this group were the Strangways,[2] Sir John (M.P. for the county in several Parliaments of James and Charles and for Weymouth in 1640) and his son Giles (M.P. for Weymouth in the Short Parliament and for Bridport in the Long). The many branches of the family had extensive marriage connections in the south-west. There are marriages to the Trenchards in four generations—(Sir John married Grace, sister of the Long Parliament Trenchards); there was an Arundell of Lanherne, a Berkeley, a Thynne, a Carew, and a Sydenham. It was through the Arundell match at the end of the fifteenth century that they came into possession of Melbury Sampford. They held lands in Abbotsbury before the dissolution, founded a chantry there, and then, for £1,096, acquired the monastic estate. At the death of Sir John Strangways

---

[1] Burke, *Landed Gentry*. Hutchins, *Dorset*, I, pp. 250-2. *Calendar of the Committee for Compounding*, p. 2873. *C.J.* 21 Sept. 1642.

[2] Hutchins, *Dorset*, II, pp. 661-5, 714, 720. *Somerset and Dorset Notes and Queries*, XII, p. 97. Burke, *Peerage* (Earl of Ilchester). *Calendar of the Committee for Compounding*, p. 1828. *Harleian Society*, XX, p. 86. S. Heath and W. C. Prideaux, *Some Dorset Manor Houses*, pp. 133 seq.

in 1593 there were 8 manors in their possession. His son, the Sir John of the Long Parliament, had refused the forced loan of 1626, but became a Straffordian in 1641.

None of these Dorset families claimed to have been in the county earlier than the fourteenth century, when the Binghams [1] of Somerset acquired by marriage the estate at Bingham's Melcombe where the Parliamentary forces had their headquarters at the beginning of the war. Colonel John Bingham, son-in-law of John Trenchard and first cousin of Sir Ralph Hopton, was the first of his family to sit in Parliament. The Trenchards [2] came into Dorset from the Isle of Wight. Under Edward IV they acquired by marriage the manor of Wolfeton near Dorchester where their principal house was built in the reign of Henry VIII. Most of their other estates were added in the sixteenth century. Warmwell, 5 miles from Wolfeton, was monastic land, and Litchet Maltravers, near Poole, was bought from the Howards. A Christopher Trenchard sat for Dorchester in 1542 and a George Trenchard in 1572. Three of George's sons became M.P.s: the eldest, Sir George, for the county in 1601; Thomas for the county in 1621, and again as a Recruiter to the Long Parliament; John of Warmwell for Wareham in November 1640. John Trenchard's daughter Grace married another Recruiter, William Sydenham [3] of Wynford Eagle, close to the estates of the Holleses and the Brownes. The family had come from Somerset, where many branches remained. One John Sydenham represented Somerset in the Parliament of 1378, another in 1460, and a third in 1554. Thomas, who acquired Wynford Eagle in 1544, was a younger son of a younger son. The family had married with some of the biggest landholders of the south-west—Arundells, Drakes, Godolphins—and another younger branch which had settled in Devonshire sent

[1] Burke, *Commoners*, IV, pp. 350-3. Hutchins, *Dorset*, IV, pp. 368-82. Bayley, *Civil War in Dorset*, p. 36. *Harleian Society*, XX, p. 15.

[2] Hutchins, *Dorset*, I, pp. 426-35; II, pp. 546-58; III, pp. 325-31. *Somerset and Dorset Notes and Queries*, XX, p. 107; XIII, p. 267. Heath and Prideaux, *Some Dorset Manor Houses*, pp. 189 seq., 209 seq. Burke, *Landed Gentry*.

[3] D.N.B. G. F. Sydenham, *History of the Sydenham Family*. Hutchins, *Dorset*, II, pp. 701-6.

a member, Sir Ralph, to the Long Parliament for Bossinney. He was disabled as a Royalist in 1642.

The Brownes[1] of Frampton had been leaseholders in that district in the fifteenth century, and acquired their monastic estate at the dissolution. Sir John Browne, father of the M.P., became Sheriff of Dorset and married a daughter of Sir Henry Portman; the son married another sister of the Trenchards. The ancestors of the Erles[2] were also Somerset men. They had been at Newton under Henry III and claimed an ancestor at Beckington who paid his scutage under Henry II. Charborough, and holdings in the Borough of Wareham, came by the marriage of Walter Erle to the coheiress of Richard Wyke. Their son Thomas held at his death in 1597 the manors of Axmouth, Charborough, East and West Morden, and many other lands and rectories. Thomas's younger son Christopher was member for Weymouth in 1621, Poole in 1626, and Lyme Regis in 1628; but the elder son Walter did not sit until November 1640. He became notorious for his failure to prove the charge against Strafford with which he was entrusted at the Trial—that of planning to bring over the Irish army. Walter's son Thomas, who sat in the Short and Long Parliaments, for Milborne Port and Wareham respectively, became a barrister of the Middle Temple and a close friend of Anthony Ashley Cooper. ('The nearest friendship betwixt us as was imaginable, never to expire but in both our deaths.')

There is one member among the Dorset gentry whose allegiance changed rapidly with the times. The ancestors of Sir Gerard Napier[3] were a Scottish family, Napier of Merchiston, who said they were descended from the Earls of Lennox. They appeared in Devonshire under Henry VII, and from there one brother settled in Bedfordshire and another at Swyre in Dorset. The founder of their fortunes was Sir Robert, younger son of

[1] Hutchins, *Dorset*, I, p. 165; II, pp. 297-9. *Calendar of the Committee for the Advance of Monies*, pp. 1291, 1321.

[2] Hutchins, *Dorset*, III, pp. 468, 499-502. Burke, *Landed Gentry*.

[3] *D.N.B.* G.E.C. *Baronetage*, II, p. 91. Burke, *Extinct Baronetage*. *Harleian Society*, XX, p. 74. Hutchins, *Dorset*, II, p. 770. G. A. Ellis, *History of Weymouth*, pp. 209-10.

Sir James of Pucknowle, who was appointed Chief Baron of the Exchequer in Ireland in 1593. He pointed out that 'there is little profit incident to the office, dealing in an honest and upright course'. Despite this difficulty he acquired fairly extensive new estates, including the main family seat at Middlemarsh Hall. He represented Dorset in 1586 and the Boroughs of Wareham and Bridport in 1601 and 1604. His son Sir Nathaniel, who built the mansion of More Crichel, represented Dorset, Wareham, and Milborne Port in the 1620s (when two of his Bedfordshire cousins sat for Weymouth and Dorchester). Sir Nathaniel's son Sir Gerard—a baronet in 1641—was also member for Wareham, in 1628, and for Weymouth in the Long Parliament.

One other member can be counted practically among the county gentry in origin. The estates of the Prideaux[1] family were in many parts of Devon and Cornwall; but Edmund, who sat for Lyme Regis in 1640, came from Netherton, near Honiton, not many miles from his Dorset borough. There were Prideaux in Cornwall in the time of the Conqueror, and they had greatly extended their possessions in the fifteenth and sixteenth centuries. Sir Edmund's father was a successful lawyer who had married an Edgecumbe and acquired a baronetcy. The son built up one of the most lucrative of London legal practices. He became Recorder of Exeter and of Bristol, a Commissioner of the Great Seal, and 'Master of the Posts Messengers and Couriers'. His wealth and offices were an easy target for the pamphleteers: the post-office was said to be worth £15,000 a year—or according to Clement Walker's more modest estimate '£100 every Tuesday night besides his supper'. He certainly amassed a large fortune, and invested some of it in his house and land at Ford Abbey, Devon.[2]

Before moving on from the well-established county families to the men of lower or more recent status, we can look at some earlier events in Dorset which throw light on the connection of several of these lesser members with their more respected colleagues. At the beginning of the reign of James I a Dorchester

[1] D.N.B. G.E.C. *Baronetage*, I, p. 200. S. Heath, *The Story of Ford Abbey*, pp. 66 seq. Foss, *Lives of the Judges.*   [2] It is now in Dorset.

rector, John White,[1] was making a national reputation for himself as a Puritan preacher. We know that Denzil Holles was one of his congregation; Denis Bond was described as his 'disciple'; John Bond, according to Wood, 'sucked in the most dangerous principles' from him.[2] White became interested in the current schemes of colonisation in North America. He was concerned both about the spiritual welfare of the Dorset fishermen who crossed the Atlantic, and about a possible refuge for the godly in case persecution in England got worse—not to mention the profits of such enterprises. White discussed these matters with some of the Dorset merchants who traded in cod and furs; and in 1624 there was founded the Dorchester Company, a joint-stock venture which combined fishing expeditions with colonisation. Among its members[3] were Sir Walter Erle of Charborough, described as the 'Governor of the New England Plantation', John Browne of Frampton, Denis Bond of Dorchester, John Hill of Poundsford, Giles Green of Affington, and William Fry of Yarty. There were also a few Devon men, including Walter Young of Colliton, and Periam son of Sir William Pole. The Dorchester Company as such did not last long; but John White, John Humphrey the Treasurer, and some of the other investors helped to start its successor the New England Company, into which as we have already seen they brought the London merchants who represented the City in the Long Parliament, and also John White's namesake the lawyer. The New England Company soon merged into the Massachusetts Bay Company, with John Winthrop as its first Governor. Humphrey was now moving in high circles: in 1630 he married the sister of Theophilus Fiennes-Clinton, 4th Earl of Lincoln, who was himself married to Bridget Fiennes, daughter of William Viscount Say and Sele, co-founder of Saybrooke and member of the Providence Island Company. Lord Say and Sele's daughter Susanna was married to Thomas Erle. The Earl of Lincoln's son, Edward Lord Clinton, member for Callington in

---

[1] F. Rose-Troup, *John White, the Patriarch of Dorchester.*

[2] Wood, *Athenae*, II, p. 115.

[3] Listed in F. Rose-Troup, *John White the Patriarch of Dorchester.*

the Long Parliament, married the sister of Denzil Holles. By the
time they appeared in the Long Parliament the Dorchester
Company adventurers were therefore well connected with the
leaders of the colonising movement, and of political Puritanism.

We can now turn to the antecedents of the remaining members, some of whom had thus found through their interest in
the New World a point of contact with their betters. The
Bonds [1] came of a family that had long been on the fringe of the
gentry. They were lessees of lands at Lutton in the Isle of Purbeck from the time of Henry VI until 1615, when they became
freeholders. One of them had sat for Weymouth in 1529.
Denis, son of John of Lutton and Margaret Pitt, was, the pamphleteers delighted to say, a 'woollen draper' in Dorchester.
Perhaps it was taunts like this that led him to draw up a pedigree
showing the Norman origin of the family. Denis's wife Joan
Gould was the sister of another of the Dorchester Company
adventurers. Their son John, member for Weymouth in 1645,
had sat as a Puritan Divine in the Westminster Assembly and
preached before the House. In 1646 he was made Master of
Trinity Hall, Cambridge, and in 1649 he became Professor of Law
at Gresham College. John Fry [2] of Iwerne Minster belonged to a
similar family from the north of the county. A Fry had sat
for Shaftesbury in 1405, and another for Lyme Regis in 1545;
and by the end of Elizabeth's reign they held the manor of
Iwerne. The Chettels of Blandford [3] and the Pynes of Curry
Malet were of Tudor origin. Blandford was a priory estate
acquired at the dissolution. The Pynes,[4] though they claimed to
be 'of ancient and honourable family, long time bearing arms',
owed their estates mainly to John's great-grandfather, an Elizabethan lawyer. His acquisitions included Crewkerne, Little

[1] *D.N.B.* Hutchins, *Dorset*, I, pp. 600-7. Burke, *Landed Gentry*. H. Mayo,
Records of Dorchester. Harleian Society, XX, p. 16. Clarendon, *History*, II, p. 27.
[2] Hutchins, *Dorset*, III, p. 537. *Harleian Society*, XX, p. 42. *Somerset and Dorset
Notes and Queries*, I, pp. 53, 73; XX, p. 187; XXIV, p. 153. *C.J.* 3 Feb. 1648-9.
[3] Hutchins, *Dorset*, I, p. 163.
[4] Burke, *Landed Gentry*. Hutchins, *Dorset*, II, p. 329. *Harleian Society*, XX, p. 78.
Somerset Archaeological Proceedings, XXXVII. *Somerset and Dorset Notes and
Queries*, X, p. 83; XIX, pp. 31, 65, 78, 115.

Windsor, and lands 'in divers counties'. John's mother and first wife both came from the Hanham family, who had bought monastic lands at Wimborne Minster and Dean's Court. Thomas, grandfather of John Pyne and of the Thomas Hanham who sat for Minehead in the Long Parliament, became a Serjeant-at-Law and married the daughter of the Lord Chief Justice, Sir John Popham. John Pyne himself was called to the Bar from the Middle Temple in 1629, when he had already sat in three Parliaments. He brings us to another group of Dorset members, the lawyers.

One of these had very close connections with the Dorchester Company. Roger Hill[1] of Poundsford, son of William and nephew of the John Hill mentioned above, was related through his mother to the Youngs of Coliton, and married the daughter of Giles Green. The Hills could trace their ancestors in Somerset back to a Sir John in the reign of Edward III, but the estate at Poundsford was acquired in the sixteenth century, when a Robert and another Roger sat for Taunton. Our Roger had sat for Taunton too, in the Short Parliament, but his Dorset connections got him both a seat for Bridport and its Recordership. Three of the other boroughs were represented by their Recorders. William Constantine,[2] member for Poole in both the 1640 Parliaments, was Recorder of both Poole and Dorchester. His great-grandfather, who bought the manor of Merley, had been Mayor of Poole in 1566 and in two later years. By the marriage of William's grandfather to Margaret Neville the Constantines claimed a connection with the Earls of Westmorland. William's mother was an Evelyn of Ditton, and through his wife Jane Hanham he was related to the Pynes. Constantine was disabled as a Royalist, and was taken into custody for attempting to bring about the surrender of Poole to the King's forces. William Whitaker,[3] Recorder of Shaftesbury, had entered the Middle Temple on the same day as Pym, and became its Treasurer in 1635. He was one of several members of the

---

[1] D.N.B. and addendum. Foss, Lives of the Judges. Collinson, Somerset, III, p. 287. Somerset Record Society, XXVIII, p. 316.

[2] Hutchins, Dorset, III, p. 304. Bayley, Civil War in Dorset, pp. 108-11.

[3] Hutchins, Dorset, III, pp. 628-31.

Parliament whose families owed their rise to service under a great man of the Tudor Court, for his father Henry had been secretary to Sir Christopher Hatton. The Whitakers, originally a Lancashire family, were then at Westbury, Wiltshire; but William acquired an estate at Motcombe near his borough. Richard King,[1] who became Recorder of Weymouth in 1629, was of a more obscure origin. His father William of Castle Cary was a mere 'gent', and it was not until 1641 that Richard had a grant of arms.

The remaining local members were townsmen. The most successful of these was Giles Green,[2] member for Corfe Castle. He first appears as a prominent citizen of Weymouth, which he represented in Parliament in 1621, 1625, and 1626. There are notes in the town records of payments to him 'towards a key and slipp which he hath built upon the town ground on the East side of his house in Hell Lane' and for delivering letters to the Privy Council. He seems to have made good use of his contacts in London, for he became Receiver of Yorkshire and, in 1645, a Commissioner of the Navy. Richard Rose,[3] Mayor of Lyme Regis in 1637, was the son of another Lyme merchant said to have come from Jersey. Thomas Ceeley [4] came to Lyme Regis from Cornwall. His mother was the aunt of John Penrose, member for Helston, but his grandmother Avis Marchant was of a Dorset family, and he was connected also with the Roses. Matthew Allen [5] was a brewer of Weymouth, son of a former Mayor and himself an Alderman. (He appears in the Court Records when his beer-cart broke the wall round a well.) George Skutt [6] came of a Poole family, several of whom were merchants

---

[1] G. A. Ellis, *History of Weymouth*, p. 231. Hutchins, *Dorset*, II, p. 440.

[2] *Somerset and Dorset Notes and Queries*, II, p. 303; III, pp. 78, 101. *Calendar of the Committee for Compounding*, p. 129.

[3] Hutchins, *Dorset*, II, p. 274. *Somerset and Dorset Notes and Queries*, IV, p. 127. *Calendar of the Committee for Compounding*, p. 523. *Calendar of State Papers Domestic*, 1637, p. 481. *Lyme Regis Mayors' Accounts*, p. 109. H. J. Moule, *Weymouth Charters*, p. 140.

[4] Vivian, *Visitation of Cornwall*, p. 82. *Calendar of the Committee for Compounding*, p. 802.

[5] *Calendar of the Committee for the Advance of Monies*, p. 1045. G. A. Ellis, *History of Weymouth*, p. 229.

[6] Hutchins, *Dorset*, I, p. 33. Bayley, *Civil War in Dorset*, p. 111.

and Mayors. Of George Starre [1] we know nothing until he appears in the Parliamentary army in 1643, as a captain under Colonel Sydenham.

Lastly there are the Royalist 'outsiders'. Two of them sat for the Borough of Corfe Castle, where the predominant local influence was now that of Sir John Bankes, whose wife was the heroine of the celebrated siege. Bankes as Attorney-General and later Chief Justice of the Common Pleas was in the highest Court circle. When Sir Francis Windebank [2] had become so closely associated with Charles's unpopular measures that 'even Oxford University' refused to elect him, Bankes gave him the Corfe Castle seat. At the end of December Windebank was declared to have 'absented himself' from the Parliament and a new writ was issued. The member returned was Bankes's son-in-law John Burlace. [3] He too had lost the seat he held in the Short Parliament, when his return for Great Marlow was declared void after a dispute. It is perhaps unjust to describe Samuel Turner [4] as an outsider, for his father had sat for Bridport, and he had himself previously represented Shaftesbury in 1626. But the family owed their remarkable careers to learning and the Court, not to Dorset. William Turner, described as the 'son of a tanner', was the distinguished pioneer of botany who became chaplain and physician to Somerset. His son Peter was also a physician and a notorious Puritan. Peter's son Samuel followed his father's profession but not his beliefs. (Wood calls him 'a man of very loose principles'—presumably because he had an illegitimate son.) In the 1626 Parliament he spoke against Buckingham; but he became physician to Charles I and in 1641 he was, like the two Strangways, a Straffordian. He joined the Royal army at the outbreak of war and sat in the Oxford Parliament.

We can now enquire what effect the twenty years' upheaval and the political and private activities in it of these thirty-two

[1] Bayley, *Civil War in Dorset*, p. 194.   [2] *D.N.B.*
[3] W. C. Borlace, *History of the Borlace Family*. G.E.C. *Baronetage*, II, p. 169. Burke, *Extinct Baronetage*. Lipscombe, *Buckinghamshire*, I, p. 309; II, p. 606. There is an account of the Great Marlow election by Mary Freer in *Journal of Modern History*, XIV.   [4] *D.N.B.* Wood, *Fasti*, I, p. 303.

members had on their fortunes and those of their descendants. There is no need to spend long on the conclusion of the Digby and Holles story. Digby as Earl of Bristol became Secretary of State to Charles II in exile, and a K.G. at the Restoration. His son John, the 3rd Earl (member for Dorset in 1675) died without heirs, but Sherborne and the other estates passed to a cousin and remained in the family until the middle of the nineteenth century. When Charles and Digby were waiting for the moment of triumphal return, there came on the Commission from the new Parliament to the Hague Denzil Holles, M.P. for Dorchester and a member of the Council of State. He was also elected by his faithful borough to the Cavalier Parliament, but he was soon raised to the peerage as Baron Holles of Ifield. In 1663 he crossed the Channel again—as ambassador to the Court of Louis XIV. His last political act was to oppose the Exclusion Bill. The barony was inherited by his son Francis—who was member for Dorchester—but in 1694 the male line was extinct, and the estates passed to the Duke of Newcastle, grandson of Denzil's elder brother.

With Holles among the Dorset members at the opening of the Cavalier Parliament were Sir John Strangways, aged seventy-six, member for Weymouth, his son Sir Giles Strangways, member for the county, and his grandson John Strangways, member for Bridport, of which the family now held a virtually hereditary High Stewardship. The parliament outlived them all; but the young John was succeeded at Bridport by his brother Waddam; and Thomas, another son of Sir Giles, succeeded a Trenchard at Poole. The Strangways, it will be gathered, had not been ruined by the imprisonment of Sir John and Giles in the Tower, nor by their losses in Goldsmiths' Hall, though their fines were fixed at £10,000.[1] They were able to retain their ancestral estate at Melbury and the lands at Waterson they bought in 1641 from the Earl of Suffolk; and in 1652 Sir John came to the help of his father-in-law, Sir Lewis Dyve, Commander-in-Chief of the King's forces in Dorset, by buying from the Treason Trustees Sir Lewis's manor of

[1] *Calendar of the Committee for Compounding*, p. 1828.

Bromham, Bedfordshire.[1] When the male line failed in the middle of the eighteenth century the estates went, by the marriage of an heiress, to the family of Fox-Strangways, Earls of Ilchester.

Sir Gerard Napier's less dogmatic Royalism also had little effect on the family fortunes. 'Notwithstanding the persecution and heavy losses he endured', says the loyal Burke, 'he still augmented the paternal property.' In 1642 he lent £500 to the Parliament; later he fought for the King, and sat at Oxford. He submitted promptly in 1644, lent more money to Parliamentary garrisons, and got off with a very small fine.[2] He then sent money to Charles II in exile—by a messenger who embezzled it. In 1662 he was rewarded with the post of Commissioner for Crown Lands in Dorset, and in 1665 he entertained the King at More Crichel. Napier's son and grandson represented Corfe Castle, Poole, and Dorchester under Charles, James, and William. His brother Robert, who had been Master of the Hanaper to Charles I and Charles II, handed on the office to his son, M.P. for Weymouth and Dorchester, for whom the third baronetcy in the family was created. The last of Sir Gerard's line sat for Bridport in the first Parliament of George III: in 1765 his baronetcy was extinct.

The lines of Windebank and Burlace ended with the grandson and son respectively; Samuel Turner had no legitimate heir; nothing is known of the successors of Richard King. The remaining Royalist, William Constantine, was restored to his place as Recorder, and was returned as member for Poole in the Cavalier Parliament. But his election was declared void after a dispute, and he was removed from the Recordership when he refused the oath. The estate at Merley remained in the family only until 1712, when it was sold to the Ashes.

Only one of the greater landed families, the Erles, identified themselves clearly with the Presbyterian side. Sir Walter, after a most active wartime career in both Army and Parliament, was

---

[1] *Calendar of the Committee for Compounding*, pp. 546, 588, 1308. *Economic History Review*, Second Series, Vol. V. p. 194.

[2] *Calendar of the Committee for Compounding*, p. 1061.

one of the commissioners for the peace negotiations in 1646, and a member of the Convention Parliament in 1660. But he was elected for both Oliver's Parliaments, and was not excluded in 1656. His son Thomas, also secluded at the Purge, died in 1650, and the estates went at Walter's death to his grandson Thomas, Marlborough's general, with whom the line ended. Among the lesser men who did not sit in the Rump only the Roses of Wootton Fitzpaine had won their way safely into the ranks of the gentry. Thomas Rose of Wootton and Frome St. Quintin, who died in 1747, had been Sheriff of Dorset. His daughter and heir married Francis Drew, and a hyphenated family of Rose-Drews continued to hold the estate until 1815. William Whitaker's son Henry succeeded him as Recorder of Shaftesbury and represented the borough in 1659 and in the Cavalier Parliament. William's grandson became Sheriff. The other non-Rumpers did not maintain their position. The Chettel estate was sold for debt in 1689 and the house demolished. Giles Green's son became Clerk of the New River Company and little more is heard of his family in Dorset. Later Skutts were Mayors of Poole; but the Starres and the Allens disappear.

For those who were ready to make the most of their opportunities the war and the Commonwealth offered the best chance of quick enrichment in land since the dissolution. There are some striking instances in Dorset of the descendants of men whose zealous hatred of monasticism had founded their estates augmenting them through their devotion to constitutional liberties. John Browne, Thomas Trenchard, Roger Hill, and others subscribed at the outbreak of war to a loan for the forces in Dorset—at eight per cent. They lent more money for provisions for Poole in 1643. Most of them lost their Dorset estates in the Royalist occupation, but they received the regular allowance of £4 weekly in compensation. They were not slow to recover their losses more adequately at the expense of malignants and delinquents. Browne and Trenchard acted together in the acquisition of many such properties, and if the *Mystery of the Good Old Cause* can be believed they did not always stop to make sure their victims were really on the wrong side.

Browne obtained (by a narrow majority) an Act of Parliament granting him £3,000 out of Sequestrations.[1] Trenchard was alleged to have got his son-in-law's estate sequestered for his own benefit, and to have denounced to the Sequestrators as a concealed debt the dowry he had promised. Another story of a pettier form of robbery is that John Trenchard and Richard Rose let lodgings to Royalists, seized their furniture, and 'secured it for themselves as belonging to such obnoxious prescribed characters'.[2] John Bingham and William Sydenham were partners in the lucrative game of discovering concealed or undervalued estates for the Committee for Compounding. On one occasion their reward was £1,000 each.[3] Walter Erle had £1,500 from delinquents' estates; Thomas Ceeley (who according to Walker had been a prisoner for debt) had £2,000— on account—from the fines of the Edgecumbes and others. A story of Ceeley's dealings revealed in Goldsmiths' Hall[4] shows something of the complex transactions that were possible between victors and vanquished. John Jeffrey of Maypowder complained that in 1644 he had sold an estate to Ceeley, and re-entered upon it when the greater part of the price was not paid, but that Ceeley 'having friends in Parliament' (he was not yet a member himself), got an order for its restitution and kept both the land and the money. Ceeley's story was that Jeffrey had concealed the debt from the Committee and tried to compound for lands which were mortgaged to Ceeley. In 1652 he paid the balance of the purchase money, though he had to sell the lands again to do it. Jeffrey, he alleged, then demanded rent and interest before he would hand over the estate.

At the sales of land after 1649 still greater opportunities arose. It was then that Roger Hill acquired the title to the Bishop of Winchester's fabulously rich manor of Taunton Deane; John Trenchard bought Wytham from Hopton's estate; and Richard Rose got his manor of Wootton Fitzpaine. Some of the acquisitions were of course forfeited at the Restoration; others, chiefly

[1] *C.J.* 12 Sept. 1649.   [2] Noble, *Lives of the Regicides*, Vol. II. p. 381.
[3] *Calendar of the Committee for Compounding*, pp. 1167, 1135.
[4] *Calendar of the Committee for Compounding*, p. 1066.

7

those from private persons, were not. But it is as dangerous with the Independents as with the Royalists to generalise about changes in family fortunes. The available information does not suggest that politics, and enterprise in exploiting the political situation, were nearly as important in determining the station in life of the successors of our M.P.s as the usual accidents of family history. A continuation of even these sketchy outlines of political and economic biography will make the point clear.

Sir Thomas Trenchard, though he is not on any of the lists of Secluded Members, did not sit after the Purge. His son Thomas represented Poole in the Cavalier Parliament. Two of his grandsons were also Dorset members, and one of them, Sir John, had a colourful career as an opponent of Catholicism and James II, which brought him into the disreputable circle of Oates and the Popish Plotters. He was rewarded under William and Mary with the office of Secretary of State for the Northern Department. Sir Thomas's great-grandson (M.P. for Wareham) left only a daughter; but she married her cousin and enabled Wolfeton to continue in the family until the beginning of the nineteenth century. The younger of the Trenchard brothers in the Long Parliament, John, became a fairly active Rumper, though he refused to act as one of the King's judges. His activities in the land market do not seem to have brought him much lasting benefit, and we last hear of him when his evasion of his debts was the subject of a protest in Chancery after the Restoration. Warmwell went at his death in 1662 to his son-in-law John Sadler, and was eventually sold to a London merchant.

John Browne's eldest son was Sheriff in 1667. Three of his younger sons became merchants, and one of them sat for Weymouth. The lands continued in the family until the end of the eighteenth century. The estate which John Bingham had built up during the war was divided at his death between his daughters and his brother; but the family remained at Bingham's Melcombe until the beginning of this century. Bingham's brother-in-law and close associate William Sydenham was less careful about his politics than most of the Dorset Independents.

He served on many Rump Committees, became Commander-in-Chief of the forces in Dorset, and a Commissioner of the Treasury. In 1653 he was one of the Council of Thirteen set up by the Army leaders, and was prominent in Barebones' Parliament and its Council of State. But he often opposed the government: he was against the abolition of the Lords, and against intolerance towards Quakers. In the last year of the Protectorate he joined the 'Wallingford House' group of officers in opposition first to Richard Cromwell and then to the restoration of the Rump. For his consistent and indiscreet support of the Army against the Parliament he was expelled from the House in January 1660.[1] The Act of Indemnity incapacitated him for life from holding any office. He died in 1661, leaving a son William who completed the ruin of his branch of the family when he was alleged to have put up Wynford Eagle for sale in a lottery and then refused to hand it over.

Denis Bond was early in the war an associate of the Republicans; but he became a friend of the Protector, presided over the Council of State in 1652, sat in the Parliaments of 1654 and 1656, and died four days before Cromwell (when 'the Devil took Bond for his soul'). His service on a total of 263 parliamentary committees may well be a record. It got him inevitably on to the list for the Trial, but he had the good sense not to act. Accordingly his son Nathaniel was able to retain the estates, and in 1686 he bought the adjoining manor of Creech Grange, where his descendants remained. Nathaniel and two of his sons sat for Dorchester, Poole, and Corfe Castle in several parliaments. Edmund Prideaux was also a good Cromwellian, and had a Protectorate baronetcy just before his death in 1659. Immediately before the Trial he gave up his post as Solicitor-General. Immediately after it he became Attorney-General. Since he was no regicide his only son was able to inherit his fortune. Some of the estates were sold; but the family—and its baronetcy—continued until 1875. Prideaux appointed as his assistant in the office of Attorney-General another lawyer who had guessed right about the wisdom of declining the invitation

[1] C.J. 17 Jan. 1659-60.

to try the King—Roger Hill. Under the Protector he became a Serjeant-at-Law and a Baron of the Exchequer. Hill seems to have been active in improving his new estates: we find him applying for permission to enclose lands at Taunton Deane, and complaining of the negligence of his predecessor the Bishop. At the Restoration he lost many of his acquisitions, and his office of Serjeant-at-Law; but a marriage five years before his death to the coheiress of Thomas Barnes of Essex did something to retrieve his fortunes. His son Sir Roger was able in 1670 to buy the manor of Denham, Buckinghamshire, which was handed on through Sir Roger's daughter Abigail to the Way family.

John Pyne, though excepted from the Act of Oblivion, eventually got his pardon. Despite financial difficulties after the Restoration he was able to keep Curry Malet, which remained in the family until the nineteenth century. But the outstanding example in Dorset of a man who suffered for his beliefs is John Fry. He told his friend Robert Frampton, later Bishop of Gloucester, that he had meant to serve the King but changed his mind when Prince Maurice came into the west and 'harshly stripped him of all he possessed'. He became a prominent Committee-man in the Rump, and sat in the first sessions of the regicide court. But he had also developed religious, or anti-religious, opinions as shocking to his own side as they would have been to the other. During the Trial, after John Downes (Arundel) had complained to the Speaker of Fry's 'blasphemies', he was suspended from sitting.[1] Eventually he satisfied the House that he did not deny the divinity of Christ or the existence of the Trinity; but he seems to have been moving like Winstanley towards faith in human reason rather than in a personal God. His offences were great enough to have him excepted after his death from the Act of Oblivion. The estates were confiscated, though some at least seem to have been bought back by the family. One of his sons became a doctor and a Quaker, another was said to be a 'grocer' in Bristol.

The limitations of this impression of 28 families whose members happened to sit for one county in one Parliament are

[1] *C.J.* 26 Jan. and 3 Feb. 1648–9, 31 Jan., 20 Feb., and 22 Feb. 1650–1.

obvious enough. Dorset has no more claim to be a normal or an abnormal county than any of the others we have dealt with; and it is not yet particularly well provided with sources of the kind of information we need. Indeed, nothing we have written about particular counties and regions can pretend to be more than a rough sketch of studies that could only be completed by working intensively on local manuscript material. If the facts about local interests and connections could in that way be made available for the whole country, it might with their help be possible to study in detail the history of the Parliament itself and to disentangle in the day-to-day work of the House and its Committees the little pushings and pullings from which the forces of the great conflict were made.

CONCLUSION

WE have tried in these pages to give, partly by figures and statements concerning all the members and partly by studies of particular areas, a factual account of the membership of the Long Parliament. We have referred only in passing to the larger questions of interpretation. But the study of the conflict in which the Long Parliament played a central part raises many problems fundamental to the understanding of English history. In the years between the first elections in 1640 and the last brief reunion of the survivors in 1660 to clear the way for the Restoration, there came into the open questions which normally go unasked, or are answered only in conventional platitudes. These are the questions about power in the organised community—who holds it, how it is shared, and how it is maintained in face of divisions and challenges. Answers to such questions can be given—and have been given both by contemporaries and by historians—in terms of the institutions through which power is exercised, and of the emotional loyalties such institutions command. Devotion to the Monarchy, to Parliament, to the Church, and to the Law were all involved in the struggle; so were the suspicions and hostilities which each of these in its different ways aroused. But explanations in such terms are not enough. Behind the institutions and the symbols are the interests and needs from which they sprang.

No one in our generation can write history uninfluenced by the work of those who have concentrated on the study of the economic forces underlying political development. We have tended here to put the emphasis on local and family connections rather than on economic groupings because the particular kind of evidence we have used convinces us of their importance. That evidence does not go far enough to enable us to make any confident generalisations on the relation of the Civil War to the great economic changes of the age. In particular, arguments for and against the Marxist view—that the war was the crisis of a class struggle from which bourgeois England emerged triumphant over feudal England—involve much wider considerations than we have raised. We can, however, indicate tentatively some of the dangers in the general assertions which both Marxists and their opponents are apt to make. The absence of any marked difference between Royalists and Parliamentarians in the numerical tests we have applied is in itself of very limited importance. It shows that of the men who went into Parliament —and we have insisted that these are not to be taken as a sample or cross-section of any larger group—those who supported the King were not superficially different in their way of life, their status, and their family histories from those who opposed him. On both sides there were merchants and lawyers; on both there were old landed families and new ones, families that prospered and families that failed. No reasonable Marxist denies this, and no reasonable anti-Marxist will regard it as proving his case. Nevertheless, if a class distinction in the accepted sense did exist between the two sides, one would expect it to have been reflected more strongly in at least some of the facts we have collected.

The question which this limited evidence leads us to ask is not so much why the M.P.s fail to fit neatly into social categories appropriate to their choice of sides as whether the accepted categories are real ones, or at least whether they are helpful to a study of the basic causes of the conflict. It is possible that there existed under Charles I 'parasitic feudal landowners', 'still keeping up lordly courts of relatives and retainers, still running their estates in the traditional way with little reference to the demands of the national market'.[1] But it is very difficult to identify them among the 200 Royalist M.P.s. The Royalists in the House, most of whom it is true were in 1640 associated with the other members in opposing Strafford and Laud, are generally, on this view, written off as 'unprogressive gentry'. Such

---

[1] Christopher Hill, *The English Revolution 1640*, p. 26. This essay is the best statement of the current Marxist interpretation of the Civil War.

a term of abuse is not without meaning; but it hardly defines them as a class in Marx's sense different from that to which the other members belonged. To show the Civil War as a struggle between the 'feudal aristocracy' and the 'bourgeoisie' it is necessary to prove a continuity if not of ancestry at least of tradition and style of life between the Royalists of 1642 and the men who formed the dominant class in the Middle Ages. Our investigation of family origins, so far as it goes, suggests that the survival of a medieval landed family was less common than is often assumed. Most Royalists and most Parliamentarians could not produce a plausible pedigree, still less an estate, dating back further than the Wars of the Roses. What is it that makes one great-grandson of a Tudor copyholder or a Tudor judge a progressive bourgeois, and another a feudal aristocrat?

For one region, the south-west, we have given tentative figures which show that there was a considerable proportion of families with a medieval record, and that a majority of their descendants became Royalists; but even if it could be shown that these descendants adhered to a feudal economy or outlook, neither the proportion of 'medieval' families among the Royalists nor the proportion of Royalists among the medieval families is high enough to carry great weight. In the rest of the country the familiar geographical boundary between the predominantly Royalist north and west and the predominantly Parliamentarian south and east has some economic significance, though it was certainly not a rigid line between two coherent and fundamentally different systems, with opposing political demands. If we had attempted a detailed examination of Cumberland and Westmorland we could have produced some specimens of medieval families who retained great local power. The Bellinghams, the Musgraves, the Dalstons, and the Curwens, who occupied the county seats in 1640, all had parliamentary records going back to the fourteenth or early fifteenth centuries. Wales too could give us several families of the same kind. But so far as there were in these regions men who still behaved like medieval barons, their tendency was to make the Civil War an opportunity for fighting out their local quarrels. The last thing they wanted was to be involved in a united war against the rising bourgeoisie. Nor did these areas produce a majority of the Royalist M.P.s. Though the Parliamentarian members came in much greater numbers from the London side of the Severn to Humber line than from the other, the Royalists were more evenly distributed. Roughly a third of them came from the north and west, another third from the south-west, and the remainder from the midlands, the east, and the south-east. Most of the leaders on the Royalist as on the Parliamentary side were southerners. The south and east were, as their greater parliamentary representation suggests, more active in national politics than the north and west. It was here that the tightly-bound nuclei of the Parliamentarian cause—the family groups round the Fienneses, the Hampdens and others, the colonising ventures, and the Puritan congregations—mainly developed. The less politically alive among the south-eastern gentry could be influenced by the leaders of such groups, through relationship or mere geographical proximity, more easily than could men of their kind in the north and west. The latter, especially during the long period without a Parliament, had less chance to become part of a national movement of resistance. But the driving force of Royalism in Parliament came from men who had such a chance and, usually at the last minute, rejected it.

The mass of Royalist M.P.s was blended from the same ingredients as the rest of the 'political nation'. There were a few large and a few smaller estates that had survived in a family from the fifteenth century or earlier with only minor gains and losses. There were many descendants of elder or younger branches of ancient families whose situation had been radically changed in the last few generations. There were many whose recorded ancestry began with one of the familiar chances of prosperity in Tudor or Stuart times. With estates went political experience appropriate to their size, in the government of the village, the county, or the nation.

Commerce contributed heavily to the mixture. There were the monopolists for whom Royalism had a special attraction;

there were the Aldermen, descendants of perhaps two or three
generations of local merchants; but there were also the numerous
landed and titled families whose mothers and grandmothers
brought in their share of City fortunes. The law contributed
heavily too: besides the Recorders and the other barristers there
were the many whose estates had been founded or preserved by
the profits of high legal office a generation or two earlier.
Among all these we can detect the things that by their proportion gave to Royalism some faint distinguishing flavour. The
Court had naturally a rather larger share of the Royalist than of
the Parliamentary mixture. Besides the few members who were
in one way or another the King's direct dependants, the sons
and grandsons of Grooms of the Bedchamber, of crown-
appointed officials in courts and councils, of Treasurers, Chan-
cellors, and even Archbishops, sometimes showed their gratitude.
The stewards, secretaries, and lawyers employed by aristocratic
patrons also account for a sprinkling of names in Royalist
pedigrees.

The impression derived from these family histories is that in
the form it usually takes the concept of a surviving 'feudal'
class is misleading. The unit formed by the main line of a family
and the estates it lived on could not in the seventeenth century
expect to survive unaided for long. It was exposed to constant
dangers. Failure of male heirs was, we have suggested, the
greatest; and perhaps the frequency of second and third
marriages is an indication of zeal in avoiding it. But there were
many others—a minority and wardship, a spendthrift heir, a
ruinous lawsuit—and if the estate escaped these it could still
perish through slow accumulation of debt. Obviously the
dangers were diminished by exploiting the estate as profitably
as possible, and increased if lands were badly cultivated and
tenants paid less than an economic rent; but the chief solution
to the problem was repeatedly to infuse new wealth into the
estate from an independent source.

' " It is impossible for a mere country gentleman ever to grow
rich or to raise his house. He must have some other vocation
with his own inheritance, as to be a courtier, lawyer, merchant,

or some other vocation. If he hath no other vocation, let him get a ship and judiciously manage her, or buy some auditors place, or be vice-admiral in his country. By only following the plough he may keep his word and be upright, but will never increase his fortune." Sir John Oglander wrote this with his own blood June the 25th 1632 then aged 48 years.'[1] Oglander became of course a prominent Royalist. Instances of such 'vocations' can be found among the members on both sides and among their near ancestors; but he might have added that a more effective method than any was to take advantage of the misfortune of others by marriage to an heiress. If by such means an estate had in 1640 preserved its identity for two or three centuries, it may well be evidence not so much of unprogressive habits as of rare good luck and good management. After a century of unprecedented opportunities for material success and failure, men of property cannot be simply divided into a 'progressive' and an 'unprogressive' class. The vast majority of families in the 'political nation' were, or had been within the memory of their older members, rising families, with cause to oppose such obsolete laws and customs as hampered their rise, and to dislike the wealth and the ways of their betters. All of them now had in some degree an interest in stability and a fear of the ambitions of their inferiors. Whether in the eventual conflict between the political forces of stability and those of change they took one side or the other could not be determined by any crude classification. Many of the factors on which it depended are matters of personal habit and outlook quite beyond the scope of a collective study. Others, as we have tried to show, can be explored by examining counties rather than classes, and alliances and hostilities on a local rather than a national scale. Looked at in this way the groups that collected round an old-established landed family are comparable, as a factor in the formation of political allegiances, with the groups that collected round a trading venture or round a religious sect. The Royal Court was the centre of one network of interests and intrigues; so was the great political connection of the

---

[1] *A Royalist's Notebook* (ed. Bamford), p. 75.

Herbert family; so too were the friendships and relationships of the Puritan colonisers; and all merged, in every county on which they impinged, into the local connections. To these personal and local factors every line of investigation eventually leads, and from these must come such answers as can be given to the big questions about the nature of the war and the society that fought it.

In 1640 nine-tenths of the Commons seemed united in opposition to the old regime of the 'evil counsellors'. In 1642 a small majority seemed united in the war against the minority who decided that opposition had now gone too far. In 1648 another small majority, of a Parliament purged of the old supporters of compromise, showed that now they themselves wanted compromise, and stability, and the King. They too were expelled. This again is often described as a 'class split'; and in the country generally there were undoubtedly the beginnings of a resistance by the small men, the propertyless, and the oppressed. But in Parliament, to which such men had not been elected, there was as little sign of a class division at Pride's Purge as at the outbreak of war. The main characteristic of the Rump was its lack of characteristics. The election of the Recruiters and the purge of the 'Presbyterians' had each increased the proportion of men outside or on the fringe of the close-knit community from which M.P.s were normally drawn; but that small community had not been greatly or permanently enlarged. Sons of ancient aristocratic families sat and worked with the notorious land-grabbers and upstart colonels. The unscrupulously ambitious and the apathetic might both prefer to go on sitting. In any case the decision to attend or stay away from a Parliament whose power and prospects of survival were so uncertain was very different from the decision that had to be taken in 1642. It might be more casual; or it might be more rational. The old influences and alignments, though not destroyed by the war, had been changed; and to them had been added new ones produced by years of service in Parliament, on national and local committees, and in the Army. But the men who abolished the monarchy and the House of Lords and passed the Navigation

Act did not find themselves doing these things because they were as a whole different in origins and interests from those who had left Westminster in 1642 or 1648.

We could perhaps have taken the process of sub-division a stage further and have attempted, from what can be ascertained of the debates and divisions in the Rump and the Council of State, to see by whom the most extreme measures were supported and opposed. But neither body devoted itself principally to carrying out a revolution. A large part of their work was more administrative than legislative. The continuity of central government, which the victorious side had symbolised in its claim to represent 'the King and Parliament' had now been decisively broken. A new and a busier administration was needed; and it was supplied to a great extent by the Rump and its committees. The whole question of the work of Parliament from 1649 to 1653, and of the groupings and rivalries within it, is one of the big neglected topics of the period.

In 1660 the compromisers who had been defeated in 1648 had their way, and the twenty-year upheaval ended more suddenly than it had begun. To discuss the general character of the Restoration settlement is again outside our range. Quite clearly immense changes had taken place in central government and in the social structure of the nation which could not be undone. But to our doubts about the difference between Royalist and Parliamentarian M.P.s at the beginning of the war we have to add doubts about its effects on them and their families. It is remarkable how few of the Royalist members, who had by their own account suffered such ruin and spoliation in the cause, failed to preserve their political influence and at least their chief estates. Some, it is true, may have prospered by learning new tricks from the temporary expropriators of their lands; others were dispossessed under the later Stuarts as their debts and mortgages grew too heavy—a process that was always going on, war or no war. Again it has to be emphasised that Royalist M.P.s were not typical of Royalists in general, and that in every region the impact of the great political events was different. In Wales and the border counties the fortunes of many Royalist members had been permanently impaired, to the benefit of a few great Presbyterian families like the Middletons and the Harleys, who found themselves on the right side at the Restoration without having been on the wrong one when some estates were being sequestered and others offered for sale. In the more prosperous eastern counties every one of the few Royalist members had a successor in the Parliaments of Charles II. In Cumberland and Westmorland the names of Bellingham, Musgrave, Dalston, and Curwen appear as usual in the Cavalier Parliament. It did not entirely belie its name, though it was, especially in its later years, an ex-Presbyterian Parliament too.

More striking than the continuance of Royalist families is the almost complete failure of the upstarts to establish political dynasties. The regicides, and the few others who fled from the expected retribution, could not hope to save much more than their lives; but with few exceptions the successors of the parvenu Recruiters, and of the few original members of lowly origin, returned to obscurity. Perhaps there is some truth in the suggestion that the period was one in which new landed families could not easily become established. Certainly it was not one in which names that had been conspicuous on the wrong side would be received into the political circle of their counties, though to those who had been in it already much was forgiven. Within that circle the new groupings and new hostilities of Restoration England and of the 'Glorious Revolution' began to work themselves out. What relation they bore to the old ones we have not attempted to discover.

We said at the beginning that we claimed for this study only a limited and largely negative value; and we are well aware that we are leaving it with only the surface of the relevant evidence touched. To say of an M.P. that he was a Royalist or an Independent shows hardly anything of his outlook or activity. Private correspondence, records of debates and divisions, minutes of committees, and notes of unofficial meetings undoubtedly survive in sufficient quantity to give at least glimpses of the complex inner tensions and forces of the Long Parliament, from a knowledge of which new interpretations of the conflict might be constructed. Similarly to say of an estate that it was lost or retained is only the beginning of its story. The answers to the important questions about the land and its owners are to be found in rentals, account-books, and surveys; in leases, mortgages, and fines; and in all the other documentary debris that the acquisition and maintenance of wealth leave behind. Such a study, extending widely and deeply enough, might perhaps reveal a pattern of social and economic development in which the Civil War would have a clear and essential place. Until we know more of these things it is well to be very guarded in explanations of the causes and consequences of the Revolution.

STATISTICAL TABLES

(For the definition of the 'regions' used in Tables 1 and 2, see Appendix V)

TABLE I

MEMBERS OF THE LONG PARLIAMENT

A. *Numbers*

	North	East	Midland	West	S.E.	S.W.	Total
Seats . .	62	64	77	60	94	150	507
Royalists . .	37	14	32	43	28	82	236
Parliamentarians	28	55	51	20	70	78	302
Unclassified .	2	0	3	1	5	3	14
'Original' members .	67	69	86	64	103	163	552
Recruiters .	40	23	39	46	38	89	275
All members .	107	92	125	110	141	252	827
Rumpers . .	36	24	35	20	38	56	209

B. *Percentages (of the total number of members in each region)*

The figures in col. 1 mean that fifty-five per cent. of the 'original' Northern members were Royalists and forty-two per cent. Parliamentarians, and that sixty per cent. of the Northern members sitting in 1648 sat in the Rump.

	North	East	Midland	West	S.E.	S.W.	Total
Royalists . .	55	20	37	67	27	50	43
Parliamentarians .	42	80	59	31	68	48	55
Rumpers . .	60	37	45	33	42	38	42

TABLE 2

AGE GROUPS

Region		Number of members born :						
		Before 1580	1580–9	1590–9	1600–9	1610–19	1620–9	Not known
North	Royalist	4	4	6	15	7	1	0
	Parliamentary	2	5	10	9	2	0	0
	Recruiter	0	3	6	8	16	5	2
	Total	6	12	22	32	25	6	2
East	Royalist	2	2	3	3	4	0	0
	Parliamentary	6	12	18	10	5	1	3
	Recruiter	0	1	8	5	4	3	2
	Total	8	15	29	18	13	4	5
Midland	Royalist	0	3	10	6	10	3	0
	Parliamentary	2	9	18	18	3	1	0
	Recruiter	0	2	5	15	11	5	1
	Total	2	14	33	39	24	9	1
West	Royalist	1	5	9	14	8	6	0
	Parliamentary	5	4	3	5	1	1	1
	Recruiter	0	0	6	6	17	10	7
	Total	6	9	18	25	26	17	8
South-east	Royalist	1	2	9	7	7	1	1
	Parliamentary	6	12	14	18	9	1	10
	Recruiter	0	1	5	9	15	3	5
	Total	7	15	28	34	31	5	16
South-west	Royalist	1	10	20	20	24	1	6
	Parliamentary	7	13	26	12	7	6	7
	Recruiter	0	9	14	21	21	14	10
	Total	8	32	60	53	52	21	23
Whole Parlia-ment	Royalist	9	26	57	65	60	12	7
	Parliamentary	28	55	89	72	27	10	21
	Recruiter	0	16	44	64	84	40	27
	Total	37	97	190	201	171	62	55

(For age-groups of the Rumpers see p. 45)

TABLE 3

PARLIAMENTARY RECORD OF THE MEMBERS OF THE LONG
PARLIAMENT

	Sitting in or before 1628		Maximum number of age in 1628		Sitting in or after 1661		Alive and not in Lords in 1661	
		%		%		%		%
Royalist	75	32	164	70	48	20	95	40
Parliamentary	128	42	265	88	25	8	139	46
Recruiter	17	6	151	55	32	12	181	66
Rumpers who were original members	31	34	78	86	4		51	56
Rumpers who were Recruiters	6		69	58	5		79	67
Total of Rumpers	37	18	147	70	9		130	62

TABLE 4

PARLIAMENTARY RECORD OF THE FAMILIES OF
MEMBERS OF THE LONG PARLIAMENT

(In this table 'relations' means fathers, sons, brothers, and *on the male side
only* grandfathers, grandsons, uncles, and nephews. 'Earlier' means in the
1628 or earlier Parliaments; 'later' means in the Cavalier or later Parliaments.)

Number of members with relations sitting	Royalists		Parliamentarians		Recruiters		Rumpers	
		%		%		%		%
Earlier . .	153	65	152	50	109	40	88	42
Later . .	125	53	138	45	82	30	73	35
Earlier and later . .	91	38	92	30	46	17	38	18
Earlier but not later . .	62	26	60	20	63	23	50	24
Later but not earlier .	34	14	46	15	36	13	35	17
Neither .	49	21	104	34	130	47	86	41
Total . .	236	100	302	100	275	100	209	100

A NOTE ON
GOODWIN v. *FORTESCUE*

THE contest between Sir Francis Goodwin, father of our member for Bucking-hamshire, and Sir John Fortescue, which arose out of the Buckinghamshire election of 1604, has received much attention from constitutional historians. But in considering the legal intricacies of the affair they have told us little about either Goodwin or Fortescue, and have thereby missed much that is significant in the dispute. It is in fact·an illustration of the dangers of separating constitutional from political history, and of failing to explore the local roots of national politics. In it we can see an ominous struggle between ministerial influence backed by local standing, and a purely local primacy.

Sir John and Sir Francis were both men of considerable importance.[1] Fortescue had in 1604 more parliamentary experience than any other councillor of James I: he had sat in the Commons since 1572, and had been Knight of the Shire for both Buckinghamshire and Middlesex. He had become a very considerable landowner in each of these counties as the result of purchases. only possible to a man of great wealth. This wealth was the natural reward of the holder under Elizabeth of three great offices—Chancellor of the Exchequer, Master of the Great Wardrobe, and Chancellor of the Duchy of Lancaster. James gave the Exchequer to a Scotsman, but left Fortescue in possession of his other offices, even giving him a patent for life of the Chancellorship of the Duchy as some consolation for the loss of the Exchequer. Mr. D. H. Willson has pointed out the importance of Fortescue to Salisbury at a time when all but two of the councillors of the old reign with parliamentary experience had been removed from the Commons by death, disgrace, or James's promotions to the Lords.[2] It is hardly surprising therefore that Salisbury called on the judges to assist him in reversing the Buckinghamshire election and securing Sir John Fortescue's presence in the House. Whether the grounds for Goodwin's exclusion were good at law is uncertain

---

[1] Both Sir John Fortescue and Sir Francis Goodwin appear in the *D.N.B.*—though Sir Francis only gains incidental mention through his son. The *V.C.H.* adds much useful information about the history of the Goodwins.

[2] *American Historical Review*, Vol. 36.

on the available evidence, but we know from evidence adduced by Mr. Willson that Salisbury told Winwood of his intention to get the election upset by the lawyers, so that the decision about Goodwin's outlawry seems at least suspicious. James may have been telling the truth when he expressed indifference about Fortescue's services in the Commons, but Salisbury was clearly not disinterested.

Whether Goodwin was an outlaw or not, there can be no doubt about his standing in the county. The Goodwins had been tenants of Upper Winchendon in 1518, and by 1546 they owned the manor. Though the family was thus a fairly new one in 1604, it held a leading—if not indeed the leading —position in the political life of Buckinghamshire. Sir Francis's father and elder brother had both been Sheriff, and Sir Francis himself had been elected Knight of the Shire before he was twenty-one, a most unusual distinction for a commoner. His position in the county was not at all damaged by the dispute, for in 1606 he was back in the House through a by-election at Buckingham, and he represented the county in four of the next six Parliaments. He died in 1634. With the death in 1643 of his son Arthur, a close friend of Hampden, the male line of the Goodwins ended—hence perhaps the failure of historians to realise their local importance.

THE STAFFORD ELECTION, 1645

THE story of the election of the two Recruiters for the Borough of Stafford,[1] though it contains many features common in any period before the secret ballot, illustrates also some of the complications introduced into local politics by the presence of military power. The background to it is a series of quarrels, which we cannot attempt to disentangle here, within the Parliamentary County Committee, between the Committee and a group of gentry who had a petition against it presented at the Assizes, and between the town and the county about their respective contributions to the war. Sir William Brereton, who, though an outsider, was now the commander chiefly concerned with the defence of Staffordshire, had in December 1644 taken possession of the town, removed some officers and soldiers whose loyalty was in doubt, and arrested the Governor, Colonel Lewis Chadwick. Charges were also brought against Colonel Simon Rugeley, Sheriff of Staffordshire and Committee member. Brereton insisted that neither Chadwick nor Rugeley was guilty of anything worse than indiscretion; but at the time of the election he was alarmed to find 'the old plots and designs still prosecuted for the strengthening and upholding of a faction against the Committee of Stafford and the honest party'.

In October 1645, when it was known that the writs for the election had been issued, the Mayor and a large number of burgesses were invited to the house of the new Governor, Captain Henry Stone, 'to drink a cup of wine with Sir William Brereton'. At this gathering Brereton expressed himself cautiously in favour of Sir Richard Skeffington—his brother-in-law—and Mr. John Swinfen who came of an old-established county family. Stone and another prominent Committee member, Captain Foxall, were strongly in their favour, and it was arranged that the 'conductors' of two of the three wards in the borough should mention their names when they announced

[1] This account is derived chiefly from the rough minutes of the Committee of Privileges (Brit. Mus. Add. MSS. 28716) and from the letter-book of Sir William Brereton (Brit. Mus. Add. MSS. 11332). The information about the County Committee comes from its minute-book in the William Salt Library, Stafford, an edition of which is shortly to be published by the Staffordshire Record Society.

the election. The third conductor was apparently less reliable, and an un-official canvasser was selected instead. Three more prospective candidates were put forward by other burgesses present, but only one of these, Edward Leigh—a Committee member, a colonel, and a puritan writer—was even-tually nominated. The fourth candidate at the election was Sir Charles Shirley. He was the choice of the Earl of Essex, Lord Lieutenant of the County, who according to Brereton usually had the nomination of one of the Stafford members.

When the election was held Brereton was absent, and he complained that he had not had notice of it. But the army was not short of representatives. Colonel Rugeley was there; so was Captain Stone, though he was not a bur-gess and the election was no concern of the Governor. Captain Foxall sat at the table beside the Mayor, and his company of soldiers, unarmed, were in the hall. (Some of them were burgesses, but many were not.) Two main parties had emerged: the supporters of Swinfen and Skeffington, with Foxall as their leader and the Mayor apparently working with them as far as he could, and the supporters of Shirley and Leigh, who included Rugeley and the Town Clerk. The voters were first asked to cry their choice, and there is naturally a conflict of evidence about the result. The Mayor then directed the supporters of Leigh and Shirley to go to one side of the hall, and those of Swinfen and Skeffington to the other. The Shirley and Leigh party de-manded that their candidates should be declared elected, but Foxall insisted on a poll. When this was conceded a dispute arose about procedure. The Mayor and Foxall wanted to put all four names to the electors together; but Rugeley declared that there ought to be two polls, with two names in each; otherwise, he said, he would complain to the Parliament. Foxall had to give way on this point, and on another argument about which candidates should be polled first. The first poll was accordingly held between Swinfen and Shirley, the town clerk calling each elector by name and recording his vote. Foxall and Stone demanded that the result should be announced forthwith, in order they said, that the unsuccessful candidate might have another chance at the second poll. Leigh's supporters again objected. Their witnesses explained afterwards that if it had become known that Shirley was beaten, his friends would have been discouraged from voting for Leigh. They may also have feared that Shirley would insist on standing at the second poll and would split the vote. Colonel Rugeley again threatened to complain to the Parliament; and as before he had his way. When the results were announced it appeared that there had been some cross-voting and abstentions: at the first poll Swinfen had been elected by 73 votes to 68, and at the second Leigh had defeated Skeffington by one vote.

Brereton was uneasy about the consequences of Leigh's success: he had been 'all along mispossessed by a rotten faction . . . and may possibly be engaged in opposition to Mr. Swinfen by those who may conceive displeasure at his carrying it against Sir Charles Shirley'. But Sir William hoped that

Leigh might be 'gained to a right understanding' and decided that despite the irregularities he would not challenge the election. Shirley's supporters, however, petitioned against it. Their main charge was that Swinfen's party 'by the influence of many gentlemen and the soldiery', and 'by threats menaces and rewards' had made many of the burgesses pledge their votes before the election. In support of the petition they produced witnesses who had heard other voters say they changed from Shirley's side to Swinfen's because they were afraid of Captain Foxall. There was a story of a little room called the Jury Chamber opening off the polling hall, where Swinfen's supporters were 'kept with beer and tobacco' and where none of the other party were admitted. Some twenty burgesses, it was alleged, went away after the voters had been divided, thinking Shirley and Leigh were elected without a poll, and when Mr. Thomas Winkle tried to fetch them back he found the great door closed against him. (A witness for Swinfen denied this, and said Winkle had started a brawl and threatened to kick him downstairs.) There were also the usual complaints about unqualified voters. Much was made of the meeting at Stone's house, the presence of the officers and soldiers, and the polling procedure. But the Committee were not impressed. After hearing counsel for each side they resolved, on 26 April 1646, that Swinfen was duly elected. It was not until July 1647 that this decision was reported to the House. Skeffington had in the meantime been elected as Knight of the Shire.

APPENDIX IV

BIBLIOGRAPHY

THE sources used in a study of this-kind are necessarily different from those on which more intensive work in a narrower field is based. Two people dealing with the lives and family histories of over eight hundred M.P.s cannot hope to see much of the manuscript material which is available to the writers of individual biographies and of big collective works like the projected Official History of Parliament. We have had to limit ourselves largely to printed information; and to some extent we have depended on the help of two groups of workers at whom historians are apt to look askance—the local antiquarians and the genealogists.

Both parish histories and pedigrees may, it is true, contain a formidable amount of fiction. The clergymen and elderly gentlefolk who used to write the history of their village were not often well-equipped for the task. But some of these works, repulsive perhaps in style and appearance, prove to have been compiled with an accuracy and an understanding of sources at which few professional historians are in a position to scoff. Occasionally a good modern municipal history exists, but even these rarely say much about the less prominent M.P.s. The best work of local historians is usually to be found in the publications of the county archaeological societies. *Archaeologia Cantiana*, the *Transactions of the Bristol and Gloucestershire Archaeological Society*, the *Wiltshire Archaeological and Natural History Magazine*, and others of their kind filled many gaps for us. The Devonshire Association for the Advancement of Science has published (in volumes 19, 32, 41-42, 59-62, and 65-67 of its *Transactions*) accounts of members for Devon boroughs. The *Transactions of the Shropshire Archaeological Society* contain H. T. Weyman's articles on Shropshire members and the Staffordshire Record Society published Josiah Wedgwood's work on Staffordshire members which is among the best of our sources. However much Col. Wedgwood's eagerness may have led him astray at other times, his work on his own county deserves greater recognition.

Genealogy is a specialised business, in which the historian may easily become a clumsy and inaccurate dabbler. We have often detected inconsistencies and improbabilities in the pedigrees we have copied; but it would be surprising if we have not made blunders in those we compiled ourselves.

Extensive use has been made of the standard works of reference in this field. Among them the new edition of G.E.C.'s *Complete Peerage* is outstanding in accuracy and, within its limits, completeness; but like the earlier edition and the *Complete Baronetage* it confines itself to the actual holders of titles. Burke, who does include ancestors and younger sons, is less cautious. Most of the works that go under his name, but especially the *Commoners* (1833-8) —and its successors the various editions of the *Landed Gentry*—the *Peerage and Baronetage*, the *Extinct and Dormant Peerage*, and the *Extinct and Dormant Baronetage*, have been consulted frequently. For our period they are seldom seriously misleading and often entertaining. Other works of similar scope, such as Collins's *Peerage* (1741), Wotton's *English Baronets* (1727) and Kimber and Johnson's *Baronetage of England* (1771) sometimes added a little. The Heralds' Visitations, printed by the Harleian Society and in other editions, vary a good deal in the quality of the original investigation and the later editing. In any case, since their chief purpose was to maintain the exclusiveness of the county hierarchy and at the same time to absorb approved new families into it, they are not an impartial authority. Nevertheless they are often good evidence for the dates of birth and the parentage of our members. J. L. Vivian's *Visitations of Cornwall* (1887) and *Visitations of Devon* (1895), and the pedigrees compiled by A. R. Maddison for Lincolnshire (Harleian Society, Vols. 50-52 and 55) and by A. Campling for East Anglia (Harleian Society, Vols. 91 and 97) are full and accurate. At the other extreme are Berry's Genealogies for various southern counties. Many articles and notes, including some of J. H. Round's demolition work, are to be found in the genealogical periodicals, *Collectanea Topographica et Genealogica* (1834-41), *The Topographer and Genealogist* (1846-58), *The Herald and Genealogist* (1863-74), *Miscellanea Genealogica et Heraldica* (1866-1938), *The Genealogist* (1877-1922) and *The Ancestor* (1902-1905). *Notes and Queries* and its various regional namesakes sometimes solved difficulties and more often showed that we were not the first to encounter them. To most of these publications, and to the pedigrees in county histories, indexes are provided by G. W. Marshall's *Genealogist's Guide* (1879) and the as yet unfinished supplement to it by J. B. Whitmore (Harleian Society, Vols. 99 and 101). Other sources can sometimes be traced through H. G. Harrison's *Select Bibliography of British Genealogy* (1937) and T. R. Thompson's *Catalogue of British Family Histories* (2nd edn., 1935). The *Interim Report of the Committee on House of Commons Personnel* (1932) contains among other bibliographical material a list of the Historical Manuscripts Commission volumes in which references to M.P.s were found.

Further help with dates of birth and occasionally with identification, as well as our figures for education, came from the printed admission registers of the Inns of Court and Universities: *Register of Admissions to Gray's Inn* (ed. J. Foster, 1889), *Records of Lincoln's Inn* (Vol. I—Admissions, 1896), *Members admitted to the Inner Temple* (1877), *Middle Temple Admission Registers*

(Vol. I, 1949), J. Foster's *Alumni Oxonienses* (1891-2) and J. and J. A. Venn's *Alumni Cantabrigienses* (1922). The last two contain brief biographical notes, of which Venn's are generally the better. Anthony Wood's *Athenae Oxonienses* (New edition, 1813-20) has good stories about some of the Oxford men.

For the information about estates, and for much genealogical material too, we have used extensively the big county histories. The Victoria County History, for the areas where it is complete, provided fully documented evidence for most of the essential facts about landed families. The Northumberland County History Committee's *History of Northumberland* is in the same class. The older county histories are of variable merit. Many of them, compiled in the eighteenth century and extensively re-written and expanded by later 'editors' were intended, or compelled by financial considerations, to subserve the vanity of local subscribers, and this sometimes detracts from the value of their family histories. At the same time it is not hard to distinguish the eulogies which assign an ancestor of every subscribing gentleman to the personal circle of William the Conqueror, or the tactful assurances that the newcomer who bought a Norfolk estate in the seventeenth century came of a Yorkshire family of immense antiquity, from serious efforts to trace the descent of manors. (The statements, and still more the omissions, made by writers of various later generations about the part played by county families in the Civil War would make an interesting study in themselves.) Of these works F. Blomefield, *Topographical History of Norfolk* (2nd edn., 1805-9), J. Hutchins, *History and Antiquities of Dorset* (3rd edn., 1861-73), and, of later date than most, W. A. Copinger, *The County of Suffolk* (1904-5), are the ones we have had most reason to use, and all three have proved second only to the *V.C.H.* in quality. R. C. Hoare's colossal but incomplete *History of Modern Wiltshire* (1822-44), J. Collinson's *History and Antiquities of Somerset* (1791), and E. Hasted's *History and Topographical Survey of Kent* (1778-99, revised edn., 1886), are among the others we have frequently consulted. For Cornwall there is no comparable county history, but J. Maclean's *Parochial and Family History of the Deanery of Trigg Minor* and the *Parochial Histories of Cornwall* by D. Gilbert (1838) and J. Polsue (1867-72) fill part of the gap. T. H. B. Oldfield's *Representative History* (1816) deals with all the counties and boroughs, but is not as informative about seventeenth-century management as about eighteenth.

Many counties have their own History of the Great Civil War. With the outstanding exception of Miss M. Coate's *Cornwall in the Great Civil War* (1933) they are disappointing, though A. R. Bayley's *The Great Civil War in Dorset* (1910) and G. N. Godwin's *The Civil War in Hampshire* (1904) contributed to some of our biographies. For some counties there are collections of parliamentary biography covering the seventeenth century. Apart from those for Devonshire, Shropshire, and Staffordshire mentioned above, the most valuable are the small volumes by W. R. Williams, *The Parliamentary History of Herefordshire* (1896), *of Worcestershire* (1897), *of Gloucestershire* (1898), *of Oxfordshire* (1899) and *of the Principality of Wales* (1895). W. P. Courtney, *History of Parliamentary Representation of Cornwall* (1889) is more useful than W. T. Lawrance, *Parliamentary Representation of Cornwall* (1924). W. W. Bean, *The Parliamentary Representation of the Six Northern Counties* (1890) and W. D. Pink and A. B. Beavan, *The Parliamentary Representation of Lancashire* (1889), were consulted for the north.

By far the most ambitious biographical collection is the unfinished *Dictionary of M.P.s* by W. D. Pink, the manuscripts of which, in various stages of completion, are in the John Rylands Library, Manchester. They provide very full biographical notes for members of the Long Parliament whose surnames come before L in the alphabet, or whose counties come before Devonshire. Other Parliaments of the Tudor and Stuart periods are also partially covered. Pink was an accurate and indefatigable worker; but he hardly ever gives the sources of his information, and he sometimes uses them uncritically. His work was consulted extensively for the south-western and south-eastern members, and occasionally for those from other regions; but only as a last resort has it been accepted as a sole source of biographical details. For the lists of other Parliaments in which our members and their relations sat he often corrected and supplemented the printed sources. The chief of these, the Blue Book of 1878 (*Official Return of Members of Parliament*) is better on the Long Parliament than on others of the period, but has many errors and gaps. John Pym is among the members it omits.

The *Dictionary of National Biography* deals with most of the important members, and with some unimportant ones, the reason for whose inclusion is not always apparent. For our purpose it proved on the whole disappointing. Many of the longer articles were written by Sir Charles Firth, who was not interested in family history. He usually omits to mention his subject's mother and makes only the briefest reference to the father and his family; nor can he be relied on for facts about education and parliamentary experience. The other entries, even when supplemented by the corrections and additions in the *Bulletin of the Institute of Historical Research*, are of very uneven merit. One contributor appears to think that a Recruiter was someone employed by the Parliament to make people join the army. The *Official History of Parliament* will of course supply these deficiencies so far as M.P.s are concerned; but next to the completion of the *V.C.H.* the wholesale revision of the *D.N.B.* seems to be the most urgent need for workers on studies of this kind.

Most of the contemporary sources that we used, either in the original form or in later editions, have been cited in footnotes. Many of the members are mentioned by writers like Clarendon, Aubrey, and Ludlow; but though it was a delight to turn to authors who brought the names to life, they offered little that was relevant to our main tasks. For the events of the Parliament itself the *Commons Journals*, which by this time were being kept on a clear and efficient system, are the main source. The indexes, particularly the entries under personal names, are hopelessly incomplete. The volumes of D'Ewes's *Journal* edited by W. Notestein and W. H. Coates, which incorporate in footnotes most of what can be added from other journals, give the best possible account of debates for the months they cover (November 1640 to March 1641, and October 1641 to January 1642). For the rest of the period the only collected accounts are the compilations in the *Old Parliamentary History* and Rushworth's *Historical Collections* (1692). Both of these rely largely on the *Journals*, on the weekly newspapers, several of which specialised in parliamentary news, and on speeches reprinted as pamphlets. Rushworth also reprints some of the lists of names which the pamphleteers drew up for their own purposes. Others are in the *Somers Tracts* (1809-15), and the originals of nearly all the pamphlets and newspapers are in the Thomason Collection in the British Museum.

Few modern secondary works deal directly with our subject. Biographies of most of the leading parliamentary figures are either inadequate or non-existent, and only one serious attempt has been made to study in detail the politics of the Parliament—J. H. Hexter's *The Reign of King Pym* (1940). Nothing on our period can compare with J. E. Neale's *The Elizabethan House of Commons* (1949), or with L. B. Namier's *The Structure of Politics at the Accession of George III* (1929). Each of these provided material for comparison and contrast, and the latter especially is an indication of the kind of more ambitious work that remains to be done on the seventeenth century.

COUNTIES AND BOROUGHS
AND THEIR MEMBERS

COUNTIES in each region, and boroughs in each county, are arranged alphabetically.

    1 = Members who sat as a result of the original elections, or of disputes arising from them.

    2 = Members elected before the outbreak of the war to replace other validly elected members.

    3 = Recruiters elected between August 1645 and Pride's Purge.

    4 = Recruiters elected after Pride's Purge.

    * = Sat after a disputed election or double return.

    † = Sat after a member chosen for two seats had preferred another.

Names in square brackets are those of members who were validly elected but are not known to have taken their seats.

Dates are those on which members ceased to be capable of sitting. Members with no date sat in the Rump.

    Exp. = Expelled.

    Dis. = 'Disabled to sit'.

    Dec. = Deceased.

    Sec. = On one of the lists of members secluded at Pride's Purge, and not afterwards re-admitted. The date '12/48' alone means that the member is not on the lists of those secluded but does not appear in the *Journals* as sitting in the Rump.

1. THE NORTH

CUMBERLAND

County

1. Sir George Dalston (3/43 Dis.). Sir Patrick Curwen (3/43 Dis.).
3. William Armine. Richard Tolson (12/48 Sec.).

Carlisle

1. William Dalston (1/44 Dis.). Richard Barwis (12/48).
3. Thomas Cholmley (12/48).
4. Edward Lord Howard of Eskrick (6/51 Exp.).

Cockermouth

1. Sir John Hippisley. Sir Thomas Sandford, Bt.* † [1] (1/44 Dis.).
3. Francis Allen.*[1]

LANCASHIRE

County

1. Roger Kirkby (8/42 Dis.).   Ralph Assheton (12/48 Sec.).
3. Richard Houghton (12/48 Sec.).

Clitheroe

1. Ralph Assheton (12/48 Sec.). Richard Shuttleworth (12/48 Dec.).

Lancaster

1. Thomas Fanshawe (9/42 Dis.). John Harrison (9/43 Dis.).
3. Thomas Fell. Sir Robert Bindlosse, Bt. (12/48 Sec.).

Liverpool

1. John Moore (6/50 Dec.). Sir Richard Wynn, Bt. (12/48 Sec.).
4. Thomas Birch.[2]

Newton

1. Peter Legh (2/42 Dec.). Sir Roger Palmer (1/44 Dis.).
2. William Ashurst (12/48).
3. Peter Brooke.*

Preston

1. Thomas Standish (11/42 Dec.). Richard Shuttleworth (12/48 Sec.).
3. William Langton (12/48).

Wigan

1. Orlando Bridgman (5/42 Exp.). Alexander Rigby (8/50 Dec.).
3. John Holcroft (12/48 Sec.).

NORTHUMBERLAND

County

1. Henry Percy (12/41 Exp.). Sir William Widdrington (8/42 Dis.).
2. Sir John Fenwick, Bt. (12/48 Sec.).[3]
3. William Fenwick (12/48 Sec.).

[1] Sandford and Allen were both returned in place of Sir John Fenwick, who elected to serve for Northumberland. Sandford was disabled to sit before the dispute was settled; Allen was admitted in 1645, and is counted as a Recruiter.

[2] In place of Sir Richard Wynn, who died in July 1649.

[3] Disabled 22 Jan. 1644, but re-admitted 26 June 1646.

Berwick

1. Sir Thomas Widdrington. Robert Scawen [1] (12/48 Sec.).

Morpeth

1. Sir William Carnaby (8/42 Dis.). John Fenwick (1/43 Dis.).
3. John Fiennes (12/48 Sec.). George Fenwick.

Newcastle-on-Tyne

1. John Blakiston (6/49 Dec.). Sir John Melton* (12/40 Dec.).
2. Sir Henry Anderson (9/43 Dis.).
3. Robert Ellison* (12/48 Sec.).

WESTMORLAND

County

1. Sir Philip Musgrave, Bt. (3/43 Dis.). Sir Henry Bellingham, Bt. (10/45 Dis.).
3. James Bellingham (12/48). Henry Lawrence (12/48 Sec.).

Appleby

1. Sir John Brooke (3/43 Dis.). Richard Boyle, Viscount Dungarvan (11/43 Dis.).
3. Henry Ireton (12/51 Dec.). Richard Salway.

YORKSHIRE

County

1. Ferdinando, Lord Fairfax (3/48 Dec.). Henry Belasyse (9/42 Dis.).

Aldborough

1. Robert Strickland (1/43 Dis.). Richard Aldeburgh (9/42 Dis.).
3. Brian Stapleton (12/48). Thomas Scott (1/48 Dec.). James Chaloner.

Beverley

1. Sir John Hotham, Bt. (9/43 Dis.). Michael Warton (1/44 Dis.).
3. James Nelthorpe. John Nelthorpe (12/48 Sec.).

Boroughbridge

1. Thomas Mauleverer. Sir Philip Stapleton (9/47 Dec.).
3. Henry Stapleton (12/48 Sec.).

Hedon

1. John Alured. Sir William Strickland.

Hull

1. Sir Henry Vane, junior. Sir John Lister (12/40 Dec.).
2. Peregrine Pelham (?/50 Dec.).

[1] In place of Sir Edward Osborne, who resigned the seat.

Knaresborough

1. Henry Benson (11/41 Exp.). Sir Henry Slingsby (9/42 Dis.).
2. Sir William Constable, Bt.* [1]
3. Thomas Stockdale.

New Malton

1. Thomas Hebblethwaite (11/44 Dis.). Henry Cholmley (12/48 Sec.).
3. Richard Darley.

Northallerton

1. Henry Darley. John Wastell.

Pontefract

1. Sir George Wentworth of Walley (9/42 Dis.). Sir George Wentworth of Wentworth Woodhouse (1/44 Dis.).
3. William White. Henry Arthington.

Richmond

1. Sir Thomas Danby (9/42 Dis.). Sir William Pennyman, Bt. (8/43 Dec.).
3. Thomas Chaloner. Francis Thorpe.

Ripon

1. John Mallory (1/44 Dis.). William Mallory (9/42 Dis.).
3. Sir Charles Egerton (12/48 Sec.). Miles Moody (3/47 Dec.). Sir John Bourchier.

Scarborough

1. John Hotham (9/43 Dis.). Sir Hugh Cholmley (4/43 Dis.).
3. Sir Matthew Boynton, Bt. (3/47 Dec.). Luke Robinson. John Anlaby.

Thirsk

1. Sir Thomas Ingram (9/42 Dis.). John Belasyse (9/42 Dis.).
3. William Ayscough (12/48 Sec.). Francis Lascelles.

York

1. Sir William Allanson. Thomas Hoyle (1/50 Dec.).

2. THE EAST

CAMBRIDGESHIRE

County

1. Sir Dudley North, K.B. (12/48 Sec.). Thomas Chicheley (9/42 Dis.).
3. Francis Russell.

[1] See *C.J.* 19 March 1642 for an account of the election.

Cambridge

1. Oliver Cromwell. John Lowry.[1]

Cambridge University

1. Henry Lucas (12/48 Sec.). Thomas Eden (8/45 Dec.).
3. Nathaniel Bacon.

ESSEX

County

1. Robert, Lord Rich, K.B. (2/41 Peer). Sir William Masham, Bt.
2. Sir Martin Lumley, Bt. (12/48 Sec.).

Colchester

1. Sir Thomas Barrington, Bt. (9/44 Dec.). Harbottle Grimston (12/48 Sec.)
3. John Sayer (12/48).

Harwich

1. Sir Harbottle Grimston, Bt. (2/48 Dec.). Sir Thomas Cheeke (12/48).
3. Capel Luckyn (12/48 Sec.).

Maldon

1. Sir Henry Mildmay. Sir John Clotworthy (12/48 Sec.).[2]

HERTFORDSHIRE

County

1. Sir William Lytton (12/48 Sec.). Arthur Capel (8/41 Peer).
2. Sir Thomas Dacres (12/48 Sec.).

Hertford

1. Charles Cecil, Viscount Cranborne (12/48). Sir Thomas Fanshawe, K.B. (11/43 Dis.).
3. William Leman.

St. Albans

1. Sir John Jennings, K.B. (8?/42 Dec.). Edward Wingate (12/48 Sec.).
2. Richard Jennings (12/48 Sec.).

HUNTINGDONSHIRE

County

1. Sir Sidney Montagu (12/42 Exp.). Valentine Walton.
3. Edward Montagu (12/48 Sec.).

---

[1] Alderman Richard Foxton is named in the return, but there is no evidence that he sat or disputed Lowry's election.

[2] See p. 127.

Huntingdon

1. George Montagu (12/48 Sec.). Edward Montagu (6/44 Peer).
3. Abraham Burrell.

LINCOLNSHIRE

County

1. Sir John Wray, Bt. (12/48). Sir Edward Ayscough (12/48 Sec.).

Boston

1. Sir Anthony Irby (12/48 Sec.). William Ellis.

Grantham

1. Thomas Hussey (3/41 Dec.). Henry Pelham (12/48 Sec.).
2. Sir William Armine, Bt.

Grimsby

1. Sir Christopher Wray (2/46 Dec.). Gervase Holles (8/42 Dis.).
3. William Wray (12/48 Sec.). Edward Rossiter (12/48 Sec.).

Lincoln

1. Thomas Grantham (12/48). John Broxholme (2/47 Dec.).
3. Thomas Lister.

Stamford

1. Geoffrey Palmer (9/42 Dis.). Thomas Hatcher (12/48 Sec.).
3. John Weaver.

NORFOLK

County

1. John Potts (12/48 Sec.). Sir Edmund Moundeford (12/45 Dec.).
3. Sir John Hobart, Bt. (11/47 Dec.). Sir John Palgrave, Bt. (12/48 Sec.).

Castle Rising

1. Sir John Holland, Bt. (12/48 Sec.). Sir Robert Hatton† (9/42 Dis.).
3. John Spelman (12/48 Sec.).

King's Lynn

1. John Perceval (?/44 Dec.). Thomas Toll.
[3. Edmund Hudson (7/47 Exp.).]
4. William Cecil, Earl of Salisbury.

Norwich

1. Richard Harman* (?/46 Dec.). Richard Catelyn* (1/44 Dis.).
3. Thomas Atkins. Erasmus Earle.

Thetford

1. Sir Thomas Woodhouse, Bt. Framlingham Gawdy (12/48 Sec.).

Great Yarmouth

1. Miles Corbet. Edward Owner (12/48).

SUFFOLK

County

1. Sir Nathaniel Barnardiston (12/48). Sir Philip Parker (12/48 Sec.).

Aldeburgh

1. William Rainsborough (2/42 Dec.). Alexander Bence (12/48 Sec.).
2. Squire Bence (11/48 Dec.).

Bury St. Edmunds

1. Sir Thomas Jermyn, K.B. (2/44 Dis.). Thomas Jermyn (9/43 Dis.).
3. Sir Thomas Barnardiston (12/48 Sec.). Sir William Spring, Bt. (12/48 Sec.).

Dunwich

1. Henry Coke (9/42 Dis.). Anthony Bedingfield (12/48).
3. Robert Brewster.

Eye

1. Sir Frederick Cornwallis, Bt. (9/42 Dis.). Sir Roger North.
3. Maurice Barrowe (12/48 Sec.).

Ipswich

1. William Cage (11/45 Dec.). John Gurdon.
3. Francis Bacon.

Orford

1. Sir Charles Le Gros (12/48). Sir William Playters, Bt. (12/48 Sec.).

Sudbury

1. Sir Simonds D'Ewes (12/48). Sir Robert Crane, Bt.* (2/43 Dec.).
3. Brampton Gurdon.

3. THE MIDLAND COUNTIES

BEDFORDSHIRE

County

1. Thomas, Lord Wentworth, K.B. (11/40 Peer). Sir Oliver Luke (12/48 Sec.).
2. Sir Roger Burgoyne, Bt. (12/48 Sec.).

Bedford

1. Sir Beauchamp St. John (12/48 Sec.). Sir Samuel Luke* (12/48 Sec.).

BERKSHIRE

County

1. John Fettiplace (1/44 Dis.). Henry Marten.
3. Sir Francis Pile, Bt. (12/48).
4. Philip Herbert, Earl of Pembroke and Montgomery (2/50 Dec.).

Abingdon

1. Sir George Stonehouse, Bt. (1/44 Dis.).
3. William Ball (5?/48 Dec.).
4. Henry Neville.

Reading

1. Sir Francis Knollys, senior (3?/48 Dec.). Sir Francis Knollys, junior (5/43 Dec.).
3. Tanfield Vachell* (12/48). Daniel Blagrave.*

Wallingford

1. Edmund Dunch.* Thomas Howard* (1/44 Dis.).
3. Robert Packer (12/48 Sec.).

New Windsor

1. Cornelius Holland.* William Taylor* (5/41 Exp.).
2. Richard Winwood* (12/48 Sec.).

BUCKINGHAMSHIRE

County

1. John Hampden (6/43 Dec.). Arthur Goodwin (?/43 Dec.).
3. Edmund West.* George Fleetwood.*

Amersham

1. William Cheyney (4/41 Dec.). Francis Drake (12/48 Sec.).
2. Sir William Drake (12/48 Sec.).

Aylesbury

1. Sir John Packington, Bt. (8/42 Dis.). Ralph Verney (9/45 Dis.).
3. Thomas Scott. Simon Mayne.

Buckingham

1. Sir Peter Temple, Bt. Sir Alexander Denton (1/44 Dis.).
3. John Dormer.

Great Marlow

1. Bulstrode Whitelocke.* Peregrine Hoby* (12/48 Sec.).[1]

Wendover

1. Robert Croke (11/43 Dis.). Thomas Fountaine (9?/46 Dec.).
3. Richard Ingoldsby.† Thomas Harrison.

[1]See the article by M. Freer in *Journal of Modern History*, Vol. 14.

Chipping Wycombe

1. Sir Edmund Verney (10/42 Dec.). Thomas Lane (12/48 Sec.).
3. Richard Browne (12/48 Sec.).

DERBYSHIRE

County

1. Sir John Curzon, Bt. (12/48 Sec.). Sir John Coke (12/48).

Derby

1. William Allestrey* (10/43 Dis.). Nathaniel Hallowes.*
3. Thomas Gell (12/48 Sec.).

LEICESTERSHIRE

County

1. Henry, Lord Grey of Ruthyn (11/43 Peer). Sir Arthur Haselrig, Bt.
3. Henry Smith.

Leicester

1. Thomas, Lord Grey of Groby. Thomas Coke (1/44 Dis.).
3. Peter Temple.

NORTHAMPTONSHIRE

County

1. Sir Gilbert Pickering, Bt. Sir John Dryden, Bt.

Brackley

1. John Crewe (12/48 Sec.). Sir Martin Lister (12/48 Sec.).

Higham Ferrers

1. Sir Christopher Hatton (9/42 Dis.).
3. Edward Harby.

Northampton

1. Richard Knightley (12/48 Sec.). Zouch Tate (12/48).

Peterborough

1. William Fitzwilliams (12/48 Sec.). Sir Robert Napier, Bt.* (12/48 Sec.).

NOTTINGHAMSHIRE

County

1. Sir Thomas Hutchinson (8/43 Dec.). Robert Sutton (12/43 Dis.).
3. John Hutchinson. Gervase Pigot.

Nottingham

1. William Stanhope (1/44 Dis.). Gilbert Millington.
3. Francis Pierrepont.

East Retford

1. Charles, Viscount Mansfield (1/44 Dis.). Sir Gervase Clifton, Bt. (?/44 Dis.).
3. Francis Thornhaugh (11/48 Dec.). Sir William Lister (12/48 Sec.).
[4. Edward Neville.]

OXFORDSHIRE

County

1. Thomas, Viscount Wenman (12/48 Sec.). James Fiennes (12/48 Sec.).

Banbury

1. Nathaniel Fiennes* (12/48 Sec.).

Oxford University

1. Sir Thomas Roe (1/44 Dec.). John Selden (12/48 Sec.).

Oxford

1. Charles, Lord Howard (11/40 Peer). John Whistler (?/44 Dis.).
2. John Smith (?/44 Dis.).
3. John Nixon (12/48 Sec.). John Doyley (12/48 Sec.).

New Woodstock

1. William Lenthall.* Sir Robert Pye† (12/48 Sec.).

RUTLANDSHIRE

County

1. Baptist Noel (8/43 Peer). Sir Guy Palmes (9/43 Dis.).
3. Sir James Harrington.* Thomas Waite.*

STAFFORDSHIRE

County

1. Sir William Bowyer (3/41 Dec.). Sir Edward Littleton, Bt. (3/44 Dis.).
2. Sir Hervey Bagot, Bt. (11/42 Dis.).
3. John Bowyer (12/48 Sec.). Sir Richard Skeffington (6/47 Dec.). Thomas Crompton.

Lichfield

1. Sir Walter Devereux (7?/41 Dec.). Michael Noble (12/48).
2. Sir Richard Cave (8/42 Dis.).
3. Michael Biddulph (12/48 Sec.).

Newcastle-under-Lyme

1. Sir Richard Leveson, K.B. (11/42 Dis.). Sir John Meyrick (12/48 Sec.).
3. Samuel Terrick (12/48 Sec.).

Stafford

1. Ralph Sneyd (5/43 Dis.). Richard Weston (10/42 Dis.).
3. John Swinfen* (12/48 Sec.). Edward Leigh* (12/48 Sec.).

Tamworth

1. Ferdinand Stanhope (3/43 Dis.). Henry Wilmott† (12/41 Exp.).
2. Sir Peter Wentworth, K.B.
3. George Abbot (12/48).

WARWICKSHIRE

County

1. James, Lord Compton* (3/43 Peer). Richard Shuckburgh (1/44 Dis.).
3. Thomas Boughton (12/48 Sec.). Sir John Burgoyne, Bt. (12/48 Sec.).

Coventry

1. John Barker.* Simon Norton* (?/41 Dec.).
2. William Jesson (12/48).

Warwick

1. Sir Thomas Lucy (12/40 Dec.). William Purefoy.
2. Godfrey Bosvile.

4. WALES AND THE WEST

CHESHIRE

County

1. Sir William Brereton. Peter Venables (1/44 Dis.).
3. George Booth (12/48 Sec.).

Chester

1. Sir Thomas Smith (1/44 Dis.). Francis Gamul (1/44 Dis.).
3. William Edwards (12/48 Sec.). John Ratcliffe (12/48 Sec.).

HEREFORDSHIRE

County

1. Sir Robert Harley, K.B. (12/48 Sec.). Fitzwilliam Coningsby (10/41 Exp.).
2. Humphrey Coningsby (5/43 Dis.).
3. Edward Harley (12/48 Sec.).

Hereford

1. Richard Weaver (7/42 Dec.). Richard Seaborne (1/44 Dis.).
2. James Scudamore (5/43 Dis).
3. Bennett Hoskins (12/48 Sec.). Edmund Weaver (12/48?).

Leominster

1. Sampson Eure (1/44 Dis.). Walter Kyrle (12/48 Sec.).
3. John Birch (12/48 Sec.).

Weobley

1. Arthur Jones (2/44 Dis.). William Tompkins (1/41 Dec.).
2. Thomas Tompkins (6/44 Dis.).
3. Robert Andrews. William Crowther (12/48).

MONMOUTHSHIRE

County

1. William Herbert (2/44 Dis.). Sir Charles Williams (3/41 Dec.).
2. Henry Herbert.
3. John Herbert.

Monmouth

3. Thomas Pury.* [1]

SHROPSHIRE

County

1. Sir Richard Lee (9/42 Dis.). Sir John Corbet, Bt. (12/48 Sec.).
3. Humphrey Edwards.*

Bishop's Castle

1. Richard More (12/43 Dec.). Sir Robert Howard (9/42 Dis.).
3. Esay Thomas (12/48 Sec.). John Corbet.

Bridgnorth

1. Thomas Whitmore (2/44 Dis.). Edward Acton (2/44 Dis.).
3. Robert Clive (12/48). Robert Charlton (12/48).

Ludlow

1. Ralph Goodwin (2/44 Dis.). Charles Baldwin (2/44 Dis.).
3. Thomas More (12/48). Thomas Mackworth.

Shrewsbury

1. Francis Newport (1/44 Dis.). William Spurstow (1/46 Dec.).
3. Thomas Hunt (12/48 Sec.). William Masham.

Much Wenlock

1. William Pierrepont (12/48 Sec.). Thomas Littleton (2/44 Dis.).
3. Sir Humphrey Briggs (12/48 Sec.).

WORCESTERSHIRE

County

1. John Wylde. Humphrey Salway.

Bewdley

1. Sir Henry Herbert* (8/42 Dis.).
3. Nicholas Lechmere.*

[1] See p. 2-3.

Droitwich

1. Endymion Porter (3/43 Dis.). Samuel Sandys (8/42 Dis.).
3. Thomas Rainsborough (10/48 Dec.). Edmund Wylde. George Wylde.

Evesham

1. Richard Cresheld (12/48). William Sandys (1/41 Exp.).
2. John Coventry (8/42 Dis.).
3. Samuel Gardner.

Worcester

1. John Cowcher ★ (12/48). John Nash ★ (12/48 Sec.).

WALES

ANGLESEY

County

1. John Bodville (2/44 Dis.).
3. Richard Wood (12/48).

Beaumaris

1. John Griffith (8/42 Dec.).
3. William Jones (12/48 Sec.).

BRECONSHIRE

County

1. William Morgan (12/48).
4. Philip Jones.

Brecon

1. Herbert Price★ (5/43 Dis.).
3. Lewis Lewis (12/48 Sec.).

CARDIGANSHIRE

County

1. Walter Lloyd (2/44 Dis.).
3. Sir Richard Pryse (12/48 Sec.).

Cardigan

1. John Vaughan (9/45 Dis.).
3. Thomas Wogan.

CARMARTHENSHIRE

County

1. Henry Vaughan (2/44 Dis.).
3. John Lloyd (12/48 Sec.).

Carmarthen

1. Francis Lloyd (2/44 Dis.).
3. William Davies (12/48).

CAERNARVONSHIRE

County

1. John Griffith (8/42 Dis.).
3. Richard Wynn (12/48 Sec.).

Caernarvon

1. Sir William Thomas★ (2/44 Dis.).
3. William Foxwist (12/48 Sec.).

DENBIGHSHIRE

County

1. Sir Thomas Middleton (12/48 Sec.).

Denbigh

1. Simon Thelwall (12/48 Sec.).

FLINTSHIRE

County

1. John Mostyn (2/43 Dis.).
3. John Trevor (12/48 Sec.).

Flint

1. John Salusbury (2/43 Dis.).
3. Thomas Middleton (12/48 Sec.).

GLAMORGANSHIRE

County

1. Philip, Lord Herbert.

Cardiff

1. William Herbert (10/42 Dec.).
3. Algernon Sidney.

MERIONETHSHIRE

County

1. William Price (2/44 Dis.).
3. Roger Pope (8?/47 Dec.). John Jones.

MONTGOMERYSHIRE

County

1. Sir John Price, Bt. (10/45 Dis.).
3. Edward Vaughan (12/48 Sec.).

Montgomery

1. Richard Herbert (9/42 Dis.).
[3. George Devereux.]

PEMBROKESHIRE

County

1. John Wogan (12/45 Dec.).
3. Arthur Owen (12/48 Sec.).

Haverfordwest

1. Sir John Stepney, Bt. (4/43 Dis.).
3. Sir Robert Needham (12/48 Sec.).

Pembroke

1. Hugh Owen (12/48).

RADNORSHIRE

County

1. Charles Price (10/42 Dis.).
3. Arthur Annesley (12/48 Sec.).

New Radnor

1. Philip Warwick (2/44 Dis.).
3. Robert Harley (12/48 Sec.).

5. THE SOUTH-EAST

HAMPSHIRE

County

1. Sir Henry Wallopp (11/42 Dec.). Richard Whitehead (12/48 Sec.).
3. Richard Norton.

Andover

1. Robert Wallopp. Sir Henry Rainsford (4/41 Dec.).
2. Sir William Waller * 1 (12/48 Sec.).

Christchurch

1. Henry Tulse (9?/42 Dec.). Matthew Davis (3/43 Dis.).
3. John Kemp (12/48). Richard Edwards.

New Lymington

1. John Button (12/48 Sec.). Henry Campion (12/48).

1 See *C.J.* 3 May 1642 for an account of the election.

Newport

1. Lucius Carey, Viscount Falkland (9/42 Dis.). Sir Henry Worsley, Bt. (12/48 Sec.).
3. William Stephens.

Newtown

1. John Meux (2/44 Dis.). Nicholas Weston (8/42 Dis.).
3. Sir John Barrington, Bt. (12/48 Sec.). John Bulkeley (12/48 Sec.).

Petersfield

1. Sir William Lewis, Bt. (12/48 Sec.). Sir William Uvedale (12/48).

Portsmouth

1. George Goring (8/42 Dis.). Edward Dowce † (11?/48 Dec.).
3. Edward Boote (12/48).

Southampton

1. George Gollop (12/48). Edward Exton (12/48).

Stockbridge

1. William Heveningham. William Jephson (12/48).

Whitchurch

1. Sir Thomas Jervoise. Richard Jervoise (10/45 Dec.).
3. Thomas Hussey.

Winchester

1. John Lisle. Sir William Ogle (6/43 Dis.).
3. Nicholas Love.

Yarmouth

1. Philip Sidney, Lord Lisle. Sir John Leigh (12/48 Sec.).

KENT

County

1. Sir Edward Dering (2/42 Dis.). Sir John Culpepper (1/44 Dis.).
2. Augustine Skinner.
3. John Boys (12/48 Sec.).

Canterbury

1. Sir Edward Masters (8/48 Dec.). John Nutt.

Maidstone

1. Sir Francis Barneham (11/46 Dec.). Sir Humphrey Tufton (12/48).
3. Thomas Twisden (12/48 Sec.).

Queenborough

1. Sir Edward Hales, Bt. (4/48 Dis.). William Harrison (6/43 Dis.).
3. Augustine Garland. Sir Michael Livesey.

Rochester

1. Richard Lee (12/48). Sir Thomas Walsingham.

MIDDLESEX

County

1. Sir Gilbert Gerard, Bt. (12/48 Sec.). Sir John Francklyn (3/48 Dec.).
3. Sir Edward Spencer (12/48).

London

1. Thomas Soame (12/48 Sec.). Isaac Pennington. Matthew Craddock (5/41 Dec.). Samuel Vassall (12/48 Sec.).
2. John Venn.

Westminster

1. John Glynn (12/48 Sec.). William Bell (12/48 Sec.).

SURREY

County

1. Sir Richard Onslow (12/48 Sec.). Sir Ambrose Browne, Bt. (12/48 Sec.).

Bletchingley

1. John Evelyn (12/48 Sec.). Edward Bysshe (12/48 Sec.).

Gatton

1. Samuel Owfield (?/44 Dec.). Thomas Sandys* (12/48 Sec.).
3. William Owfield (12/48 Sec.).

Guildford

1. Sir Robert Parkhurst (12/48). George Abbot (?/45 Dec.).
3. Nicholas Stoughton (3/48 Dec.). Henry Weston* (12/48).

Haslemere

1. Poynings Moore* (12/48). John Goodwin.
4. Carew Raleigh.[1]

Reigate

1. William, Viscount Mounson. Sir Thomas Bludder (1/44 Dis.).
3. George Evelyn (12/48 Sec.).

Southwark

1. Edward Bagshawe (1/44 Dis.). John White (1/45 Dec.).
3. George Thomson. George Snelling.

SUSSEX

County

1. Sir Thomas Pelham, Bt. (12/48 Sec.). Anthony Stapley.

[1] In place of Sir Poynings Moore, who died in April 1649.

Arundel

1. Sir Edward Alford (1/44 Dis.). Henry Garton (10/41 Dec.).
2. John Downes.*
3. Herbert Hay (12/48 Sec.).

Bramber

1. Sir Thomas Bowyer, Bt.* (11/42 Dis.). Arthur Onslow* (12/48 Sec.).
3. James Temple.

Chichester

1. Sir William Morley (11/42 Dis.). Christopher Lewkenor (9/42 Dis.).
3. Sir John Temple (12/48 Sec.). Henry Peek (12/48 Sec.).

East Grinstead

1. Richard Sackville, Lord Buckhurst* (2/43 Dis.). Robert Goodwin.*
3. John Baker.*

Horsham

1. Thomas Middleton (12/48). Hall Ravenscroft (12/48 Sec.).

Lewes

1. James Rivers (6/41 Dec.). Herbert Morley.
2. Henry Shelley (12/48).

Midhurst

1. William Cawley.* Thomas May (11/42 Dis.).
3. Sir Gregory Norton, Bt.

Shoreham

1. John Alford (12/48 Sec.). William Marlott (?/46 Dec.).
3. Herbert Springate (12/48 Sec.).

Steyning

1. Thomas Leedes* (11/42 Dis.). Sir Thomas Farnefold* (3/43 Dec.).
3. Edward Apsley. Herbert Board (?/48 Dec.).

THE CINQUE PORTS

Dover

1. Sir Peter Heyman (2/41 Dec.). Sir Edward Boys (8/46 Dec.).
2. Benjamin Weston.
3. John Dixwell.

Hastings

1. Thomas Eversfield (2/44 Dis.). John Ashburnham (2/44 Dis.).
3. John Pelham (12/48 Sec.). Roger Gratwick.

Hythe

1. John Harvey (4/45 Dec.). Henry Heyman.
3. Thomas Westrow.

New Romney

1. Thomas Webb† (1/41 Exp.). Sir Norton Knatchbull (12/48 Sec.).
2. Richard Browne (12/48).

Rye

1. Sir John Jacob (1/41 Exp.). John White (2/44 Dis.).
2. William Hay.
3. John Fagge.

Sandwich

1. Sir Thomas Peyton, Bt. (2/44 Dis.). Sir Edward Partridge (12/48 Sec.).
3. Charles Rich (12/48 Sec.).

Seaford

1. Sir Thomas Parker (12/48). Francis Gerard (12/48 Sec.).

Winchelsea

1. Sir Nicholas Crispe (2/41 Exp.). John Finch (9/42 Dec.).
2. William Smith (1/44 Dis.).
3. Henry Oxenden (12/48 Sec.). Samuel Gott (12/48 Sec.).

6. THE SOUTH-WEST

CORNWALL

County

1. Sir Bevil Grenville (9/42 Dis.). Alexander Carew (9/43 Exp.).
3. Hugh Boscawen (12/48 Sec.). Nicholas Trefusis (12/48).

Bodmin

1. Anthony Nichols★ (12/48). John Arundell (1/44 Dis.).
3. Thomas Waller★ (12/48 Sec.).

Bossinney

1. Sir Christopher Yelverton★ (12/48). Sir Ralph Sydenham★ (9/42 Dis.)
3. Lionel Copley (12/48 Sec.).

Callington

1. George Fane (1/43 Dis.). Sir Arthur Ingram (8/42 Dec.).
3. Edward, Lord Clinton (12/48 Sec.). Thomas Dacres (12/48 Sec.).

Camelford

1. Piers Edgecumbe (1/44 Dis.). William Glanville (1/44 Dis.).
3. William Say.

Fowey

1. Jonathan Rashleigh (1/44 Dis.). Sir Richard Buller (11/42 Dec).
3. Nicholas Gould. Gregory Clement (5/52 Exp.).

Grampound

1. James Campbell (12/48 Sec.). Sir John Trevor.†

Helston

1. Sidney Godolphin (2/43 Dec.). Francis Godolphin (1/44 Dis.).
3. John Penrose (12/48). John Thomas (12/48 Sec.).

Launceston

1. [William Coryton (8/41 Exp.)]. Ambrose Manaton (1/44 Dis.). John Harris (12/48 Sec.).
3. Thomas Gewen (12/48 Sec.).

Liskeard

1. John Harris (1/44 Dis.). Joseph Jane (1/44 Dis.).
3. George Kekewich (12/48 Sec.). Thomas Povey (12/48 Sec.).

East Looe

1. Francis Buller (12/48 Sec.). Thomas Lower (1/44 Dis.).
3. John Moyle.

West Looe

1. Thomas Arundell (11/48 Dec.). Henry Killigrew (1/44 Dis.).
3. John Arundell (12/48 Sec.).
4. Robert Bennett.

Lostwithiel

1. Richard Arundell (1/44 Dis.). John Trevanion (7/43 Dec.).
3. Sir John Maynard, K.B. (12/48). Francis Holles (12/48 Sec.).

Mitchell

1. William Chadwell (1/44 Dis.). Robert Holborne† (8/42 Dis.).
3. Charles, Lord Carr (12/48 Sec.). [Thomas Temple.]

Newport

1. Richard Edgecumbe (1/44 Dis.).[1]
3. Sir Philip Perceval† (11/47 Dec.). Nicholas Leach (5/47 Dec.). William Prynne (12/48 Sec.). Alexander Pym (12/48).

Penryn

1. Sir Nicholas Slaning (8/42 Dis.). John Bampfield (12/48).

St. Germans

1. John Moyle (12/48). Benjamin Valentine (?/52 Dec.).
3. [William Scawen.]

St. Ives

1. Edmund Waller (7/43 Exp.). Francis Godolphin (12/48).
3. John Feilder.

[1] Newport had two seats, but only one member seems to have been returned.

St. Mawes

1. Richard Erisey (12/48 Sec.). George Parry (1/44 Dis.).
3. William Priestley (12/48 Sec.).

Saltash

1. Edward Hyde (8/42 Dis.). George Buller (12/46 Dec.).
3. John Thynne (12/48 Sec.). Henry Wills (12/48 Sec.).

Tregony

1. Sir Richard Vivian (1/44 Dis.). John Polwhele (1/44 Dis.).
3. Sir Thomas Trevor, Bt. (12/48 Sec.). John Carew.

Truro

1. John Rolle (11/48 Dec.). Francis Rous.

DEVONSHIRE

County

1. Thomas Wise (3/41 Dec.). Edward Seymour (1/43 Dis.).
2. Sir Samuel Rolle (12/47 Dec.).
3. Sir Nicholas Martyn (12/48 Sec.). [William Morice (12/48 Sec.)].

Ashburton

1. Sir Edmund Fowell (12/48 Sec.). Sir John Northcote, Bt. (12/48 Sec.).

Barnstaple

1. George Peard (?/44 Dec.). Richard Ferris* (1/44 Dis.).
3. Philip Skippon. John Doddridge (12/48 Sec.).

Berealston

1. William Strode (9/45 Dec.). Hugh Pollard† (12/41 Exp.).
2. Charles Pym (12/48 Sec.).
3. Sir Francis Drake, Bt. (12/48 Sec.).

Dartmouth

1. John Upton (9/41 Dec.). Roger Matthew (2/44 Dis.).
2. Samuel Browne (12/48 Sec.).
3. Thomas Boone.

Exeter

1. Robert Walker (3/43 Dis.). Simon Snow (12/48 Sec.).
3. Samuel Clarke (12/48).

Honiton

1. William Poole (6/43 Dis.). Walter Yonge (12/48).
3. Charles Vaughan (12/48 Sec.).

Okehampton

1. Edward Thomas (12/48 Sec.). Lawrence Whitaker.

Plymouth

1. Robert Trelawney (3/42 Exp.). John Waddon (12/48 Sec.).
2. Sir John Yonge (12/48 Sec.).

Plympton Earl

1. Sir Thomas Heale, Bt. (1/44 Dis.). Hugh Potter† (12/48 Sec.).
3. Christopher Martyn.*

Tavistock

1. William, Lord Russell (5/41 Peer). John Pym (12/43 Dec.).
2. John Russell (1/44 Dis.).
3. Elisha Crimes (12/48 Sec.). Edward Fowell (12/48 Sec.).

Tiverton

1. Peter Sainthill (1/44 Dis.). George Hartnall (1/44 Dis.).
3. John Elford (12/48). Robert Shapcote (12/48 Sec.).

Totnes

1. Oliver St. John. John Maynard (12/48 Sec.).

DORSET

County

1. George, Lord Digby (6/41 Peer). Richard Rogers (9/42 Dis.).
2. John Browne.
3. Sir Thomas Trenchard (12/48).

Bridport

1. Giles Strangways (1/44 Dis.). Roger Hill.
3. Thomas Ceeley (12/48 Sec.).

Corfe Castle

1. Sir Francis Windebank (12/41 Exp.). Giles Green (12/48 Sec.).
2. John Burlace (3/44 Dis.).
3. Francis Chettel (12/48).

Dorchester

1. Denzil Holles (12/48 Sec.). Denis Bond.

Lyme Regis

1. Edmund Prideaux. Richard Rose (12/48).

Poole

1. John Pyne. William Constantine (9/42 Dis.).
3. George Skutt (12/48 Sec.).

Shaftesbury

1. William Whitaker (10/46 Dec.). Samuel Turner (1/44 Dis.).
3. John Bingham. George Starre (10?/47 Dec.). John Fry (2/51 Exp.).

Wareham

1. John Trenchard. Thomas Erle★ (12/48 Sec.).

Weymouth and Melcombe Regis

1. Sir John Strangways (9/42 Dis.). Sir Walter Erle (12/48 Sec.). Gerard Napier (1/44 Dis.). Richard King (2/43 Dis.).
3. Matthew Allen (12/48 Sec.). John Bond (12/48 Sec.). William Sydenham.

GLOUCESTERSHIRE

County

1. John Dutton (1/44 Dis.). Nathaniel Stephens (12/48 Sec.).
3. Sir John Seymour (12/48 Sec.).

Bristol

1. Humphrey Hooke (5/42 Exp.). Richard Longe (5/42 Exp.).
2. John Glanville (9/45 Dis.). John Taylor (2/44 Dis.).
3. Richard Aldworth. Luke Hodges.

Cirencester

1. Sir Theobald Gorges (1/44 Dis.). John George (1/44 Dis.).
4. [Sir Thomas Fairfax★.] Nathaniel Rich.★

Gloucester

1. Thomas Pury. Henry Brett (2/44 Dis.).
3. John Lenthall.

Tewkesbury

1. Sir Robert Cooke★ (8/43 Dec.). Edward Stephens★ (12/48 Sec.).
3. John Stephens.

SOMERSET

County

1. Sir John Poulett (8/42 Dis.). Sir John Stawell, K.B. (8/42 Dis.).
3. John Harrington★ (12/48). George Horner★ (12/48 Sec.).

Bath

1. William Bassett (2/42 Dis.). Alexander Popham.
3. James Ashe.

Bridgwater

1. Sir Peter Wroth (5/44 Dec.). Edmund Wyndham (1/41 Esp.).
2. Thomas Smith (8/42 Dis.).
3. Sir Thomas Wroth. Robert Blake.

Ilchester

1. Robert Hunt★ (2/44 Dis.). Edward Phillipps★ (2/44 Dis.).
3. William Strode (12/48 Sec.). Thomas Hodges (12/48 Sec.).

Milborne Port

1. John Digby† (8/42 Dis.). Edward Kyrton (8/42 Dis.).
3. Thomas Grove (12/48 Sec.). William Carent.

Minehead

1. Alexander Luttrell (6/42 Dec.). Sir Francis Popham (8/44 Dec.).
2. Thomas Hanham (1/44 Dis.).
3. Edward Popham (12/48). Walter Strickland.

Taunton

1. George Searle. Sir William Portman, Bt. (2/44 Dis.).
3. John Palmer.

Wells

1. Sir Ralph Hopton (8/42 Dis.). Sir Edward Rodney (8/42 Dis.).
3. Lislibone Long. Clement Walker (12/48 Sec.).

WILTSHIRE

County

1. Sir Henry Ludlow (12/45 Dec.). Sir James Thynne (2/43 Dis.).
3. James Herbert (12/48 Sec.). Edmund Ludlow.

Great Bedwin

1. Sir Walter Smith (2/44 Dis.). Richard Harding (1/44 Dis.).
3. Edmund Harvey. Henry Hungerford (12/48).

Calne

1. George Lowe (2/44 Dis.). Hugh Rogers.
3. Rowland Wilson (2/50 Dec.).

Chippenham

1. Sir Edward Baynton.* Sir Edward Hungerford (10/48 Dec.).
3. William Eyre.

Cricklade

1. Robert Jenner (12/48 Sec.). Thomas Hodges (12/48).

Devizes

1. Edward Baynton (12/48 Sec.). Robert Nicholas.

Downton

1. Anthony Ashley Cooper*† (Admitted 1/60).[1] Sir Edward Griffin (2/44 Dis.).
3. Alexander Thistlethwaite (12/48 Sec.).

Heytesbury

1. Thomas Moore (12/48 Sec.). Edward Ashe.

[1] See p. 22.

Hindon

1. Sir Miles Fleetwood (3/41 Dec.). Robert Reynolds.
2. Thomas Bennett* (?/44 Dis.).
3. [George How.] [1]

Ludgershall

1. William Ashburnham (12/41 Exp.). Sir John Evelyn (12/48 Sec.).
2. Walter Long (12/48 Sec.).

Malmesbury

1. Sir Neville Poole (12/48 Sec.). Anthony Hungerford (6/44 Dis.).
3. Sir John Danvers.

Marlborough

1. John Francklyn (?/45 Dec.). Sir Francis Seymour (2/41 Peer).
2. Philip Smith.
3. Charles Fleetwood.

Old Sarum

1. Robert Cecil (12/48). Edward Herbert (1/41 Attorney-General).
2. Sir William Saville, Bt. (9/42 Dis.).
3. Roger Kirkham (11/46 Dec.). Sir Richard Lucy, Bt.

Salisbury

1. Robert Hyde* (8/42 Dis.). Michael Oldsworth.*
3. John Dove.

Westbury

1. William Wheeler (12/48 Sec.). John Ashe.

Wilton

1. Sir Henry Vane, senior. Sir Benjamin Rudyard (12/48 Sec.).

Wootton Bassett

1. William Pleydall (2/44 Dis.). Edward Poole (12/48 Sec.).
3. Edward Massey (12/48 Sec.).

[1] See p. 23.

ALPHABETICAL LIST OF MEMBERS

Col. 1.

    R = Royalist.[1]
    S = Straffordian.[2]
    Py = Parliamentarian.
   Rec = Recruiter.
    x = Died too early to be classified as Royalist or Parliamentarian.

Col. 2.

    P = Secluded at Pride's Purge.[3]
    p = Ceased to sit at Pride's Purge.[4]
    d = Expelled or disabled before Pride's Purge.
    L = In House of Lords before Pride's Purge.
    x = Died before Pride's Purge.
    I = Sat in the Rump.[5]
    w = Signed the death-warrant of Charles I.

Col. 3.

    b = Sat in Parliament before 1640.
    x = Too young to have sat before 1640.

Col. 4.

    a = Sat in the Cavalier Parliament or later.
    x = Died before the Cavalier Parliament.
    L = In House of Lords before the Cavalier Parliament.

[1] For the definition of 'Royalist' see p. 14.

[2] This includes all names that appear either on the list posted in Old Palace Yard, and reprinted in Rushworth, *Historical Collections*, Part III, Vol. I, p. 248, or in Verney's *Notes of Proceedings* (Camden Society, 31, p. 57). Where the lists give only a surname which could indicate one of two or more members, each member is marked 's'.

[3] This includes members who appear on any of the lists of those secluded and were not re-admitted.

[4] I.e. members who could have sat in the Rump but do not appear in the *Journals* as taking part in its proceedings.

[5] For the definition of these 'Independents' see p. 41.

		1	2	3	4
ABBOT, George	Tamworth	Rec	*p*	.	x
ABBOT, George	Guildford	Py	x	.	x
ACTON, Edward	Bridgnorth	R	d	.	x
ALDEBURGH, Richard	Aldborough	RS	d	b	x
ALDWORTH, Richard	Bristol	Rec	I	.	x
ALFORD, Sir Edward	Arundel	RS	d	b	x
ALFORD, John	Shoreham	PyS	P	.	x
ALLANSON, Sir William	York	Py	I	.	x
ALLEN, Francis	Cockermouth	Rec	I	.	x
ALLEN, Matthew	Weymouth & M.R.	Rec	P	.	x
ALLESTREY, William	Derby	R	d	.	x
ALURED, John	Hedon	Py	Iw	.	x
ANDERSON, Sir Henry	Newcastle-on-Tyne	R	d	b	x
ANDREWS, Robert	Weobley	Rec	I	.	.
ANLABY, John	Scarborough	Rec	I	x	.
ANNESLEY, Arthur	RADNORSHIRE	Rec	P	x	L
APSLEY, Edward	Steyning	Rec	I	.	x
ARMINE, Sir William, Bt.	Grantham	Py	I	b	x
ARMINE, William	CUMBERLAND	Rec	I	x	.
ARTHINGTON, Henry	Pontefract	Rec	I	x	.
ARUNDELL, John	Bodmin	R*s*	x	x	x
ARUNDELL, John	W. Looe	Rec	P	.	.
ARUNDELL, Richard	Lostwithiel	R*s*	d	x	a
ARUNDELL, Thomas	W. Looe	Py	x	.	x
ASHBURNHAM, John	Hastings	R	d	.	a
ASHBURNHAM, William	Ludgershall	R	d	.	a
ASHE, Edward	Heytesbury	Py	I	.	x
ASHE, James	Bath	Rec	I	x	.
ASHE, John	Westbury	Py	I	.	x
ASHURST, William	Newton	Py	*p*	.	x
ASSHETON, Ralph	LANCASHIRE	Py	P	.	x
ASSHETON, Ralph	Clitheroe	Py	P	.	a
ATKINS, Thomas	Norwich	Rec	I	.	.
AYSCOUGH, Sir Edward	LINCOLNSHIRE	Py	P	b	x
AYSCOUGH, William	Thirsk	Rec	P	x	.
BACON, Francis	Ipswich	Rec	I	.	.
BACON, Nathaniel	Cambridge Univ.	Rec	I	.	x
BAGOT, Sir Hervey	STAFFORDSHIRE	R	d	b	x
BAGSHAWE, Edward	Southwark	R	d	.	.
BAKER, John	E. Grinstead	Rec	I	.	.
BALDWIN, Charles	Ludlow	R	d	.	.
BALL, William	Abingdon	Rec	x	.	x
BAMPFIELD, John	Penryn	Py	*p*	x	x

		1	2	3	4
BARKER, John	Coventry	Py	I	.	.
BARNARDISTON, Sir Nathaniel	SUFFOLK	Py	p	b	x
BARNARDISTON, Sir Thomas	Bury St. Edmunds	Rec	P	x	.
BARNEHAM, Sir Francis	Maidstone	Py	x	b	x
BARRINGTON, Sir John, Bt.	Newtown	Rec	P	x	a
BARRINGTON, Sir Thomas, Bt.	Colchester	Py	x	b	x
BARROWE, Maurice	Eye	Rec	P	.	.
BARWIS, Richard	Carlisle	Py	p	b	x
BASSETT, William	Bath	R	d	.	x
BAYNTON, Sir Edward	Chippenham	Py	I	b	x
BAYNTON, Edward	Devizes	Py	P	x	a
BEDINGFIELD, Anthony	Dunwich	Py	p	.	x
BELASYSE, Henry	YORKSHIRE	R	d	b	x
BELASYSE, John	Thirsk	R	d	x	L
BELL, William	Westminster	Py	P	.	.
BELLINGHAM, Sir Henry, Bt.	WESTMORLAND	R	d	b	x
BELLINGHAM, James	WESTMORLAND	Rec	p	x	x
BENCE, Alexander	Aldeburgh	Py	P	.	.
BENCE, Squire	Aldeburgh	Py	x	.	x
BENNET, Robert	W. Looe	Rec	I	.	.
BENNETT, Thomas	Hindon	R	d	.	.
BENSON, Henry	Knaresborough	R	x	b	x
BIDDULPH, Michael	Lichfield	Rec	P	.	x
BINDLOSSE, Sir Robert, Bt.	Lancaster	Rec	P	x	.
BINGHAM, John	Shaftesbury	Rec	I	x	.
BIRCH, John	Leominster	Rec	P	x	a
BIRCH, Thomas	Liverpool	Rec	I	.	.
BLAGRAVE, Daniel	Reading	Rec	Iw	.	.
BLAKE, Robert	Bridgwater	Rec	I	.	x
BLAKISTON, John	Newcastle-on-Tyne	Py	Iw	.	x
BLUDDER, Sir Thomas	Reigate	R	d	b	x
BOARD, Herbert	Steyning	Rec	x	.	x
BODVILLE, John	ANGLESEY	R	d	x	.
BOND, Denis	Dorchester	Py	I	.	x
BOND, John	Weymouth & M.R.	Rec	P	x	.
BOONE, Thomas	Dartmouth	Rec	I	x	.
BOOTE, Edward	Portsmouth	Rec	p	.	x
BOOTH, George	CHESHIRE	Rec	P	x	L
BOSCAWEN, Hugh	CORNWALL	Rec	P	x	a
BOSVILE, Godfrey	Warwick	Py	I	.	x
BOUGHTON, Thomas	WARWICKSHIRE	Rec	P	.	.
BOURCHIER, Sir John	Ripon	Rec	Iw	b	x
BOWYER, John	STAFFORDSHIRE	Rec	P	x	.

		1	2	3	4
Bowyer, Sir Thomas, Bt.	Bramber	R	d	.	x
Bowyer, Sir William	STAFFORDSHIRE	Py	x	b	x
Boyle, Richard, Viscount Dungarvan	Appleby	R	L	x	L
Boynton, Sir Matthew, Bt.	Scarborough	Rec	x	b	x
Boys, Sir Edward	Dover	Py	x	b	x
Boys, John	KENT	Rec	P	b	x
Brereton, Sir William, Bt.	CHESHIRE	Py	I.	b	.
Brett, Henry	Gloucester	R	d	.	.
Brewster, Robert	Dunwich	Rec	I	.	.
Bridgman, Orlando	Wigan	RS	d	.	.
Briggs, Sir Humphrey	Much Wenlock	Rec	P	x	.
Brooke, Sir John	Appleby	R	d	b	x
Brooke, Peter	Newton	Rec	I	x	.
Browne, Sir Ambrose, Bt.	SURREY	Py	P	b	.
Browne, John	DORSET	Py	I	b	x
Browne, Richard	New Romney	Py	p	.	x
Browne, Richard	Wycombe	Rec	P	.	a
Browne, Samuel	Dartmouth	Py	P	.	.
Broxholme, John	Lincoln	Py	x	.	x
Bulkeley, John	Newtown	Rec	P	x	a
Buller, Francis	E. Looe	Py	P	b	.
Buller, George	Saltash	Py	x	.	x
Buller, Sir Richard	Fowey	Py	x	b	x
Burgoyne, Sir John, Bt.	WARWICKSHIRE	Rec	P	.	x
Burgoyne, Sir Roger, Bt.	BEDFORDSHIRE	Py	P	x	.
Burlace, John	Corfe Castle	R	d	x	a
Burrell, Abraham	Huntingdon	Rec	I	.	x
Button, John	New Lymington	Py	P	b	.
Bysshe, Edward	Bletchingley	Py	P	.	a
Cage, William	Ipswich	Py	x	b	x
Campbell, James	Grampound	Py	P	.	x
Campion, Henry	New Lymington	Py	p	b	x
Capel, Arthur	HERTFORDSHIRE	R	L	b	x
Carent, William	Milborne Port	Rec	I	.	.
Carey, Lucius, Viscount Falkland	Newport I.o.W.	R	x	x	x
Carew, Alexander	CORNWALL	R	x	x	x
Carew, John	Tregony	Rec	Iw	x	x
Carnaby, Sir William	Morpeth	RS	x	b	x
Carr, Charles, Lord	Mitchell	Rec	P	x	a
Catelyn, Richard	Norwich	R	x	.	x
Cave, Sir Richard	Lichfield	R	x	.	x

			1	2	3	4
CAWLEY, William	Midhurst		Py	Iw	b	.
CECIL, Charles, Viscount Cranborne	Hertford		Py	*p*	x	x
CECIL, Robert	Old Sarum		Py	*p*	x	.
CECIL, William, Earl of Salisbury	King's Lynn		Rec	I	b	L
CEELEY, Thomas	Bridport		Rec	P	.	.
CHADWELL, William	Mitchell		R	d	.	.
CHALONER, James	Aldborough		Rec	I	.	x
CHALONER, Thomas	Richmond		Rec	Iw	.	.
CHARLTON, Robert	Bridgnorth		Rec	*p*	.	x
CHEEKE, Sir Thomas	Harwich		Py	*p*	b	x
CHETTEL, Francis	Corfe Castle		Rec	*p*	.	x
CHEYNEY, William	Amersham		x	x	x	x
CHICHELE, Thomas	CAMBRIDGESHIRE		RS	d	x	a
CHOLMLEY, Henry	New Malton		Py	P	b	.
CHOLMLEY, Sir Hugh	Scarborough		R	d	b	x
CHOLMLEY, Thomas	Carlisle		Rec	*p*	.	x
CLARKE, Samuel	Exeter		Rec	*p*	.	x
CLEMENT, Gregory	Fowey		Rec	Iw[1]	.	x
CLIFTON, Sir Gervase, Bt.	E. Retford		RS	d	b	a
CLINTON, Edward, Lord	Callington		Rec	P	x	x
CLIVE, Robert	Bridgnorth		Rec	*p*	.	x
CLOTWORTHY, Sir John	Maldon		Py	P	.	.
COKE, Henry	Dunwich		R	d	b	.
COKE, Sir John	DERBYSHIRE		Py	*p*	.	x
COKE, Thomas	Leicester		RS	d	x	x
COMPTON, James, Lord	WARWICKSHIRE		RS	L	x	L
CONINGSBY, Fitzwilliam	HEREFORDSHIRE		R	d	b	.
CONINGSBY, Humphrey	HEREFORDSHIRE		R	d	x	.
CONSTABLE, Sir William, Bt.	Knaresborough		Py	Iw	b	x
CONSTANTINE, William	Poole		R	d	x	.
COOKE, Sir Robert	Tewkesbury		Py	x	.	x
COOPER, Sir Anthony Ashley, Bt.	Downton		2	.	x	L
COPLEY, Lionel	Bossinney		Rec	P	.	.
CORBET, Sir John, Bt.	SHROPSHIRE		Py	P	.	.
CORBET, Miles	Great Yarmouth		Py	Iw	b	.
CORBETT, John	Bishop's Castle		Rec	I	x	.
CORNWALLIS, Sir Frederick, Bt.	Eye		RS	d	x	L
COVENTRY, John	Evesham		RS	d	x	x

[1] Signature afterwards erased.
[2] Admitted in January 1660. See p. 22.

		1	2	3	4
COWCHER, John	Worcester	Py	*p*	b	x
CRADDOCK, Matthew	London	Py	x	.	x
CRANE, Sir Robert, Bt.	Sudbury	Py	x	b	x
CRESHELD, Richard	Evesham	Py	*p*	b	x
CREWE, John	Brackley	Py	P	b	L
CRIMES, Elisha	Tavistock	Rec	P	x	.
CRISPE, Sir Nicholas	Winchelsea	R	d	.	a
CROKE, Robert	Wendover	R	d	x	a
CROMPTON, Thomas	STAFFORDSHIRE	Rec	I	.	.
CROMWELL, Oliver	Cambridge	Py	Iw	b	x
CROWTHER, William	Weobley	Rec	*p*	.	x
CULPEPPER, Sir John	KENT	R	d	.	x
CURWEN, Sir Patrick	CUMBERLAND	RS	d	b	a
CURZON, Sir John, Bt.	DERBYSHIRE	Py	P	b	.
DACRES, Thomas	Callington	Rec	P	x	.
DACRES, Sir Thomas	HERTFORDSHIRE	Py	P	b	.
DALSTON, Sir George	CUMBERLAND	R	d	b	x
DALSTON, William	Carlisle	R	d	x	.
DANBY, Sir Thomas	Richmond	RS	d	x	x
DANVERS, Sir John	Malmesbury	Rec	Iw	b	x
DARLEY, Henry	Northallerton	Py	I	b	.
DARLEY, Richard	New Malton	Rec	I	.	.
DAVIES, William	Carmarthen	Rec	*p*	.	x
DAVIS, Matthew	Christchurch	R	d	b	.
DENTON, Sir Alexander	Buckingham	R	x	.	x
DERING, Sir Edward, Bt.	KENT	R	x	b	x
DEVEREUX, Sir Walter	Lichfield	Py	x	b	x
DEWES, Sir Simonds	Sudbury	Py	*p*	b	x
DIGBY, George, Lord	DORSET	RS	L	x	L
DIGBY, John	Milborne Port	RS	d	x	.
DIXWELL, John	Dover	Rec	Iw	.	.
DODDRIDGE, John	Barnstaple	Rec	P	x	.
DORMER, John	Buckingham	Rec	I	x	.
DOVE, John	Salisbury	Rec	I	.	.
DOWCE, Edward	Portsmouth	Py	x	b	x
DOWNES, John	Arundel	Py	Iw	.	.
DOYLEY, John	Oxford	Rec	P	.	x
DRAKE, Francis	Amersham	Py	P	.	.
DRAKE, Sir Francis, Bt.	Berealston	Rec	P	x	a
DRAKE, Sir William	Amersham	Py	P	.	a
DRYDEN, Sir John, Bt.	NORTHAMPTONSHIRE	Py	I	.	x
DUNCH, Edmund	Wallingford	Py	I	b	.
DUTTON, John	GLOUCESTERSHIRE	R	d	b	x

		1	2	3	4
EARLE, Erasmus	Norwich	Rec	I	.	.
EDEN, Thomas	Cambridge Univ	Py	x	b	x
EDGECUMBE, Piers	Camelford	R*s*	d	b	a
EDGECUMBE, Richard	Newport, C'wall	R*s*	d	x	x
EDWARDS, Humphrey	SHROPSHIRE	Rec	Iw	.	x
EDWARDS, Richard	Christchurch	Rec	I	.	x
EDWARDS, William	Chester	Rec	P	.	.
EGERTON, Sir Charles	Ripon	Rec	P	.	.
ELFORD, John	Tiverton	Rec	*p*	.	.
ELLIS, William	Boston	Py	I	x	a
ELLISON, Robert	Newcastle-on-Tyne	Rec	P	x	.
ERISEY, Richard	St. Mawes	Py	P	.	.
ERLE, Thomas	Wareham	Py	P	x	x
ERLE, Sir Walter	Weymouth & M.R.	Py	P	.	.
EURE, Sampson	Leominster	R	d	b	x
EVELYN, George	Reigate	Rec	P	x	a
EVELYN, Sir John	Ludgershall	Py	P	b	.
EVELYN, John	Bletchingley	Py	P	b	.
EVERSFIELD, Thomas	Hastings	R	d	x	x
EXTON, Edward	Southampton	Py	*p*	x	.
EYRE, William	Chippenham	Rec	I	x	
FAGGE, John	Rye	Rec	I	x	a
FAIRFAX, Ferdinando, Lord	YORKSHIRE	Py	x	b	x
FAIRFAX, Sir Thomas	Cirencester	Rec	1	x	.
FANE, George	Callington	R	d	x	a
FANSHAWE, Sir Thomas	Hertford	RS	d	b	a
FANSHAWE, Thomas	Lancaster	R	d	.	x
FARNEFOLD, Sir Thomas	Steyning	R	x	b	x
FEILDER, John	St. Ives	Rec	I	.	.
FELL, Thomas	Lancaster	Rec	I	.	x
FENWICK, George	Morpeth	Rec	I	.	x
FENWICK, John	Morpeth	RS	x	x	x
FENWICK, Sir John, Bt.	NORTHUMBERLAND	Py	P	b	x
FENWICK, William	NORTHUMBERLAND	Rec	P	x	a
FERRIS, Richard	Barnstaple	R	d	.	x
FETTIPLACE, John	BERKSHIRE	RS	d	b	.
FIENNES, James	OXFORDSHIRE	Py	P	b	.
FIENNES, John	Morpeth	Rec	P	x	.
FIENNES, Nathaniel	Banbury	Py	P	.	.
FINCH, John	Winchelsea	Py	x	.	x
FITZWILLIAMS, William, Lord	Peterborough	Py	P	x	x
FLEETWOOD, Charles	Marlborough	Rec	I	x	.

[1] Election declared valid 17 Feb. 1649, but he probably did not take his seat.

		1	2	3	4
FLEETWOOD, George	BUCKINGHAMSHIRE	Rec	Iw	x	.
FLEETWOOD, Sir Miles	Hindon	x	x	b	x
FOUNTAINE, Thomas	Wendover	Py	x	.	x
FOWELL, Sir Edmund	Ashburton	Py	P	.	.
FOWELL, Edward	Tavistock	Rec	P	.	.
FOXWIST, William	Caernarvon	Rec	P	x	.
FRANCKLYN, Sir John	MIDDLESEX	Py	x	b	x
FRANCKLYN, John	Marlborough	Py	x	.	x
FRY, John	Shaftesbury	Rec	I	x	x
GAMUL, Francis	Chester	R	d	.	x
GARDNER, Samuel	Evesham	Rec	I	.	.
GARLAND, Augustine	Queenborough	Rec	Iw	.	.
GARTON, Henry	Arundel	x	x	.	x
GAWDY, Framlingham	Thetford	Py	P	b	x
GELL, Thomas	Derby	Rec	P	.	x
GEORGE, John	Cirencester	R	d	b	a
GERARD, Francis	Seaford	Py	P	x	.
GERARD, Sir Gilbert, Bt.	MIDDLESEX	Py	P	b	.
GEWEN, Thomas	Launceston	Rec	P	b	.
GLANVILLE, John	Bristol	R	d	b	.
GLANVILLE, William	Camelford	R	d	x	.
GLYNNE, John	Westminster	Py	P	.	.
GODOLPHIN, Francis	St. Ives	Py	p	.	x
GODOLPHIN, Francis	Helston	R	d	b	.
GODOLPHIN, Sidney	Helston	RS	x	b	x
GOLLOP, George	Southampton	Py	p	b	x
GOODWIN, Arthur	BUCKINGHAMSHIRE	Py	x	b	x
GOODWIN, John	Haslemere	Py	I	.	.
GOODWIN, Ralph	Ludlow	R	d	b	x
GOODWIN, Robert	E. Grinstead	Py	I	b	.
GORGES, Sir Theobald	Cirencester	R	x	.	x
GORING, George	Portsmouth	R	d	.	x
GOTT, Samuel	Winchelsea	Rec	P	x	.
GOULD, Nicholas	Fowey	Rec	I	.	.
GRANTHAM, Thomas	Lincoln	Py	p	x	x
GRATWICK, Roger	Hastings	Rec	I	.	x
GREEN, Giles	Corfe Castle	Py	P	b	x
GRENVILLE, Sir Bevil	CORNWALL	R	x	.	x
GREY, Henry, Lord, of Ruthyn	LEICESTERSHIRE	Py	L	.	x
GREY, Thomas, Lord, of Groby	Leicester	Py	Iw	x	x
GRIFFIN, Sir Edward	Downton	R	d	.	.

		1	2	3	4
GRIFFITH, John	CAERNARVONSHIRE	RS	d	x	x
GRIFFITH, John	Beaumaris	RS	x	b	x
GRIMSTON, Sir Harbottle, Bt.	Harwich	Py	x	b	x
GRIMSTON, Harbottle	Colchester	Py	P	b	a
GROVE, Thomas	Milborne Port	Rec	P	.	.
GURDON, Brampton	Sudbury	Rec	I	.	.
GURDON, John	Ipswich	Py	I	.	.
HALES, Sir Edward, Bt.	Queenborough	R	d	b	x
HALLOWES, Nathaniel	Derby	Py	i	.	.
HAMPDEN, John	BUCKINGHAMSHIRE	Py	x	b	x
HANHAM, Thomas	Minehead	R	d	.	x
HARBY, Edward	Higham Ferrers	Rec	I	.	.
HARDING, Richard	Great Bedwin	R	d	.	.
HARLEY, Edward	HEREFORDSHIRE	Rec	P	x	a
HARLEY, Sir Robert	HEREFORDSHIRE	Py	P	b	x
HARLEY, Robert	New Radnor	Rec	P	x	a
HARMAN, Richard	Norwich	Py	x	.	x
HARRINGTON, Sir James	RUTLAND	Rec	I	.	.
HARRINGTON, John	SOMERSET	Rec	p	.	x
HARRIS, John	Liskeard	R	d	b	x
HARRIS, John	Launceston	Py	P	b	x
HARRISON, John	Lancaster	R	d	.	a
HARRISON, Thomas	Wendover	Rec	Iw	.	x
HARRISON, William	Queenborough	R	x	.	x
HARTNALL, George	Tiverton	R	d	.	.
HARVEY, Edmund	Great Bedwin	Rec	I	.	.
HARVEY, John	Hythe	Py	x	.	x
HASELRIG, Sir Arthur, Bt.	LEICESTERSHIRE	Py	I	.	.
HATCHER, Thomas	Stamford	Py	P	b	.
HATTON, Sir Christopher	Higham Ferrers	R	d	b	L
HATTON, Sir Robert	Castle Rising	RS	d	b	x
HAY, Herbert	Arundel	Rec	P	.	x
HAY, William	Rye	Py	I	.	.
HEALE, Sir Thomas, Bt.	Plympton Earl	R	d	b	a
HEBBLETHWAITE, Thomas	New Malton	R	x	.	x
HERBERT, Edward	Old Sarum	R	d	b	x
HERBERT, Sir Henry	Bewdley	R	d	b	a
HERBERT, Henry	MONMOUTHSHIRE	Py	I	x	x
HERBERT, James	WILTSHIRE	Rec	P	x	a
HERBERT, John	MONMOUTHSHIRE	Rec	I	x	x
HERBERT, Philip, Earl of Pembroke	BERKSHIRE	Rec	I	b	x
HERBERT, Philip, Lord	GLAMORGANSHIRE	Py	I	x	L

		1	2	3	4
HERBERT, Richard	Montgomery	Rs	d	.	x
HERBERT, William	MONMOUTHSHIRE	Rs	x	x	x
HERBERT, William	Cardiff	Rs	x	x	x
HEVENINGHAM, William	Stockbridge	Py	I	.	.
HEYMAN, Henry	Hythe	Py	I	x	x
HEYMAN, Sir Peter	Dover	x	x	b	x
HILL, Roger	Bridport	Py	I	.	.
HIPPISLEY, Sir John	Cockermouth	Py	I	b	x
HOBART, Sir John, Bt.	NORFOLK	Rec	x	b	x
HOBY, Peregrine	Great Marlow	Py	P	.	a
HODGES, Luke	Bristol	Rec	I	.	x
HODGES, Thomas	Cricklade	Py	p	.	.
HODGES, Thomas	Ilchester	Rec	P	.	x
HOLBORNE, Robert	Mitchell	RS	x	.	x
HOLCROFT, John	Wigan	Rec	P	.	x
HOLLAND, Cornelius	New Windsor	Py	I	.	.
HOLLAND, Sir John, Bt.	Castle Rising	Py	P	.	a
HOLLES, Denzil	Dorchester	Py	P	b	a
HOLLES, Francis	Lostwithiel	Rec	P	x	a
HOLLES, Gervase	Grimsby	R	d	.	a
HOOKE, Humphrey	Bristol	R	d	.	x
HOPTON, Sir Ralph	Wells	R	d	b	x
HORNER, George	SOMERSET	Rec	P	.	.
HOSKINS, Bennett	Hereford	Rec	P	x	.
HOTHAM, Sir John, Bt.	Beverley	R	x	b	x
HOTHAM, John	Scarborough	R	x	x	x
HOUGHTON, Richard	LANCASHIRE	Rec	P	x	.
HOWARD, Charles, Lord	Oxford	R	L	x	L
HOWARD, of Escrick, Edward, Lord	Carlisle	Rec	I	b	L
HOWARD, Sir Robert	Bishop's Castle	R	d	b	x
HOWARD, Thomas	Wallingford	R	d	x	.
HOYLE, Thomas	York	Py	I	b	x
HUNGERFORD, Anthony	Malmesbury	R	d	.	x
HUNGERFORD, Sir Edward	Chippenham	Py	x	b	x
HUNGERFORD, Henry	Great Bedwin	Rec	p	x	.
HUNT, Robert	Ilchester	R	d	x	.
HUNT, Thomas	Shrewsbury	Rec	P	.	.
HUSSEY, Thomas	Grantham	R	x	x	x
HUSSEY, Thomas	Whitchurch	Rec	I	.	x
HUTCHINSON, John	NOTTINGHAMSHIRE	Rec	Iw	x	.
HUTCHINSON, Sir Thomas	NOTTINGHAMSHIRE	Py	x	b	x
HYDE, Edward	Saltash	R	d	x	L

		1	2	3	4
HYDE, Robert	Salisbury	RS	d	.	.
INGOLDSBY, Richard	Wendover	Rec	Iw	x	a
INGRAM, Sir Arthur	Callington	Py	x	b	x
INGRAM, Sir Thomas	Thirsk	R	d	x	a
IRBY, Sir Anthony	Boston	Py	P	b	a
IRETON, Henry	Appleby	Rec	Iw	x	x
JACOB, Sir John	Rye	R	d	.	.
JANE, Joseph	Liskeard	RS	d	b	x
JENNER, Robert	Cricklade	Py	P	.	x
JENNINGS, Sir John	St. Albans	Py	x	b	x
JENNINGS, Richard	St. Albans	Py	P	x	a
JEPHSON, William	Stockbridge	Py	p	.	x
JERMYN, Sir Thomas	Bury St. Edmunds	R	x	b	x
JERMYN, Thomas	Bury St. Edmunds	R	d	b	x
JERVOISE, Richard	Whitchurch	Py	x	.	x
JERVOISE, Sir Thomas	Whitchurch	Py	I	b	x
JESSON, William	Coventry	Py	p	.	x
JONES, Arthur	Weobley	R	d	x	.
JONES, John	MERIONETHSHIRE	Rec	Iw	.	x
JONES, Philip	BRECONSHIRE	Rec	I	x	.
JONES, William	Beaumaris	Rec	P	.	.
KEKEWICH, George	Liskeard	Rec	P	.	.
KEMP, John	Christchurch	Rec	p	.	x
KILLIGREW, Henry	W. Looe	R	x	.	x
KING, Richard	Weymouth & M.R.	R	x	.	x
KIRKBY, Roger	LANCASHIRE	R	d	.	x
KIRKHAM, Roger	Old Sarum	Rec	x	.	x
KNATCHBULL, Sir Norton	New Romney	Py	P	.	a
KNIGHTLEY, Richard	Northampton	Py	P	x	.
KNOLLYS, Sir Francis, senior	Reading	Py	x	b	x
KNOLLYS, Sir Francis, junior	Reading	Py	x	b	x
KYRLE, Walter	Leominster	Py	p	.	x
KYRTON, Edward	Milborne Port	RS	d	b	x
LANE, Thomas	Wycombe	Py	P	b	x
LANGTON, William	Preston	Rec	p	x	x
LASCELLES, Francis	Thirsk	Rec	I	x	.
LAWRENCE, Henry	WESTMORLAND	Rec	P	.	.
LEACH, Nicholas	Newport, C'wall	Rec	x	x	x
LECHMERE, Nicholas	Bewdley	Rec	I	x	.
LEE, Sir Richard, Bt.	SHROPSHIRE	RS	d	.	x
LEE, Richard	Rochester	Py	p	x	.
LEEDES, Thomas	Steyning	R	x	.	x
LEGH, Peter	Newton	R	x	x	x

9

		1	2	3	4
Le Gros, Sir Charles	Orford	Py	p	b	x
Leigh, Edward	Stafford	Rec	P	.	.
Leigh, Sir John	Yarmouth, I.o.W.	Py	P	.	.
Leman, William	Hertford	Rec	I	.	.
Lenthall, John	Gloucester	Rec	I	x	.
Lenthall, William	Woodstock	Py	I	b	.
Leveson, Sir Richard	Newcastle, Staffs	R	d	b	.
Lewis, Lewis	Brecon	Rec	P	x	.
Lewis, Sir William, Bt.	Petersfield	Py	P	.	a
Lewkenor, Christopher	Chichester	R	d	b	x
Lisle, John	Winchester	Py	I	x	.
Lister, Sir John	Hull	x	x	b	x
Lister, Sir Martin	Brackley	Py	P	.	.
Lister, Thomas	Lincoln	Rec	I	.	x
Lister, Sir William	E. Retford	Rec	P	.	.
Littleton, Sir Edward, Bt.	STAFFORDSHIRE	R	d	.	x
Littleton, Thomas	Much Wenlock	R	d	x	a
Livesey, Sir Michael, Bt.	Queenborough	Rec	Iw	x	.
Lloyd, Francis	Carmarthen	RS	d	x	.
Lloyd, John	CARMARTHENSHIRE	Rec	P	x	.
Lloyd, Walter	CARDIGANSHIRE	RS	d	.	.
Long, Lislibone	Wells	Rec	I	x	x
Long, Walter	Ludgershall	Py	P	b	.
Longe, Richard	Bristol	R	d	.	x
Love, Nicholas	Winchester	Rec	I	x	.
Lowe, George	Calne	R	d	b	a
Lower, Thomas	E. Looe	R	d	x	.
Lowry, John	Cambridge	Py	I	.	.
Lucas, Henry	Cambridge Univ.	Py	P	.	.
Luckyn, Capel	Harwich	Rec	P	x	a
Lucy, Sir Richard, Bt.	Old Sarum	Rec	I	.	.
Lucy, Sir Thomas	Warwick	x	x	b	x
Ludlow, Edmund	WILTSHIRE	Rec	Iw	x	.
Ludlow, Sir Henry	WILTSHIRE	Py	x	b	x
Luke, Sir Oliver	BEDFORDSHIRE	Py	P	b	x
Luke, Sir Samuel	Bedford	Py	P	.	.
Lumley, Sir Martin, Bt.	ESSEX	Py	P	.	x
Luttrell, Alexander	Minehead	Py	x	x	x
Lytton, Sir William	HERTFORDSHIRE	Py	P	b	x
Mackworth, Thomas	Ludlow	Rec	I	x	.
Mallory, John	Ripon	Rs	d	x	x
Mallory, William	Ripon	Rs	x	b	x
Manaton, Ambrose	Launceston	R	d	b	x

		1	2	3	4
MANSFIELD, Charles, Viscount	E. Retford	R	d	x	x
MARLOTT, William	Shoreham	Py	x	b	x
MARTEN, Henry	BERKSHIRE	Py	Iw	.	.
MARTYN, Christopher	Plympton Earl	Rec	I	.	.
MARTYN, Sir Nicholas	DEVONSHIRE	Rec	P	?.	x
MASHAM, Sir William, Bt.	ESSEX	Py	I	b	x
MASHAM, William	Shrewsbury	Rec	I	x	x
MASSEY, Edward	Wootton Bassett	Rec	P	.	a
MASTERS, Sir Edward	Canterbury	Py	x	.	x
MATTHEW, Roger	Dartmouth	R	x	b	x
MAULEVERER, Thomas	Boroughbridge	Py	Iw	.	x
MAY, Thomas	Midhurst	R	d	.	x
MAYNARD, John	Totnes	Py	P	b	a
MAYNARD, Sir John	Lostwithiel	Rec	p	b	x
MAYNE, Simon	Aylesbury	Rec	Iw	x	.
MELTON, Sir John	Newcastle-on-Tyne	x	x	.	x
MEUX, John	Newtown	R	d	x	x
MEYRICK, Sir John	Newcastle, Staffs.	Py	P	.	x
MIDDLETON, Sir Thomas	DENBIGHSHIRE	Py	P	b	.
MIDDLETON, Thomas	Flint	Rec	P	x	a
MIDDLETON, Thomas	Horsham	Py	p	.	?
MILDMAY, Sir Henry	Maldon	Py	I	b	.
MILLINGTON, Gilbert	Nottingham	Py	Iw	.	.
MONTAGU, Edward	HUNTINGDONSHIRE	Rec	P	x	L
MONTAGU, Edward	Huntingdon	Py	L	x	L
MONTAGU, George	Huntingdon	Py	P	x	a
MONTAGU, Sir Sidney	HUNTINGDONSHIRE	R	x	.	x
MOODY, Miles	Ripon	Rec	x	.	x
MOORE, John	Liverpool	Py	Iw	.	x
MOORE, Poynings	Haslemere	Py	p	b	x
MOORE, Thomas	Heytesbury	Py	P	x	a
MORE, Richard	Bishop's Castle	Py	x	b	x
MORE, Thomas	Ludlow	Rec	p	.	.
MORGAN, William	BRECONSHIRE	Py	p	.	x
MORICE, William	DEVONSHIRE	Rec	P[1]	.	a
MORLEY, Herbert	Lewes	Py	I	x	a
MORLEY, Sir William	Chichester	R	d	b	x
MOSTYN, John	FLINTSHIRE	R	x	b	x
MOUNDEFORD, Sir Edmund	NORFOLK	Py	x	b	x
MOUNSON, William, Viscount	Reigate	Py	I	x	.
MOYLE, John	St. Germans	Py	p[2]	x	x

[1] Elected August 1648, but probably did not take his seat before Pride's Purge, when he was secluded.   [2] Perhaps deceased. See p. 22.

		1	2	3	4
MOYLE, John	E. Looe	Rec	I	.	.
MUSGRAVE, Sir Philip, Bt.	WESTMORLAND	R	d	.	a
NAPIER, Gerard	Weymouth & M.R.	R	d	b	.
NAPIER, Sir Robert, Bt.	Peterborough	Py	P	b	.
NASH, John	Worcester	Py	P	.	.
NEEDHAM, Sir Robert	Haverfordwest	Rec	P	.	.
NELTHORPE, James	Beverley	Rec	I	x	.
NELTHORPE, John	Beverley	Rec	P	x	.
NEVILLE, Edward	E. Retford	Rec	.¹	x	.
NEVILLE, Henry	Abingdon	Rec	I	x	.
NEWPORT, Francis	Shrewsbury	RS	d	x	L
NICHOLAS, Robert	Devizes	Py	I	.	.
NICHOLS, Anthony	Bodmin	Py	p	x	x
NIXON, John	Oxford	Rec	P	.	.
NOBLE, Michael	Lichfield	Py	p	.	x
NOEL, Baptist	RUTLAND	RS	L	x	L
NORTH, Sir Dudley	CAMBRIDGESHIRE	Py	P	b	.
NORTH, Sir Roger	Eye	Py	I	b	x
NORTHCOTE, Sir John, Bt.	Ashburton	Py	P	.	a
NORTON, Sir Gregory, Bt.	Midhurst	Rec	Iw	x	x
NORTON, Richard	HAMPSHIRE	Rec	I	x	a
NORTON, Simon	Coventry	x	x	.	x
NUTT, John	Canterbury	Py	I	.	.
OGLE, Sir William	Winchester	R	d	.	.
OLDSWORTH, Michael	Salisbury	Py	I	b	.
ONSLOW, Arthur	Bramber	Py	P	x	a
ONSLOW, Sir Richard	SURREY	Py	P	b	.
OWEN, Arthur	PEMBROKESHIRE	Rec	P	.	a
OWEN, Hugh	Pembroke	Py	p	b	.
OWFIELD, Samuel	Gatton	Py	x	b	x
OWFIELD, William	Gatton	Rec	P	.	.
OWNER, Edward	Great Yarmouth	Py	p	b	x
OXENDEN, Henry	Winchelsea	Rec	P	x	.
PACKER, Robert	Wallingford	Rec	P	x	a
PACKINGTON, Sir John, Bt.	Aylesbury	R	d	x	a
PALGRAVE, Sir John	NORFOLK	Rec	P	.	.
PALMER, Geoffrey	Stamford	R	d	.	.
PALMER, John	Taunton	Rec	I	.	x
PALMER, Sir Roger	Newton	R	d	b	x
PALMES, Sir Guy	RUTLAND	R	d	b	x
PARKER, Sir Philip	SUFFOLK	Py	P	.	.

¹ Elected 21 Dec. 1648, but took no active part in the Rump.

		1	2	3	4
PARKER, Sir Thomas	Seaford	Py	p	.	.
PARKHURST, Sir Robert	Guildford	Py	p	b	x
PARRY, George	St. Mawes	RS	d	.	x
PARTRIDGE, Sir Edward	Sandwich	Py	P	.	.
PEARD, George	Barnstaple	Py	x	.	x
PEEK, Henry	Chichester	Rec	P	.	.
PELHAM, Henry	Grantham	Py	P	b	.
PELHAM, John	Hastings	Rec	P	x	a
PELHAM, Peregrine	Hull	Py	Iw	.	x
PELHAM, Sir Thomas, Bt.	SUSSEX	Py	P	b	x
PENNINGTON, Isaac	London	Py	I	.	x
PENNYMAN, Sir William, Bt.	Richmond	RS	x	.	x
PENROSE, John	Helston	Rec	p	x	x
PERCEVAL, John	King's Lynn	Py	x	.	x
PERCEVAL, Sir Philip	Newport, Cornwall	Rec	x	.	x
PERCY, Henry	NORTHUMBERLAND	R	d	b	x
PEYTON, Sir Thomas, Bt.	Sandwich	R	d	x	a
PHILLIPPS, Edward	Ilchester	R	d	x	a
PICKERING, Sir Gilbert, Bt.	NORTHAMPTONSHIRE	Py	I	x	.
PIERREPONT, Francis	Nottingham	Rec	I	x	x
PIERREPONT, William	Much Wenlock	Py	P	.	.
PIGOT, Gervase	NOTTINGHAMSHIRE	Rec	I	x	.
PILE, Sir Francis, Bt.	BERKSHIRE	Rec	p	x	x
PLAYTERS, Sir William, Bt.	Orford	Py	P	.	.
PLEYDALL, William	Wootton Bassett	R	d	.	.
POLLARD, Hugh	Berealston	RS	x	b	x
POLWHELE, John	Tregony	R	d	.	.
POOLE, Edward	Wootton Bassett	Py	P	x	a
POOLE, Sir Neville	Malmesbury	Py	P	b	x
POOLE, William	Honiton	R	x	x	x
POPE, Roger	MERIONETHSHIRE	Rec	x	.	x
POPHAM, Alexander	Bath	Py	I	.	a
POPHAM, Edward	Minehead	Rec	p	x	x
POPHAM, Sir Francis	Minehead	Py	x	b	x
PORTER, Endymion	Droitwich	RS	d	.	x
PORTMAN, Sir William, Bt.	Taunton	RS	x	x	x
POTTER, Hugh	Plympton Earl	Py	P	.	a
POTTS, John	NORFOLK	Py	P	.	.
POULETT, Sir John	SOMERSET	R	d	x	L
POVEY, Thomas	Liskeard	Rec	P	x	.
PRICE, Charles	RADNORSHIRE	RS	x	b	x
PRICE, Herbert '	Brecon	Rs	d	.	a
PRICE, Sir John, Bt.	MONTGOMERYSHIRE	R	d	.	x

9*

		1	2	3	4
Price, William	Merionethshire	R*s*	d	x	a
Prideaux, Edmund	Lyme Regis	Py	I	.	x
Priestley, William	St. Mawes	Rec	P	.	.
Prynne, William	Newport, Cornwall	Rec	P	.	a
Pryse, Sir Richard, Bt.	Cardiganshire	Rec	P	x	x
Purefoy, William	Warwick	Py	Iw	b	x
Pury, Thomas	Gloucester	Py	I	.	.
Pury, Thomas	Monmouth	Rec	I	x	.
Pye, Sir Robert	New Woodstock	Py	P	b	.
Pym, Alexander	Newport, Cornwall	Rec	p	x	.
Pym, Charles	Berealston	Py	P	x	.
Pym, John	Tavistock	Py	x	b	x
Pyne, John	Poole	Py	I	b	.
Rainsborough, Thomas	Droitwich	Rec	x	x	x
Rainsborough, William	Aldeburgh	Py	x	.	x
Rainsford, Sir Henry	Andover	x	x	.	x
Raleigh, Carew	Haslemere	Rec	I	.	.
Rashleigh, Jonathan	Fowey	R	d	b	a
Ratcliffe, John	Chester	Rec	P	x	a
Ravenscroft, Hall	Horsham	Py	P	.	.
Reynolds, Robert	Hindon	Py	I	.	.
Rich, Charles	Sandwich	Rec	P	x	.
Rich, Nathaniel	Cirencester	Rec	I	x	.
Rich, Robert, Lord	Essex	R	L	x	x
Rigby, Alexander	Wigan	Py	I	.	x
Rivers, James	Lewes	x	x	.	x
Robinson, Luke	Scarborough	Rec	I	x	.
Rodney, Sir Edward	Wells	R	d	b	x
Roe, Sir Thomas	Oxford Univ.	Py	x	b	x
Rogers, Hugh	Calne	Py	I	.	x
Rogers, Richard,	Dorset	R	d	x	x
Rolle, John	Truro	Py	x	b	x
Rolle, Sir Samuel	Devonshire	Py	x	b	x
Rose, Richard	Lyme Regis	Py	p	.	x
Rossiter, Edward	Grimsby	Rec	P	x	.
Rous, Francis	Truro	Py	I	b	x
Rudyard, Sir Benjamin	Wilton	Py	P	b	x
Russell, Francis	Cambridgeshire	Rec	I	x	.
Russell, John	Tavistock	R	d	x	.
Russell, William, Lord	Tavistock	R	L	x	L
Sackville, Richard, Lord Buckhurst	E. Grinstead	RS	d	x	L
Sainthill, Peter	Tiverton	R	x	.	x

		1	2	3	4
St. John, Sir Beauchamp	Bedford	Py	P	b	.
St. John, Oliver	Totnes	Py	I	.	.
Salusbury, John	Flint	R	d	x	.
Salway, Humphrey	WORCESTERSHIRE	Py	I	.	x
Salway, Richard	Appleby	Rec	I	x	.
Sandford, Sir Thomas	Cockermouth	R	d	x	x
Sandys, Samuel	Droitwich	R	d	x	a
Sandys, Thomas	Gatton	Py	P	.	x
Sandys, William	Evesham	R	d	x	a
Saville, Sir William, Bt.	Old Sarum	R	x	x	x
Say, William	Camelford	Rec	Iw	.	.
Sayer, John	Colchester	Rec	p	.	x
Scawen, Robert	Berwick	SPy	P	.	a
Scott, Thomas	Aldborough	Rec	x	.	x
Scott, Thomas	Aylesbury	Rec	Iw	.	x
Scudamore, James	Hereford	R	d	x	a
Seaborne, Richard	Hereford	R	d	.	.
Searle, George	Taunton	Py	I	.	.
Selden, John	Oxford Univ.	SPy	P	b	x
Seymour, Edward	DEVONSHIRE	R	d	x	a
Seymour, Sir Francis	Marlborough	R	L	b	L
Seymour, Sir John	GLOUCESTERSHIRE	Rec	P	.	.
Shapcote, Robert	Tiverton	Rec	P	x	a
Shelley, Henry	Lewes	Py	p	.	x
Shuckburgh, Richard	WARWICKSHIRE	R	d	.	x
Shuttleworth, Richard	Clitheroe	Py	x	x	x
Shuttleworth, Richard	Preston	Py	P	.	.
Sidney, Algernon	Cardiff	Rec	I	x	.
Sidney, Philip, Lord Lisle	Yarmouth, I.o.W.	Py	I	.	.
Skeffington, Sir Richard	STAFFORDSHIRE	Rec	x	b	x
Skinner, Augustine	KENT	Py	I	.	.
Skippon, Philip	Barnstaple	Rec	I	.	x
Skutt, George	Poole	Rec	P	.	.
Slaning, Sir Nicholas	Penryn	RS	x	.	x
Slingsby, Sir Henry, Bt.	Knaresborough	RS	d	b	x
Smith, Henry	LEICESTERSHIRE	Rec	I	x	.
Smith, John	Oxford	R	d	.	x
Smith, Philip	Marlborough	Py	I	x	.
Smith, Sir Thomas	Chester	R	d	x	a
Smith, Thomas	Bridgwater	R	x	.	x
Smith, Sir Walter	Great Bedwin	R	x	.	x
Smith, William	Winchelsea	R	d	x	a
Snelling, George	Southwark	Rec	I	.	x
Sneyd, Ralph	Stafford	R	d	x	x

		1	2	3	4
SNOW, Simon	Exeter	Py	P	.	.
SOAME, Thomas	London	Py	P	.	.
SPELMAN, John	Castle Rising	Rec	P	.	.
SPENCER, Sir Edward	MIDDLESEX	Rec	p	b	x
SPRING, Sir William, Bt.	Bury St. Edmunds	Rec	P	x	x
SPRINGATE, Herbert	Shoreham	Rec	P	x	a
SPURSTOW, William	Shrewsbury	Py	x	.	x
STANDISH, Thomas	Preston	Py	x	b	x
STANHOPE, Ferdinand	Tamworth	R	x	x	x
STANHOPE, William	Nottingham	R	d	.	.
STAPLETON, Brian	Aldborough	Rec	p	x	x
STAPLETON, Henry	Boroughbridge	Rec	P	x	.
STAPLETON, Sir Philip	Boroughbridge	Py	x	.	x
STAPLEY, Anthony	SUSSEX	Py	Iw	b	x
STARRE, George	Shaftesbury	Rec	x	.	x
STAWELL, Sir John	SOMERSET	R	d	b	a
STEPHENS, Edward	Tewkesbury	Py	P	.	.
STEPHENS, John	Tewkesbury	Rec	I	x	a
STEPHENS, Nathaniel	GLOUCESTERSHIRE	Py	P	b	x
STEPHENS, William	Newport, I.o.W.	Rec	I	x	x
STEPNEY, Sir John, Bt.	Haverfordwest	R	d	.	x
STOCKDALE, Thomas	Knaresborough	Rec	I	.	x
STONEHOUSE, Sir George, Bt.	Abingdon	R	d	.	a
STOUGHTON, Nicholas	Guildford	Rec	x	b	x
STRANGWAYS, Giles	Bridport	R	d	x	a
STRANGWAYS, Sir John	Weymouth & M.R.	RS[1]	d	b	a
STRICKLAND, Robert	Aldborough	R	d	b	.
STRICKLAND, Walter	Minehead	Rec	I	.	a
STRICKLAND, Sir William	Hedon	Py	I	.	.
STRODE, William	Berealston	Py	x	b	x
STRODE, William	Ilchester	Rec	P	.	.
SUTTON, Robert	NOTTINGHAMSHIRE	R	d	b	L
SWINFEN, John	Stafford	Rec	P	x	a
SYDENHAM, Sir Ralph	Bossinney	R	d	.	.
SYDENHAM, William	Weymouth & M.R.	Rec	I	x	x
TATE, Zouch	Northampton	Py	p	.	x
TAYLOR, John	Bristol	R	x	.	x
TAYLOR, William	New Windsor	RS	d	x	.
TEMPLE, James	Bramber	Rec	Iw	.	.
TEMPLE, Sir John	Chichester	Rec	P	.	.
TEMPLE, Sir Peter, Bt.	Buckingham	Py	I	.	x
TEMPLE, Peter	Leicester	Rec	Iw	.	.

[1] Listed as Straffordian, but he claimed to have been absent from the vote. See Verney's *Notes of Proceedings*, p. 57.

		1	2	3	4
TEMPLE, Thomas	Mitchell	Rec	P¹	x	.
TERRICK, Samuel	Newcastle, Staffs	Rec	P	.	.
THELWALL, Simon	Denbigh	Py	P	.	x
THISTLETHWAITE, Alexander	Downton	Rec	P	x	.
THOMAS, Edward	Okehampton	Py	P	b	.
THOMAS, Esay	Bishop's Castle	Rec	P	.	.
THOMAS, John	Helston	Rec	P	.	.
THOMAS, Sir William	Caernarvon	R	d	.	x
THOMSON, George	Southwark	Rec	I	.	.
THORNHAUGH, Francis	E. Retford	Rec	x	x	x
THORPE, Francis	Richmond	Rec	I	.	.
THYNNE, Sir James	WILTSHIRE	R	d	x	a
THYNNE, John	Saltash	Rec	P	.	.
TOLL, Thomas	King's Lynn	Py	I	.	x
TOLSON, Richard	CUMBERLAND	Rec	P	x	.
TOMPKINS, Thomas	Weobley	R	d	.	a
TOMPKINS, William	Weobley	R	x	b	x
TREFUSIS, Nicholas	CORNWALL	Rec	p	b	x
TRELAWNEY, Robert	Plymouth	R	x	.	x
TRENCHARD, John	Wareham	Py	I	b	.
TRENCHARD, Sir Thomas	DORSET	Rec	p	b	x
TREVANION, John	Lostwithiel	RS	x	x	x
TREVOR, Sir John	Grampound	Py	I	b	.
TREVOR, John	FLINTSHIRE	Rec	P	x	a
TREVOR, Sir Thomas, Bt.	Tregony	Rec	P	x	.
TUFTON, Sir Humphrey	Maidstone	Py	p	.	.
TULSE, Henry	Christchurch	x	x	b	x
TURNER, Samuel	Shaftesbury	RS	d	b	x
TWISDEN, Thomas	Maidstone	Rec	P	.	.
UPTON, John	Dartmouth	x	x	b	x
UVEDALE, Sir William	Petersfield	Py	p	b	x
VACHELL, Tanfield	Reading	Rec	p	.	x
VALENTINE, Benjamin	St. Germans	Py	I	b	x
VANE, Sir Henry, senior	Wilton	Py	I	b	x
VANE, Sir Henry, junior	Hull	Py	I	x	.
VASSALL, Samuel	London	Py	P	.	.
VAUGHAN, Charles	Honiton	Rec	P	.	.
VAUGHAN, Edward	MONTGOMERYSHIRE	Rec	P	b	a
VAUGHAN, Henry	CARMARTHENSHIRE	R	d	b	a
VAUGHAN, John	Cardigan	R	d	b	a
VENABLES, Peter	CHESHIRE	R	d	.	a
VENN, John	London	Py	Iw	.	x
VERNEY, Sir Edmund	Wycombe	R	x	b	x

¹ No evidence that he took his seat.

		1	2	3	4
VERNEY, Ralph	Aylesbury	R	d	x	a
VIVIAN, Sir Richard	Tregony	R	d	x	a
WADDON, John	Plymouth	Py	P	.	x
WAITE, Thomas	RUTLAND	Rec	Iw	x	.
WALKER, Clement	Wells	Rec	P	.	x
WALKER, Robert	Exeter	R	d	.	a
WALLER, Edmund	St. Ives	R	d	b	a
WALLER, Thomas	Bodmin	Rec	P	x	.
WALLER, Sir William	Andover	Py	P	.	.
WALLOPP, Sir Henry	HAMPSHIRE	Py	x	b	x
WALLOPP, Robert	Andover	Py	I	b	.
WALSINGHAM, Sir Thomas	Rochester	Py	I	b	.
WALTON, Valentine	HUNTINGDONSHIRE	Py	Iw	.	.
WARTON, Michael	Beverley	R	x	.	x
WARWICK, Philip	New Radnor	RS	d	x	a
WASTELL, John	Northallerton	Py	I	.	x
WEAVER, Edmund	Hereford	Rec	p^1	x	.
WEAVER, John	Stamford	Rec	I	.	.
WEAVER, Richard	Hereford	Py	x	b	x
WEBB, Thomas	New Romney	R	d	.	x
WENMAN, Thomas, Viscount	OXFORDSHIRE	Py	P	b	.
WENTWORTH, Sir George (of Walley)	Pontefract	RS	d	.	x
WENTWORTH, Sir George (of Wentworth Woodhouse)	Pontefract	RS	d	x	.
WENTWORTH, Sir Peter	Tamworth	Py	I	.	.
WENTWORTH, Thomas, Lord	BEDFORDSHIRE	R	L	x	L
WEST, Edmund	BUCKINGHAMSHIRE	Rec	I	.	.
WESTON, Benjamin	Dover	Py	I	x	.
WESTON, Henry	Guildford	Rec	p	x	.
WESTON, Nicholas	Newtown	RS	d	x	.
WESTON, Richard	Stafford	RS	d	.	x
WESTROW, Thomas	Hythe	Rec	I	x	.
WHEELER, William	Westbury	Py	P	.	.
WHISTLER, John	Oxford	R	x	b	x
WHITAKER, Lawrence	Okehampton	Py	I	b	x
WHITAKER, William	Shaftesbury	Py	x	b	x
WHITE, John	Southwark	Py	x	.	x
WHITE, John	Rye	RS	d	.	.
WHITE, William	Pontefract	Rec	I	.	.
WHITEHEAD, Richard	HAMPSHIRE	Py	P	b	.

[1] A 'Mr. Weaver' was re-admitted, and Edmund Weaver appears on Masson's list (*Milton*, V, p. 453); but he is not in the *Journals* and may have been confused with John Weaver.

		1	2	3	4
WHITELOCKE, Bulstrode	Great Marlow	Py	I	.	.
WHITMORE, Thomas	Bridgnorth	R	d	x	x
WIDDRINGTON, Sir Thomas	Berwick	Py	I	.	a
WIDDRINGTON, Sir William	NORTHUMBERLAND	RS	d	x	x
WILLIAMS, Sir Charles	MONMOUTHSHIRE	x	x	b	x
WILLS, Henry	Saltash	Rec	P	.	.
WILMOT, Henry	Tamworth	R	L	x	x
WILSON, Rowland	Calne	Rec	I	x	.
WINDEBANK, Sir Francis	Corfe Castle	R	x	.	x
WINGATE, Edward	St. Albans	Py	P	.	.
WINWOOD, Richard	New Windsor	Py	P	.	a
WISE, Thomas	DEVONSHIRE	x	x	b	x
WODEHOUSE, Sir Thomas, Bt.	Thetford	Py	I	.	x
WOGAN, John	PEMBROKESHIRE	Py	x	b	x
WOGAN, Thomas	Cardigan	Rec	Iw	x	.
WOOD, Richard	ANGLESEY	Rec	p	x	.
WORSLEY, Sir Henry, Bt.	Newport, I.o.W.	Py	P	x	.
WRAY, Sir Christopher	Grimsby	Py	x	b	x
WRAY, Sir John, Bt.	LINCOLNSHIRE	Py	p	b	x
WRAY, William	Grimsby	Rec	P	x	.
WROTH, Sir Peter	Bridgwater	Py	x	.	x
WROTH, Sir Thomas	Bridgwater	Rec	I	b	.
WYLDE, Edmund	Droitwich	Rec	I	x	x
WYLDE, George	Droitwich	Rec	I	.	x
WYLDE, John	WORCESTERSHIRE	Py	I	b	.
WYNDHAM, Edward	Bridgwater	R	d	b	a
WYNN, Richard	CARNARVONSHIRE	Rec	P	x	a
WYNN, Sir Richard, Bt.	Liverpool	SPy	P	b	x
YELVERTON, Sir Christopher	Bossinney	Py	p	b	x
YOUNG, Sir John	Plymouth	Py	P	.	.
YOUNG, Walter	Honiton	Py	p	b	x

The following members appear as Rumpers in the lists mentioned on p. 41, but not in the *Journals* or the lists of dissents to the vote of 5 Dec. 1648. 1649 : William Edwards, Brian Stapleton. 1652: Robert Cecil, John Bond, William Fenwick, Thomas Gell, William Jephson, William Lewis. 1659 : Charles Cecil.

INDEX

[ONLY the names of members of the Long Parliament are followed by the letters 'M.P.'. Their relations are not usually indexed separately under Christian names or titles, but are grouped together under the family surname.]